Exploring Aging Masculinities

Exploring Aging Masculinities

The Body, Sexuality and Social Lives

David Jackson
Independent Researcher, UK

EXPLORING AGING MASCULINITIES: THE BODY, SEXUALITY AND SOCIAL LIVES
© David Jackson, 2016
Foreword © Jeff Hearn 2016
Softcover reprint of the hardcover 1st edition 2016 978-1-137-52756-1

First published 2016 by
PALGRAVE MACMILLAN

The author has asserted his right to be identified as the author of this work in accordance with the Copyright, Designs and Patents Act 1988.

Palgrave Macmillan in the UK is an imprint of Macmillan Publishers Limited, registered in England, company number 785998, of Houndmills, Basingstoke, Hampshire, RG21 6XS.

Palgrave Macmillan in the US is a division of Nature America, Inc., One New York Plaza, Suite 4500, New York, NY 10004-1562.

Palgrave Macmillan is the global academic imprint of the above companies and has companies and representatives throughout the world.

ISBN 978-1-349-70781-2
E-PDF ISBN: 978-1-137-52757-8
DOI: 10.1057/9781137527578

Library of Congress Cataloging-in-Publication Data
Names: Jackson, David, 1940–
Title: Exploring aging masculinities : the body, sexuality and social lives / David Jackson, Independent Researcher, UK.
Description: New York : Palgrave Macmillan, 2016. | Includes bibliographical references and index.
Identifiers: LCCN 2015032827 |
Subjects: LCSH: Older men—Great Britain—Psychology. | Masculinity—Great Britain. | Aging—Great Britain. | Lifestyles—Great Britain.
Classification: LCC HQ1064.G7 J33 2016 | DDC 305.26/10941—dc23
LC record available at http://lccn.loc.gov/2015032827

A catalogue record for the book is available from the British Library.

Contents

Foreword: Research with Older Men, Slowly

Aging: Age, aging, aged; gender, gendering, gendered – note the differences: aging means getting older, while gendering means many different relations to gender; aged means old, while gendered means many things and relations. The temptation to follow the singular time line of age is strong and embedded in language. Age is still naturalized. We all die, but in the meantime a lot of differences persist in how ages, agings, and agednesses work.

Time: I am nearly 68, not so different from some of the men you will shortly meet in this book...

As you age, you get nearer your own death, increasingly so. As you age, the probability of hearing of the deaths of friends and colleagues gets greater, unless you get very old in which case it may be that most or all of your contemporaries have died.

Time gets more precious; it speeds up; we are on an accelerating escalator.

At the same time, life often slows down in some ways, physically, socially, mentally. Yet the idea that aging is simply a time of emptiness is surely misplaced.

Time speeds up and slows down at the same time.

Gender: And then add to this gender, in this case the gendering of men... images of men and masculinity are so dominated by young men and men of middle years that it is hardly noticed that the meanings of men and masculinities differ at 18 and 80.

Men do not, usually at least, suddenly become old or very old, or younger old, or older old. This builds on their earlier lives as workers, fathers, singles, unemployed, and so on – and also on their embodied, ethnic, class, sexual, intersectional and emotional lives. They are simultaneously old and not old, men and not men. It is wrong to define these people as only men or only anything, whatever the structural advantages men hold.

Writing, ... and reading: How on earth can you write about aging, that is old and older aging? And when this happens to be focused on aging that is the aging of older men what happens then? Is this yet another male sexual narrative or a deep fissure from that? How do you put all this into words on the page? David Jackson's book dares to do just that, with a subtle and nuanced analysis of the complexity, the ambiguous, bodily fragmented complexity, of older men's lives. It is based primarily and importantly on very unusual, perhaps unique, set of data on a diverse selection of older men's lives, through no less than a five-fold interview or conversation process, what the author calls "intimate conversations". As the author points out, this focus on intimate conversations between the research participants and the researcher is probably the most distinctive feature of this book.

The book is exceptional in terms of the length of time of these intimate conversations and this "slow research" as a whole process. This shows the importance of developing new, different, politically informed methodologies in researching on and with older, slower, less speedy people, sometimes with clear disabilities, sometimes not or less visibly so. It also speaks to the need for careful, slower reading, not the ridiculous sound bite of the headline or the fetishized academic article.

Biography and history: This extended work is contextualized in relation to three main bodies of work: first, broader critical research studies of men and masculinities; second, intersections of age, class and gender; and, third, historical, political-economic change over the lifetimes of the men interviewed.

Men's lives as older men or older old men are to be understood both biographically and historically, in their gendered historical-biographical contexts. This study lays the basis for a broader biographical approach to men, aging and gender. There is thus a special focus of issues of aging, work, health, disability and the body more generally.

Old age is also the time when material resources fork – from the protected and cushioned very rich old to the desperate and very poor old – hence the significance of older, 'grey' and pensioner activisms. These blatant divergences may die with the individuals, yet are continued through and for the inheritors of the rich.

Please read it: The book disrupts thinking and practice on men and masculinities, on age, class, gender and sexuality, and is important for policy and politics, for carers, professionals, and of course older people themselves and ourselves.

Burning: 'Old age should burn and rage at close of day' wrote Dylan Thomas.

Jeff Hearn, Helsinki, April 2015

Preface

In an article I wrote for the *Auto/Biography* journal called, 'Beyond one-dimensional models of masculinity: A life-course perspective on the processes of becoming masculine' (2003), I talk about the historically unique, social space (between retirement and death) that is slowly emerging in the lives of older men. I also suggest that this unique, social space might prove to be a creative space for re-thinking old age together with a critical re-assessment and possible re-formulation of conventional, masculine identities.

In some ways, this is what I have tried to do in this book. At the age of 75 I have started to connect old age studies with the critical men and masculinity field. As one reviewer commented, 'There has been insufficient attention devoted to the intersection between aging and masculinity in both the gerontological and the masculinity academic literature and this book addresses the gap.'

The form of research methodology that I have chosen for this investigation – a qualitative, 'intimate conversation' type of research process – is a deliberately appropriate form of research to use with aging men. The extended interview processes keeps pace with the daily rhythms and deepening ages of the research participants.

In writing this book I have also become aware of a new, reading public, particularly in the 50+ section of the population. There is a broader, more diverse reading public now taking shape out there who are thoughtful and curious and want to make sense of their changing lives. This emerging group are not just younger academics but older women and men who want to engage with the dilemmas and opportunities of the aging process. I very much hope this book reaches out to these new voices in reading groups as well as in Higher Education.

Looking again at the inter-relations between old age and masculinities, I need to acknowledge that old age is unignorably present in my everyday life in all its sudden swerves, alterations and movements. As a result, I have expanded and deepened my research interests in aging men's lived experiences and also in the complex biographies of eight, other, aging men as well as a living curiosity about my own life.

In terms of critical men and masculinities, I think readers probably need a wider background of gender relations and sexual politics to introduce them to how the author has gradually developed an interest in the culturally and socially constructed topic of men and masculinities, rather than taking for granted a supposed 'natural' form of being a man. That is why the rest of the Preface will focus on 'A short history of critical, men and masculinity studies and practices.'

A Short History of Critical, Men and Masculinity Studies and Practices

This short history is based on a mixture of theoretical insights and more personal reflections on some of my pro-feminist, personal experiences in the UK. In this brief space, I am interested in setting my critical approach to aging men into a wider background of gender, men and masculinities and sexual politics. My selective focus will be on the 'most feminist and politically progressive wing of the men's movement' (Flood, 2007), that is, pro-feminist, male experiences instead of dealing with the anti-feminist movements.

To start with, it is important to recognise that before the Second Wave of feminism, dominant and unreconstructed models of male identity were viewed as normal (Ashe, 2007). Generic man was still seen as the human norm (Brod, 1987), and it took until the late 1960s and early 1970s before the emergence of feminism and alternative sexualities began to unsettle and question the traditional position of men. At this time, a critical interrogation of men's normative, gendered power and privilege began in earnest and men started to be seen differently, as more fallible, gendered subjects rather than patriarchal norms. Michael Flood comments about this significant, historical moment in this way:

> In the early 1970s, anti-sexist men's groups, inspired directly by the women's movement, adopted consciousness-raising in small all-male groups to reflect critically on their involvement in sexism and to build non- or anti-sexist identities. (Flood, 2007)

This early 1970s and 1980s emphasis on exploring masculine identities (Ashe, 2007) within a supportive context of building friendship and seeking intimacy from other men, was true of my own personal experience in an anti-sexist, men's group called 'Men for Change' in Nottingham in the East Midlands. Many of the men in these groups were experiencing a great deal of personal pain, grief and confusion from broken relationships, separation and divorce and lost children. But other men wanted to sort out practical, social problems involving child care, fathering, relationships, family problems, issues of emotional literacy, sexual difficulties, loneliness, anger, competitive rivalry and violence. Within these groups there was always a contradictory tension present between changing masculine identities and a wider concern with gender inequality and the position of women and some men's gendered power and control. The personal and the political were always inter-related.

Looking back on some of these early encounters, I now recognise that I thought masculinity was single, innate and unchanging. I believed in the illusion of fixity, of being born a monolithic oppressor of women and staying that way through my lifetime. I did not have the alternative experiences of twisting and turning and discovering shifts and changes as you went along in your life. Later, of course, that illusion was deeply subverted by different emotional realities and vantage points that generated new forms of masculinity and change.

As the group developed, connections with other men's groups in different parts of the UK were established mainly through the publication of its own, small magazine also called *Men for Change*. The members' group continued meeting once a fortnight, with regular attendance from roughly a dozen men. Some of this contact was useful for men who were feeling bewildered about their current situation, but other more political members of the group were also becoming frustrated about the general direction of the group. This mood of gathering frustration comes through strongly in one member's letter to the rest of the group:

> I am a man who goes to a men's group and recently started helping produce MFC. But I do not want to be part of a 'men's movement'. I am also white, able-bodied, heterosexual and middle class but do not want to be part of a white's movement. A heterosexuals' movement, or a middle-class movement. My support goes to anti-racism, disabled people's campaigns, gay liberation and democratic socialism. And it goes to feminism and the anti-sexist struggle. Sexism is an oppression and it oppresses women. I am fed up with all this self-indulgent, navel gazing men's liberation oriented stuff. (*Men for Change*, issue 18, Winter 1991)

Several developments were made in the early 1990s in response to the cry for greater social justice and gender equality for women. The first response was an anti-violence and anti-abuse campaign organised around domestic violence. This anti-violence group was first called MOVE and then re-named AGENDA, based in Nottingham. I worked closely with Jon Salisbury in becoming two of the group counsellors from 1990 to 1995. Over that time we both worked with several perpetrator groups of about 6–8 members who wanted to stop being domestically violent.

I also gained confidence in starting to write about men and masculinity issues, writing film criticisms for *Men for Change* and from 1987 to 1997 I also wrote varied articles for *Achilles Heel*, the main men's magazine in the UK on unemployment and retirement, sport and men, socialism and masculinity issues, Clint Eastwood in *High Plains Drifter*, mothers and sons, and dancing towards sixty. I also began to see the bewildering variety of different masculinities. As a result I started to pluralise 'masculinities' and understood the multiplicity of possible options that went into the construction of diverse masculinities.

The other developments were working on providing a gender equity curriculum for secondary schools (Ashe, 2007). With Jon Salisbury I co-wrote and edited *Challenging Macho Values: Practical ways of working with adolescent boys* (Falmer Press and Routledge, 1996). I was also a group member of the 'Men, Masculinities and Socialism group', meeting in Sheffield from 1988 to 1990. From all these fresh initiatives I started to become much more critically aware of gender relations and sexual politics. Some of these new insights can be found in an article I wrote with Jeff Hearn on socialist masculinities published in *Achilles Heel* in Autumn 1990.

One of the main points we looked at is 'A renewal of socialist politics is unthinkable without a simultaneous reworking of conventional masculinities.' In critiquing the conventionally macho style of socialist men's politics this comment was made: 'Loud and pushy argument is a common feature of many socialist men. Through abrupt invasion of the rules of turn-taking, sudden subject shifts, frequent interruptions, some socialist men seem to be more intent on making their point than in building conversations.'

What I learnt from all these group experiences was that pro-feminist men were diverse, multiple, shifting, mobile and contradictory. They were not fixed with their feet set for ever in granite. Some of these complexities surfaced in our anti-male violence work. When the group started, I was able to define male violence as being linked to issues of gender, masculinity and power: 'Through their journeys of becoming masculine, many men learn to expect the same kind of dominating, controlling position in the home as they do in the wider society outside. As a result, male violence often comes out of a masculine need to re-assert power and control over women often in circumstances where men feel that their traditional authority is being challenged or questioned.'

A brief snapshot of what went on inside the anti-male violence group is to be found in a report on the third group that met between May and September, 1993:

> As group leaders we stressed the value of mutual aid and emphasised the importance of keeping contact by phone or in person between sessions. When the individuals in the group begin to trust each other, there is a much greater willingness to accept constructive criticism and some quite blunt honesty. Keith was into his head, making all sorts of connections and justifications about his conduct. He was using long words as a screen. "Don't bullshit us, Keith!" was Leslie's response. This straightforward remark cut through the mountains of words and Keith was able to look more self-critically at his own patterns of avoidance. (From Nottingham MOVE: Men Overcoming Violence: A Group Counselling Approach – Jonathan Salisbury and David Jackson)

Jonathan and I were beginning to understand our limitations in a 20 week programme. The full complexity of the relationship of stopping men's violence and the family relations between the man and wife were brought home forcefully to us:

> We want to re-emphasise the fact that to ensure the safety of women, anger management is not enough... We noted that Reg's partner moved back to him because she thought Nottingham Agenda (the anti-male violence group) was doing such a good job. We regarded this as a dangerous move since after only a handful of weeks the dangers to the partner are still frighteningly close. We would advocate a much more up front attempt to contact, inform and support partners. We feel that 'Agenda' should be doing more to try to ensure their safety. (Jonathan Salisbury and David Jackson: January 1994)

About this time I was a part of two different men's groups; one trying to stop male violence to women and the other on men's health. The relationship between men and masculinities and men's health practices became the central focus of three men's health groups that I participated in from 1991 to 2005.

The first was the Men's Health Awareness Project. The five-strong group published a report, working from personal experience and providing striking stories to a wider analysis of men's health, titled 'The crisis in men's health.' The second group was the European Institute of Men's

Health (1996–2001), while the third was the Nottinghamshire Men's Health Group (1997–2005). I would like to give the reader a flavour of what happened in these groups by focusing on some of the work done in the second and third groups.

First, here is a statement of some key principles linked to the Men's Health Awareness Project:

> As a group of five men we have found it essential to start by looking at our own experiences and we are now trying to link these experiences to other men's experiences taking account of the influences of class, race, education, poverty etc. Developing better health for men is linked to increasing their awareness about the emotional and social costs of striving to be a 'Real Man'. Deeper awareness can show men that they can create health-giving choices. Part of these changes is about letting go of 'Real Man' power and control and actively seeking mutual support.

Also the range of events, activities and workshops gives the reader some idea of what went on in The Nottinghamshire Men's Health Group. Here is a brief list of some of the events organised in 2003–04:

1. A four day course and workshop on men and health that included themes like 'Positive Mental Health for Men', 'Men and Help-seeking,' 'Why Don't Men Visit their GPs?', 'Men and Addictive Behaviours', 'How can Men age Well?'.
2. A group event on hearing loss, where aging men shared their own stories of 'Pretending to hear when they could not hear' with openness, humour and honesty.
3. A shared workshop with the Nottingham Prostate Cancer Support Group on prostate cancer.
4. A group event on gay men and sexual health.

The key, theoretical shifts in critical studies on men and masculinities came for me in 1995 with Connell's critical undermining of monolithic, one-dimensional models of masculinity (Connell, 1995). Unchanging, universalist notions of patriarchy and power have viewed men as a monolithic, homogeneous, stable category rather than a constantly shifting, variable, and from about 2000 onwards I have focused my attention on aging men's issues: setting up an aging men's group in 1999 (still going in 2015); starting a memory work group in 2002 with the support of two other men, based on the work of Frigga Haug and others (Haug et al., 1987).This group is now completing its work in 2015 and publishing its findings later on in the year.

Exploring Aging Masculinities emerges out of that complex, social web of collective interactions and gradually building alternative social networks for nurturing and supporting changing, aging men. From 2005 I have been conducting an independent, small scale, research project investigating the lived, embodied experiences of aging men (60-75) using a life history, narrative approach.

Subordinated masculinities, like aging and disabled men, exist outside the oppressively, dominant regime of men and masculinities that often displays the values of achievement, aggression, toughness and domination over women (Torres, 2007). Instead, subordinated masculinities are constructed in opposition and at the margins of society, often neglected and excluded, such as 'the groups of men located within particular, subordinated classes, ethnic or racial minorities, as well as disabled and aged groups' (Howson, 2007). These experiences of being excluded and marginalised often create a keen distrust of established authority and, sometimes, provoke a subversive challenge to dominant, masculinity forms of able-bodied, heterosexual complacency.

To finish, I want to stress the importance for me in emotionally investing in the aging men's stories and beginning to understand the links between socially situated experiences/knowledges and the work of Donna Haraway (1991), Connell's (1995) innovatory work on 'Subordinated masculinities' and Thomas Gerschick's bodily perspective on 'Masculinities and Degrees of Bodily Normativity in Western Culture' (Kimmel, Hearn and Connell, 2005). These potential links create connections between situated differences in forms of masculinity of lesser power, either in deteriorating masculine bodies or a loss of social status. I developed an intense interest in investigating gay masculinities, working-class masculinities, some black masculinities that are poor, vulnerable and at the bottom of the hierarchical ladder of masculinities, and disabled and aging men.

Gerschick (2005) comments that 'less-normative bodies contravene many of the beliefs associated with being a man'. Although he acknowledges that 'what is considered normative varies across time and space', he goes on to show how people's bodies are measured comparatively in terms of the current, cultural ideals ascendant in society at that particular moment. He also makes clear the social consequences of such a position: 'people with less-normative bodies are vulnerable to being denied social recognition and validation and . . . avoided, ignored and marginalized.' The complexity of this process of denied social recognitions is illustrated by Jenkins 2013) in exploring transgendered men. Some men want to assert their newly acquired masculinities in a hegemonic manner that sometimes seems to invalidate their real, gender and sexual politics.

This marginalisation of aging men's less-normative bodies works, as Gerschick suggests through the implied, cultural contrasts between dominant, vigorous and virile masculine bodies and the fragmentary, diminishing loss of physical function and capacity in many aging men's bodies. However, as I have already made clear in my discussion of what I call 'creative discontinuities and radical disruptions' (see page 50) this is not entirely a negative story. These physical losses, changes and traumatic, bodily disruptions in aging and disabled men's lives, can provoke and generate a more self-critical, reflexive re-positioning from which some aging men can interrogate and possibly re-assess the masculine habits of a lifetime. Sometimes, aging men can move beyond younger and middle-aged legacies of work obsession, successful careers and selfish sexualities and perhaps begin to change their practices and masculine subjectivities.

Acknowledgements

I am deeply grateful to the eight research participants who seriously engaged with the project and made this social investigation possible. I owe them a great deal through their wit, perceptive insights and tolerance. I learnt a huge amount about the lives of aging men through them.

I owe Bren, my wife, a great debt of gratitude for supporting me during the project, physically, emotionally and politically. Without her concern and caring this book would have never seen the light of day.

I would also like to thank the following people for generously taking part in an informed dialogue with me through the project:

Jeff Hearn – I want to thank Jeff for his consistent, generous support and thoughtful insights during the whole ten years of my research project. Without his shrewd comments I might have given up.

John Brown – I am deeply indebted to John's unwavering, emotional support and his perceptive remarks about the manuscript.

Claire Jenkins – A big thank you for the subtlety of our frequent dialogue about this project, her reading of different chapters and for tidying up my general presentation.

Vic Blake – Vic helped me to develop, particularly in the early parts of the project, a critical, self-reflexive awareness of the aging process in aging men. His electronic expertise also helped the recording process.

Richard Johnson – Richard helped me to understand the complexities of my research project through a perceptive critique of different parts of the manuscript.

Michael Luck – I want to thank Michael for giving me sustained, emotional support especially in the early days of the project.

Brendan Gough – Brendan supported me at a difficult time in the life of the project to renew my engagement with the writing through helping me to write a publishing proposal.

Andy Sparkes – I am very grateful to Andy for continuously supporting me and helping me to value my attempts at critical autobiography by publishing it in *Auto/Biography*.

Randy Barber – I want to thank Randy for a combination of informed dialogue about aging and continuous, electronic support.

John McLuskey – I'm indebted to John for helping me to formulate my original research plan and connected decisions about pacing myself.

Harriet Gross and Antonia Lyons – Both Harriet and Antonia helped me to believe in engaging in my research project. Also Harriet encouraged me by sending me relevant research papers.

Zbyszek Lucynski – At the point of the research when I wanted to expand the range and diversity of the research participants, Zbyszek helped me to make contact with aging men of ethnic and racial diversity.

I am very grateful for permission to publish a slightly altered version of 'Older men's embodied selves: Rethinking relationships of change,' previously published in 2008 in the *Auto/Biography Yearbook*, published by the Auto/Biography Study Group and edited by Andrew C. Sparkes.

I am also grateful to the following publishers for their generous giving of permission to use these varied excerpts from their published books:

Charmaz, K. 'Identity dilemmas of chronically ill men' in Sabo, D. and Gordon, D. (Eds.) *Men's health and illness: Gender, power and the body* (pp. 266–91). Sage, 1995.

Hazan, H. *Old Age: Constructions and Deconstructions*. Cambridge University Press, 1994.

Williams, C. 'Introduction' in Williams, C. (Ed.) *Doing Women's Work: Men in Non-traditional Occupations*. Sage, 1993.

1
Introduction

The main purposes of this book are to challenge the stagnant representations of aging men[1] in the UK; to investigate the daily, lived experiences of aging men from 60 to 75 years of age; and to explore the ingenuity and inventiveness of some aging men in defining their own terms within a social and historical context. Another key feature in this book is to acknowledge the centrality of older, masculinised bodies in the continuing attempts to connect gender and aging (Arber, 2003). All these different purposes represent ways of changing the voicelessness, marginalisation and sense of occasional uselessness experienced by some aging men following their departure from paid employment and taken for granted relationships and identities. Also it needs to be remembered that the majority of aging men live in systems of patriarchal power that still privilege men, despite their confrontations with ageism and loss, and stigmatise, penalise and oppress women (Kaufman, 1994). Therefore one of the objectives of this book is to contribute to change in creating greater gender equality.

The key aim of the book is to explore the complexity of the lived, embodied experiences of aging men as a counterpoint to the existing stereotypical notions of aging men. Conventionally, aging men in Western culture[2] are seen as inevitably in decline and in a state of decay. This book sets out to challenge these distorted assumptions through a detailed analysis of the life stories of eight aging men. These arguments are framed within a wider global context that recognises the importance of labour migration, de-industrialisation, imperial legacies and the social and political effects of a free market economy.

The male research participants in this study have not been directly involved in de-industrialisation (except for Ray) but a rapidly shifting work culture has affected them in terms of an uncertain cultural climate of emotional insecurity, anxiety and loss (Walkerdine and Jimenez, 2012).

In writing this book, I am very much aware that studies of aging, embodied men have the potential to radically subvert and destabilise conventional theories of men and masculinities (Silver, 2003; Thompson, 1994). Old age, ageism, bodily changes and disruptions, and disability pose considerable problems to the established authority, social power and status of many aging men (particularly elitist, aging men from business and political hierarchies) and to their gendered, embodied identities. Old age for many men is a place of frequent change, life review and re-assessment, although for some it is also a time of avoidance and self-protection. In this book I want to be alert to the potential signs of emancipatory possibilities in the later lives of aging men and the ways that these signs might help to shift damaging gender relations both in younger and middle-aged men.

The key distinctive features of the book are the continuous presence of change in aging men's lives and the possibility of personal and social re-invention. To make this clearer I need to explain the personal and wider theoretical background to 'situated differences' in the following section.

Change and Situated Differences in Aging Men's Everyday Lives

The historical origins of aging men's changing lives in the UK come from the late 1960s and early 1970s. With the gendered and sexual disruptions of second-wave feminism and alternative sexualities and the politics of lesbians, gays, bisexuals and transgendered activists emerged a wider destabilising of British men's social status and normative, dominant positions. Fidelma Ashe (2007) in her book, 'The New Politics of Masculinity' talks of men's traditional, masculine identities and dominant, social position becoming interrogated and problematized. Some men's conventional centre stage positions as main breadwinners, providers and heads of households were in the process of being undermined.

Alongside these changes went a general restructuring of the family in the UK. The patriarchal, nuclear family had begun to be replaced by the development of diverse relationships between married and cohabiting partners and children (Ashe, 2007; Giddens, 1992). Many female partners began to be disappointed by their emotionally distant and frequently detached partners. As a result, divorce rates in the UK had started to increase (Ashe, 2007).

Changing patterns in the workplace also demonstrated these wider shifts and sense of precariousness in men's lives in the UK. Against a general background of de-industrialisation, started in the 1980s, working-class masculinities were disorientated and fragmented. As a result, many working-class men had been forced to confront the rapid decline of manufacturing industry (Mac an Ghaill and Haywood, 2007) and to face up to these new economic and social changes. Traditional labour markets were now shrinking and in their place was a steadily rising service sector employment. New working practices have come along with these economic changes such as downsizing, part-time, low paid contracts, out-sourcing of industrial work to countries where labour is less expensive and more docile, and long-term unemployment. The collapse and dislocation of the old manufacturing base has contributed to aging men's sense of anxiety, insecurity and occasional depression about feeling useless (Mac an Ghaill and Haywood, 2007).

However, with a new interrogative space beginning to emerge in aging men's lives and a much longer life span (between retirement and death) than in previous generations, alternative narratives about men and masculinities in later life are starting to emerge. These collapses of their normative, dominant positions in society have opened up the possibility of new ways of reflecting on changing and different, masculine identities with more care about increased social justice for women. The damaging restrictions and false ideals of one-dimensional models of masculinity have become more visible. This increasing visibility has called into question the notion that masculinity is a fixed, unitary and stable category rather than a constantly shifting variable, existing in a socially located position.

Along with these fresh insights went the developing awareness of the subordination of some men of lesser power (Connell, 1995), such as gay, disabled, working-class, black masculinities, caring men and, partly, the lives of aging men. Despite living through the contradictions of being partly privileged in heterosexual terms and the retaining of some aspects of social dominance, most aging men also have to confront the humiliation of ageism and stereotyping (Bytheway, 1995) as well as bodily and sexual deterioration and fragmentation.

The out of date focus on a narrow, exclusive dominance (Ashe, 2007) of white, young, middle class, heterosexual men has now been superseded by critical attention and re-focusing on the more problematical and contradictory varieties of men – in this case, disabled, aging and gay men. These changes in focus have now exposed the possible links between feminist studies like Donna Haraway's emphasis on 'socially situated knowledges and experiences' (Haraway, 1991) and the critical re-positioning of aging men. Therefore, subordinated groups, like aging men, construct different versions of social reality arising out of their own situated experiences and knowledges (Johnson, Chambers, Raghuram and Tincknell, 2004). Put another way, where one stands shapes what one can see and how it is understood (Pease, 1998).

The specific, situated experiences and developing knowledges of aging men involve very different, changing circumstances of everyday life. Indeed, it is not too much to say that aging men have a unique potential for change in their later years. However, there is still great variety in some aging men's reactions to these shifting experiences. Some aging men still cling defensively to traditional forms of manhood, and other men are blocked by depression, alcoholism, violence, addictive behaviours or damaging illness. But for other aging men there are new spaces emerging, created by the deconstruction and disruption of normative understandings of masculinity.

Aging men's lived situations often include the experiences of loss, physical disruption and failure. As well as losing social power and status, as we have already observed in the changing family and workplace, aging, retired men are typically seen as economically non-productive. However, this negative impression needs to be moderated and balanced by a recognition of aging men's new social productivity, seen in active grandfathering, voluntary work and in the increased practices of care found in some aging men like Brian's informal, spousal caring for his ill wife in Chapter six.

Changes in the material bodies of aging men also involve the often traumatic experiences of sudden alteration and loss of physical function and capacity. As Peter, in my research evidence, remarks about living with Parkinson's disease, the unpredictability of his bodily shaking and shuffling often makes him feel that his bodily fragility is uncontrollable in chapter five. Also as Robert learns to do, loss of physical strength and bodily power means re-assessing your traditional grip on your masculine identities in chapter 8. Sometimes a loss can be deceptive and, later, opens up different possibilities. For example, in Roy's sexual experience, his loss and personal critique of the dominant, penetrative sex model led him to value touching, cuddling and hugging rather than being addicted to orgasm in chapter 4.

These losses, physical changes, the close proximity of death and dying, differences and traumatic disruptions in aging men's lives, can generate a more self-critical, reflexive, re-positioning from which some aging men can move beyond earlier, younger and middle-aged obsessions with work, successful careers and selfish sexualities. In some cases, these processes of re-positioning also entail a loosening attachment to patriarchal values and relations. In their place, sometimes, comes a fresh focus on, 'seeking connections with others' (Thompson, 2006), like in Dennis's late discovery of his other-related, empathetic, sexual selves as a man. These changes can also lead to the first stirrings of an anti-patriarchal standpoint in some curious and thoughtful, aging men.

Research Questions in this Study of Old Age

- How far can the aging process contribute to changes in the gender relations of men?
- How far can aging men re-position themselves in a different form of masculine identity in their later lives?
- What can be learnt from a close study of aging men's embodied identities and sexualities in old age?

The Neglected Links Between Old Age, Men and Masculinities

One of the most significant gaps in our knowledge and understanding about old age is the subtle reality of aging men's embodied and lived experiences. According to Calasanti (2004), Fennel and Davidson (2003), Fleming (1999), Hearn (1995), and Thompson (1994), most previous research on men and masculinities has largely ignored aging men. Although the work of Arber, Davidson and Ginn (2003), Emslie et al. (2004), and Sandberg (2011), have played a part in rectifying this situation, the nuanced, complex lives of aging men remain notable by their absence in the research literature on men and masculinities.

Similarly, the domain of aging studies has generally neglected the links between the processes of aging and men and masculinities. The last twenty years have seen important advances in our understandings of the lives of older women (Arber and Ginn, 1995; Bernard et al. 2000; Calasanti and Slevin, 2006). However, research on aging men has not kept up with these women-centred advances (Fennel and Davidson, 2003). Given this relative neglect, this book project represents an attempt to fill some of the empty spaces surrounding our limited understandings of the embodied lives of aging men.

The Personal Roots of my Project

My current research into the lived experiences of aging men has personal roots in the shattering destabilisation in 1986 of my own normative, embodied, masculine subjectivities. As I have documented elsewhere, in my critical autobiography, 'Unmasking masculinity', (Jackson, 1990) I went through a physical and emotional collapse that resulted in major heart surgery. This traumatic bodily and biographical disruption to how I thought I was as a man later generated in me a painful reassessment of my previously taken for granted, gendered ways of being in the world.

What I gradually learnt from these disorientating experiences and troubling bodily sensations was a more self-critical, reflexive perspective on aging processes, masculine identities, physical impairment and disability, bodily shifts and betrayals, and emotional transitions and turning points. In my active retirement at 75. I have sustained my interest in the lived experiences of aging men (myself included). Accordingly, my interests in aging processes have deepened and intensified as well as widened. In some ways I have wanted to share my new book on aging men with a broad, diverse reading public, not just younger academics but with many thoughtful older people who want to make sense of their changing lives.[3] My developing curiosity in the greying of Western, industrial nations has developed my understandings of the interactions between the local conditions of the UK and the wider, global context. I have now expanded my research interests through engagement with the lives of eight diverse, aging men as well as continuing my own interests in critical autobiography.

From 2005 to 2008 I organised a small-scale, independent research project in the North-East Midlands in the UK that utilises a biographical, narrative, research approach (Roberts, 2002; Chamberlayne, Bornat and Wengraf, 2000) to explore eight aging men's lived and embodied experiences. The rich data that this research project produced form the backbone of this book. I now intend to make clear some of the key, conceptual frames of understanding that organise the main themes of the book. This will start with the cultural construction of old age, then will move on to the inter-connectedness of gender and age, and will finish with separate sections on embodiment and identity.

The Cultural Construction of Old Age

I would like to start by looking closely at two life stories that were spoken, shared, collected and transcribed during the research interviews of the project on aging men. (See later in this chapter, 'Introducing the Research Participants' for snapshots of Brian's and Michael's [pages 12–15] life histories.) The first life story focuses on Brian's (all names are pseudonyms) response to one of his daughter's comments that he needed to fully recognise how old he is. She starts by saying:

Daughter: But, Dad, you're 70!
Brian: So?
Daughter: Well you have to...
Brian: No, I don't.

The second life story is an answer by Michael to my question:

Is there anything else you want to say about your present experiences of being an older man?

This is how Michael responded:

'...yeah, having only just had my sixtieth birthday I remember saying to a couple of people that I'm now an official, old fart. And then I thought about it afterwards and thought: "Why am I saying that? I'm proud that I am 60. It's not a problem. I can do sod all about it. As I said before, I mean, I didn't choose to be here, it was chosen for me and one thing we can't stop is the clock or time and the issue for me is attitudinal really and how I feel about myself and how I feel about what I want to do with the rest of the life I've got left..."'

Although Brian's daughter will possibly have different perceptions and meanings, it appears that she expects her father to conform to a certain set of cultural norms about age-appropriate behaviour (Vincent, 2003) in her comment, ' But, dad, you're 70!' There's also anxiety and concern expressed about his risky behaviour but she seems to believe that people like her father need to go along with 'a normal old age' that has been socially regulated and imposed from without.

These negative cultural norms and cultural imperatives are what Margaret Gullette calls 'decline ideology' (Gullette, 2004) which creates barriers in aging struggles. In some ways, you could argue that Brian's daughter is using 'decline ideology' to persuade her father to play safe and toe the line but Brian refuses to accept these normative ways of doing age, and he does this in a culturally disobedient way.

In Michael's life story, at first he internalises the 'decline ideology' by embracing the jokey, ironic, self-deprecatory label of 'an official, old fart.' Later, however, after standing back and reflecting on: 'Why am I saying that?' Michael starts to question the wisdom of doing this:

> Why am I saying that? I'm proud that I'm 60. It's not a problem.

Retirement and becoming 60 have thrown his previous work-related identities into confusion and he is beginning to confront the possibility of other alternative selves, including age, and not all ruled by inevitable decline and decay. In the second half of Michael's story he shows that 'decline ideology' can be challenged and opposed. It seems as if he is distancing himself from a negative narrative and awakening to a 'critical, age-conscious perspective' (Gullette, 2004) through exploring his feelings about being 60, and acknowledging the importance of cultural attitudes in partly shaping his age-identity and growing awareness of mortality and time passing.

The questions arising out of these life stories are 'where does Brian's daughter, in all her difference, get these expectations about age-appropriate behaviour' and 'where does Michael get his internalised version of being an "old fart" at 60?' Part of the answer to both these questions is that they get it from the dominant culture that often imposes ageist stereotypes onto the actual, varied, lived experiences of aging men.

Age is not an essentialised, over-naturalised condition. Instead, aging men are primarily aged by culture (Gullette, 2004). Their bodies become more fragile as they age but the ways in which 'Western culture (1) both marginalises and stigmatises aging individuals is a socially constructed phenomenon' (Drummond, 2007). It is from the realm of the socio-cultural that aging men learn to devalue themselves as 'official, old farts.'

Cultural ageism focuses on the undervaluing of aging men's lives through taken for granted representations and narratives. In Western culture, aging men are wrongly assumed to lose their human resilience at a certain age or to become men of a limited or inferior kind as they age. However, it is also important to recognise that for some aging men, the aging process is a long and hard struggle to preserve their vitality and to restore their humanity in age.

Western myths and stereotypes of 'grumpy old men', or, 'dirty old men', are often depicted on film or television, as moaning, angry, messy or miserable, making it extremely difficult to get to grips with the more diverse and unexpected lives of aging men. These myths often render invisible the hidden realities of, for example, the relatively unseen worlds of respected black elders; the daily caring routines of older male spouses looking after ill partners; the active campaigning of some men in their seventies and eighties for better pension rights; engaged and nurturing grandfathering and the rich, social networks of many older, gay men (Jackson, 2007).

Age Relations

However, age is not just a cultural construct. It is also influenced by institutional practices and social structures of segregation and exclusion. Calasanti and Slevin (2006) in their book, 'Age matters: realigning feminist thinking', examine three critical dimensions of age relations that 'underlie the devaluation of old age.'

The Social and Institutional Regulation of Age in the UK.

In Western culture and society, aging men know their age because society regulates public life according to chronological age (Vincent, 2003). Institutions organise access and prescribe and proscribe certain behaviours by age, from bus companies issuing passes to both school children and to older people, and public houses organising age-based restrictions on the sale of alcohol.

The ways societies are organised in the West in terms of work, health, welfare, retirement and pensions, also play a part in allocating aging men into the category, 'old.' Some aging men experience these institutional divisions as increasingly segregated barriers to active participation in all aspects of society.

Different Age Groups Gain Identities and Power in Relation to One Another

Memories of being young leave shadowy traces in aging men's lives. This relation between young men and old men not only operates as a system of dominance and inequality that discriminates against the old and privileges the 'not-old' (Calasanti, 2003), but also sets up an internal conversation within some aging men about their earlier mistakes and the need to settle, and sometimes to atone for, unresolved dilemmas.

Old age can also be seen as a relational construct created through the othering and dehumanising of aging men. The relatively dominant discourse of young, active, virile masculinities is constructed through the unequal and relational subordination and exclusion of older and disabled masculinities. Some of the things that are threatening and disruptive to the internal composure of the not-old, such as physical and psychological changes and the processes of growing old and dying, is split off and projected outside itself on to a severely limited and inferior version of older masculinities (Jackson, 2007).

Age Relations Intersect With Other Power Relations

Age is not a single analytical category. Recent work has focused on complex inter-relationships between multiple and fluid dimensions of social relations and subject formations (McCall, 2005). These multiple inter-relationships are referred to as intersectionality, so that age relations intermingle with other power relations.

In my present study, age relations have mixed with other social divisions, such as class, disability, sexuality, ethnicity and race, nationality and occupation (Hearn, 2007). These processes of inter-relationship with other social forces modify all the social divisions involved in these dynamic processes. Nothing stays still or static in these shifting, multiple relations and reconstructions. Also the different contexts of these varied social forces reveal different meanings, ambiguities and, sometimes, conflicting experiences. For example, age-identity for one of my research participants can be seen as an adventurous challenge, viewed from a middle-class, masculine perspective rather than a time of troubled defensiveness, seen from a different, working-class, manual labourer's standpoint.

Age and Masculinities

Aging men are often perceived as living without gender (Emslie, Hunt and O'Brien, 2004) or ungendered (Hearn, 1995). This, however, is a mistake as older men age in highly gendered ways so that it is possible to suggest that masculinities and aging are inextricably intertwined (Arber and Ginn, 1995). In this study I look explicitly and critically at aging men as masculine social beings (Brod, 1987), and focus on their embodied, masculine identities as they shift contradictorily through a life course. I also look carefully at the processes through which aging men construct these changing identities through social practices, narratives and discursive regimes.

Aging men, in Western culture, inhabit an ambiguous, social category (Spector-Mersel, 2006). Many aging men are still privileged (e.g. heterosexual, white, middle class, able-bodied, rich) as well as some having had experience of business and political hierarchies, but simultaneously they are marginalised by ageism, bodily fragility and loss of sexual potency. Thus, in many aging men's lives there is a strange, contradictory mixture of some legacies of masculine and heterosexual privilege and power interacting with some reduction and loss in their social and bodily power. For example, aging men who are economically non-productive after retirement, disabled, aging men with an unreliable, deteriorating, changing body etc, as they grow older.

Embodiment

Bodies are of central importance in my exploration of aging men's lives, both in terms of their intimate experiences and sensations of their lived bodies and the manner in which these are connected to and shaped by their social or discursive bodies. However, the lived bodies of aging men have largely been absent from the gerontological and sociological literature (Fleming, 1999; Oberg, 1996; Tulle-Winton, 2000). Although most men are actively embodied (Hearn, 2012) there is a deceptive culture of masculine disembodiment that is probably best illustrated in the working lives of British men in mid-life that has perpetuated to some extent the illusion of rational, masculine detachment and disembodiment. So it is my intention to challenge that appearance of rational detachment and to move the lived, aging bodies of these men more into the central spotlight of critical interrogation.

I think Fleming (Fleming, 1999) is right to argue that the critical lens through which the complex inter-relationship between age, masculinity and embodied identities can be formulated and understood is to study aging men's embodiment, or the experiences and physical sensations of their lived and fluctuating, older, masculine bodies.

As Fleming comments:

> ... 'exploring embodiment with aging men will capture the actual practices of being old and the ways in which the body works and doesn't work ... the struggles with bodily betrayals, stigmatisation and various modes of disempowerment' (Featherstone and Wernick, 1995, cited in Fleming (1999)

Gendered Identities

A gendered identity is not something we are born with. It is not innate and essentialised. It is now well recognised that identity is something that is socially produced through the narratives and social practices people use to make sense of and understand their lives. As Lawler (2008) points out, most of us keep on telling stories, both to ourselves and others, about our embodied experiences, and the key transitions and critical turning points confronted in our life courses. Through these dynamic processes of re-ordering, selecting and re-assembling the random flux of our lives, we constitute an identity as aging men by shaping a narrative account of how we got to be the way that we are.

Furthermore, there is no single unified, coherent narrative that sums up our identity but a diverse multiplicity of possible narrative identities that often compete and clash with each other for a dominant representation in varied contexts and circumstances.

In terms of aging men's lives, my selective focus in this present book will be on 'body narratives' (Sparkes, 1999; Sparkes and Smith, 2002). In the sharing of stories about myself and others, physical disruptions and fractured life events are re-constructed in personal narratives that make sense of our lives and, simultaneously, shape and re-shape our identities over time.

Introducing the Research Participants

These following vignettes of the eight, research participants who contributed so much to my research study offer brief snapshots of their life histories.

RAY was born in the North-East Midlands to working-class parents. He is now a 70-year-old, heterosexual man but he became an asthmatic and labelled as a 'delicate' boy from the ages of 7 and 8. He trained as an electrical apprentice for five years from 1952–57. Later he worked for a variety of companies as an electrician. The longest time he spent working for one firm was from 1976–93 when he was employed as an electrician for a mining equipment firm. The miners' strike (1984–85) had a knock-on effect on the production of mining equipment and the company closed its East Midlands branch in 1993.

Ray was temporarily unemployed and then he worked for a security firm from 1993–98. He retired with ill-health in 1998. He went to Spain for two years and, on coming back to Britain, he became actively engaged in a pensioners' action group and an elders' forum.

BRIAN is a 70-year-old, white, middle-class, heterosexual man. He experienced a disrupted childhood and education as a result of the Second World War and the divorce of his parents. Later he received a public school education at a boarding school. At 16 he joined the army apprentice school and trained as a control equipment technician. Afterwards he spent three years in the Middle East from 1956–59. He was involved in the Suez invasion where he was refurbishing tanks that would have been used if the conflict had continued.

Subsequently, Brian worked as a technical sales engineer and export sales manager for a number of international companies. After retiring in 1988, he became involved as an informal caregiver, as his wife's health deteriorated with a multiple sclerosis-related condition.

DENNIS comes from Jamaica and is a 72-year-old, Afro-Caribbean, working-class man. When he arrived in Britain from Jamaica in 1959 he worked in various construction industry jobs as a semi-skilled mason and labourer. In 1960 he married and had two children. Since 1966 Dennis has been caring for his wife who has mental health problems. He experienced unemployment for nine months before he started to work as a market cleaner in a large shopping centre from 1979–93. He was forced into early retirement at the age of 62. In 2004 Dennis underwent a stomach cancer operation. Since then he has started a health and fitness regime that involves regular exercise, gym work, and a carefully maintained diet.

MICHAEL was born to working-class parents in 1946 in a Derbyshire village. His father was a self-employed property repairer and his mother was a devout Christian. I interviewed him at the age of 60 when he identified himself as a gay man.

Between the ages of 17–21 his brother, father and mother all died leaving Michael in sole charge of the family house. These personal losses contributed to a great deal of confusion in his life during his late teens, including a worried concern about his sexual and gender identities. Indeed, peer group pressure persuaded him to become engaged to an older woman while simultaneously experimenting with his emerging, gay, sexual identities.

In his twenties, however, Michael became much more confident and self-accepting about his sexuality. Through his work as a social worker he was involved in setting up specialised gay support helplines and groups in some of the largest cities in the East Midlands. He established his main career direction by field-working for social services for 17 years, and then worked in the NHS as a HIV specialist until his retirement at the age of 60.

ROBERT was born to working class parents in 1945. His father worked for British rail as head shunter and his mother was a nurse. Robert went to a secondary modern school after failing the 11+ and he left at the age of 15. When I interviewed him he was a 60-year-old, heterosexual man living in retirement.

He has never been married or lived with a woman and has lived alone in a council flat for the last twenty years. In his work he has mainly focused on outdoor, manual labour and for the last twenty years of his working life he worked as a British rail platelayer until being forced to retire through ill-health – the result of a severe neck injury incurred while at work.

Since then, Robert has been an active volunteer. He has also been a panel member of his local borough council and has become involved in a community housing association and other environmental and church issues.

HANIF is a 67-year-old, Pakistani, Muslim man. He was born in Pakistan in 1940. After doing well educationally in Pakistan he became a junior clerk. In 1962 he came to Britain and encountered racist barriers in the Post Office. He first worked on a building site for an engineering firm and then for British Rail. Later he found more long-term work as a bus driver for the local bus company. He became engaged in community and political activist projects. His hard work in the local Pakistani community led to Hanif co-founding the Pakistan Friends' League and then in 1985 he got elected as a county councillor. He developed disc problems in his back and in 1986 he retired through ill-health. From then on he concentrated on community work managing a housing project and advice centre. Most recently he has been involved in a Muslim community group, focusing on youth groups. At home or in the mosque he worships four or five times a day.

ROY comes from working class parents and he was born in 1933 in South Wales. When I interviewed him he was 72 and self-identified as a gay man. He left school at 15 without any educational qualifications, but after working as a general labourer for two years he decided to train as a psychiatric nurse. Over six years Roy trained and widened his experience by working in Chelmsford, London, Montreal and New York, and he gained four nursing qualifications. In 1972 he became assistant matron in a large hospital in the North-East Midlands where he was the senior nursing officer in charge of general divisions.

During the 1980s Roy became actively involved in AIDS' organisations, setting up an AIDS information project at his hospital and also working as a telephone counsellor. Later he became a group member of a gay bereavement group. Roy retired early in 1992 through stress brought on by the pressures of the job and also caring for a dying partner during a period of eight years. Now he has a much younger partner whom he sees four days a week.

PETER is a 64-year-old, white, middle-class, disabled man. He was diagnosed with Parkinson's disease six years ago. He is married with two children. He was born into a middle-class family and has followed his father in becoming a vicar in the Church of England.

After working in the church in community-orientated schemes in an urban context, he became the director of a large voluntary organisation and then later worked for the city council in educational affairs. As a disabled, retired man, Peter was still putting his considerable work, organisational and leadership skills to socially useful effect. He was the driving force behind a local disability group where he was the chairperson. The group had successfully bid for and was awarded a £90,000 research grant for improving the treatment of people with his form of disability, and he also played a major part in creating a hospital exercise programme for disabled survivors.

The Importance of History in Biographical Research

Masculine identities and sexual subjectivities for aging men are not intelligible without an historical dimension. Their present behaviours and practices are directly influenced by the dominant, gendered and sexual standards of their youth (Gott and Hinchcliff, 2003). Sometimes the intensity of their adolescent, emotional investments, in particular masculine and sexual identities, can linger and stay with aging men's fantasies and desires through a long and complex lifetime. The specific historical circumstances shaping their early formative experiences, the shifts and changes in society and cultural contexts that they have lived through all affect how aging men were when they were interviewed and how they are now in 2016.

If we are to do justice to the multi-layered and conflicted, gendered and sexual subjectivities of aging men, we need to chart 'how actual men, with their unique biographies and particular psychic formations' (Jefferson, 2002) construct their masculine identities over their turning and twisting lives. Instead of viewing aging men's identities as natural, unitary and fixed, my research approach wants to stress their diverse and changing forms within historical periods and movements. Aging men's lives are too often seen as settled and over-determined. Often the dynamic volatility and variety of their lives are ignored.

I have made an attempt to link together macro (public histories) and micro (personal stories) forms of analysis that do not deal with abstract structures alone but deliberately move towards an historical dynamic, interweaving of the vitality of everyday, lived experiences within changing, public histories. Also I have adopted biographical and life history methods 'as an emancipatory tool,' (Chamberlayne, Bornat and Wengraf, 2000) that are capable of empowering the hitherto unheard voices of marginalised and invisible aging men, working-class men like Roy, Robert, Ray, Afro-Caribbean working-class men like Dennis and Pakistani Muslims like Hanif.

As such, my engagement with life history methods represents a wider commitment to the biographical 'turn' in the social sciences (see 'research methodology' in chapter two). Chamberlayne, Bornat and Wengraf make clear how important it is to deepen our historical and cultural understandings of people's everyday lives and experiences. They point out that:

> ... to understand oneself and others, we need to understand our own histories and how we have come to be what we are. We make our own history but not under conditions of our own choosing, and we need to understand these conditions of action more if our future making of our own history is to produce outcomes closer to our intentions and projects. (Chamberlayne, Bornat and Wengraf, 2000)

However, the hugely demanding challenges of this kind of historical study are beyond the scope of my more limited and selective research. What I have done is to provide two brief and necessarily simplified historical and cultural contexts for both gay and heterosexual aging men in the UK. These histories and cultural contexts are included in my chapter called, 'An Cultural and Historical Analysis of Aging Men's Sexualities in the UK'. Also in chapter six on aging men and spousal caring I include an historical perspective on, 'The changing meanings of caring in the UK.' I have done this so that readers can examine the eight, research participants' biographical, gendered, sexual histories against the socio-economic background of the last sixty years so that, hopefully, some inter-connections can be made between the broad sweeps of public histories and the eight men's diverse and personal narratives.

I am also aware of the limitations of a strictly linear and chronological approach to these public histories and I acknowledge that there are many more contradictions and reversals in these historical accounts. But for clarity's sake I have identified four main historical periods for both heterosexual and gay aging men from the 1950s to the present day. However, I do not want to view these historical transitions as rigidly linear but wish to take into account the overlapping fluidities between these different periods. In all of this I want to recognise the active adaptations and sheer contradictory variety going on in these aging men's lives. Also I want to pay special attention to the critical turning points (Schiavi, 1999) of these gendered and sexual narratives.

Broadening My Investigation: Setting the Lived Experiences of Aging Men in the UK in a More Global Context

In addition I want to take both a global and local perspective on aging men's masculinities in this book. There is a need to challenge, 'monolithic essentialist visions of an eternal, unchanging masculinity' (Connell, 2007) so that both diversity and commonalities, (Ruspini et al., 2011) in terms of global masculinities, interact with each other. In the world context of global aging, developed, industrial nations like Italy, Japan and the UK are rapidly greying (over the period 1985–2010 the number of people aged 65 and over in the UK increased by 20% to 10.3 million-(Office for national statistics, 2012). There has grown a progressive disparity in wealth between nations, and the less developed nations in Africa, Asia and Latin America are not only relatively poor but are also generating most of the world's population growth (United Nations, 2002).

It is important to understand this wide, international context within which, more local, aging men's masculinities are shaped. Individual lives are influenced by these global forces, such as legacies of imperialism and colonialism, de-industrialisation, global markets, multinational corporations and labour migrations (Connell, 2007).

One of the most powerful influences coming from the global context is the world dominance of the free market economy/political regime (Connell, 2011) over the last twenty-five years. The aging men in my study have all had to confront or endorse some of the key features of the free market economy in their lives, which include a belief in 'free markets' within a climate of economic deregulation that was supposed to open up markets – particularly capital markets. Public assets such as land, railways and electricity have been privatised, the welfare state has been severely eroded, community and collective living seems to have collapsed, and in its place a neoliberal, masculine subject has been constructed, very much an autonomous individual and consumer, self-regulating, reflexive, mobile and infinitely adaptable one (Johnson and Steinberg, 2004).

More locally, in the UK, the break-up of a social-democratic consensus and the introduction of a free market, economic regime started in the 1980s with Thatcherite deregulation of the economy, her adoption of market-led policies and a refusal to offer any state support to halt the decline of heavy industry (Beynon, 2002). The seismic shocks of the Thatcherite deregulation were also experienced in the North-East Midlands of the UK, in the region where my study is based.

One of the largest cities in the North-East Midlands has an estimated city population of 275,100 according to the 2001 census. Its industrial history is based around lace-making, hosiery and coal-mining, little of which now remains. Since the decline of coal-mining in the 1980s and early 1990s, this region has moved towards a more service-based and knowledge-based economy.

Mining jobs that depended on physical strength and robust, bodily toughness rapidly disappeared after the collapse of the miners' strike in 1984–85. It has been estimated that there were about 200,000 mining jobs in the UK before the strike and around 8,000 jobs today (Henshaw, 2005). Many ex-miners are now confronted by a precarious form of living and working. They are either unemployed, seriously injured or working through short-term contracts, low pay and part-time work.

As a result, the subject of masculine embodiment in a global context is too important to ignore here. Embodiment is of central importance to both older, global masculinities and more local contexts like miners' bodies. A hierarchical division of bodies in a global context has not only worked through contrasts of bodily strength, virility and vigour but also by 'constructing particular male bodies as normal or natural while others are seen as pathological or unnatural' (Petersen, 1998). As a result, normalising the bodies of white, able-bodied, heterosexual, European men and constructing them as superior to the supposedly natural different bodies of more diverse, black, gay and non-European bodies is the way that embodied hierarchy works.

Later I show, more specifically, how that embodied hierarchy works through the 'feminization of colonised men' (Connell, 2000). In Hanif's case history this embodied hierarchy is visible where his personal sense of his own bodily 'weakness' is perhaps partly linked to his historical sense of comparative subordination in moving from a recently dominated Pakistan to England where old, imperial attitudes were only slowly fading.

To give a flavour of how both global and local forces have intertwined and shaped the lived experiences of diverse, aging men living in the North-East Midlands of the UK, I want to focus here on three life history snapshots taken from my interviews with some of the research participants (see pages 12–15).

In Brian's case it is possible to discern how he has been partly shaped by global forces such as the free-market economy and the historical legacies of an English, imperialist discourse. At twenty he was engaged in the preparations for the Suez crisis. This individual act needs to be located in the wider, global context that was very much about the decline of the

British Empire, the rise of the US and the final death throes of English supremacy. However, the imprint of imperial manliness still left their indelible mark on Brian in the form of being strong, authoritative, decisive, disciplined and independently resourceful. Brian's arrogant sense of authority seemed to carry over later into his management style while working as an export sales' manager for a number of transnational corporations. In terms of a free-market economy, he was also influenced to become a strongly competitive individualist and a self-regulating, autonomous, masculine subject (Laliberte Rudman, 2006; Sandberg, 2007). I discuss this further and at greater depth in my chapter on 'Aging men's embodied selves: rethinking relationships of change' (Jackson, 2008).

In contrast to Brian's life history, Dennis is a 72-year-old Jamaican, working-class man. He came to the UK in 1959 as a part of the main period of migration from the West Indies to Britain from 1955–62 (Blakemore and Boneham, 1994). He came from a rural background of farming and fishing in Jamaica, responding both to a demand for labour in the Western, industrial world and also as a reaction to decline in rural work opportunities in Jamaica.

Dennis's subordinated position as a migrant worker was both racialised and exploited in a variety of low-paid, insecure, construction industry jobs as a semi-skilled mason and unskilled labourer. His memories and experiences are tinged with having to confront continuous racism and feelings of being unwanted in Britain. But he also expressed pride in his labouring body: 'I was strong and I was able to shovel and concrete and there would be no problem.'

This embodied pride was undermined in Dennis's later life when he was diagnosed with stomach cancer. Dennis was confronted with the shock of not having a physically robust, healthy body anymore. Slowly he became aware that it was possible to move towards a different way of being masculine in the world. It is perhaps through the physical shocks and dislocations in many working-class, aging men's lives that the dominant ideals of embodied, masculine identities and gendered expectations begin to become destabilised, unsettled and more open to possible change.

The complicated processes of labour migration were also the primary, global influences on Hanif's life history. He is a 67-year-old, Pakistan Muslim with an ambivalent class position. After doing well educationally in Pakistan he became a junior clerk but migrated to the UK in 1962 because of personal ambition and family connections already existing in the East Midlands.

At first, Hanif encountered British racism in the Post Office. He was turned down for a job that he could easily have handled. He then experienced a mixture of unskilled labouring jobs, working on a building site in the construction industry. Later he worked in an engineering firm and, briefly, became a British Rail shunter working in Sheffield. Later he found a long-term job working as a bus driver for the local bus company. In all these jobs, he felt that his actual resources and intellectual abilities were not fully recognised by the companies he worked for.

As it has already been noted in our discussion of Dennis's masculine embodiment, it is important to recognise that, 'the formation of masculinities and the meaning of men's bodies is persistently connected with the racialization of global society' (Connell, 2000). In Hanif's case this means the historical legacies of the 'feminization of colonised men' partly negatively influences his attitudes towards his own body. In my interviews with him, his personal owning up of possessing a 'weak body' keeps on coming up. He comments that 'I wasn't a very well-built lad,' and 'I was very young and weak.' He is very much aware of his physical frailty against a wider background of his colonial past. But Hanif is also able to turn this feature to his positive advantage. He says:

> I think being weak has kept me out of a lot of trouble. Being weak has overwhelming benefits for me. Being weak you don't become too aggressive towards others.

Later on in his work as a bus driver, Hanif developed a disc problem in his back and in 1986 he retired through ill health. Very aware of his physical vulnerability as a man, he chose an alternative strategy to restore his masculine pride and status when he admits that he's 'never been a physical fighter':

> I've always been a mental fighter.

What Hanif was referring to, more specifically, was his community and political activism, as he became a county councillor and co-founded the Pakistan Friends' League in his middle-age.

What this local and global interplay has given to my study is a critique of supposedly monolithic, fixed, singular, forms of masculine identity. Instead, there are many different, multiple patterns of masculinity existing within diverse, cultural traditions in many parts of the globe. The influence of global processes is always to be found amongst the specific details of local conditions. As a result, the greying of industrial nations has a mixture of common features about changing masculine identities and specific local traditions.

The Contents of the Book: A Road Map to Specific Chapters.

Chapter 1: Introduction

Here the author explains the context of the book. Its main purpose is to challenge the negative representation of aging men in the UK through exploration of their lived, embodied experiences using detailed interviews and commentaries.

Crucially, in 'Change and Situated Differences in Aging Men's Everyday Lives', the links between socially situated experience and knowledge (in this case older men's experience) and the critical re-positioning of aging men are interwoven. The frequent losses and disruptions of aging men's lives can lead to self-critical change.

Finally, the varied conceptual frames and themes of the book are clarified, including the cultural construction of old age, gender and age, embodiment and identity, the importance of history in biographical research and setting local conditions into a global context.

Chapter 2: Research Methodology

A distinctive feature of this book is the original set of primary data on a variety of older men's experiences. This has been achieved through an unusually extended interview process called, 'intimate conversations.' The author sees this as 'slow research,' appropriate to the daily rhythm and age of the participants. (Thanks to the anonymous reviewer for suggesting this 'slow research' insight.)

The biographical, narrative method is also investigated. The strength of this qualitative methodology lies in the way it allows the researcher to scrutinise the aging process, masculine identities and subjective complexities.

Lastly, the author explores the importance of reflexivity for both researcher and participant, the practical strategies used in the research and alternative forms of enquiry into the subject such as critical autobiography

Chapter 3: Aging Men's Embodied Selves: Rethinking Aging Men's Relationship with their Changing Bodies

Bodies are of central importance in the exploration of aging men's lives. However, the lived bodies of aging men have largely been absent from old age studies, gender studies and sociological literature. In an attempt to fill this void, this chapter specifically focuses on an analysis of the embodied life stories of three aging men.

This analysis reveals the following narratives of aging in action: the biomedical, the positive aging discourse, and the alternative narrative of creative discontinuities and disruptions. Each of these key discourses are critiqued and investigated, and illustrate how studies of aging men have the potential to radically destabilise but also to enrich our conventional practices and theories of men and masculinities.

Chapter 4: A Historical and Cultural Analysis of Aging Men's Sexualities in the UK

Conventionally aging men as sexual beings are seen as past it and worn out. Ageist myths and normative assumptions still obscure our understandings of aging men's sexualities.

This chapter challenges these stale ideas by looking closely at the research evidence of four diverse subjects. This diversity embraces the different worlds of two gay and two heterosexual aging men, as well as one Jamaican man. The new evidence is set within a broader, historical context of different, sexual subjectivities, shifting and changing within a life-course perspective over the last sixty years.

This careful analysis reveals the following key narratives of aging men's sexualities: sex drive; sexual reputation; non-penetrative sex and relationship-focused; sexual retirement and withdrawal; hypersexual; erotic adventure and romantic love narrative.

Chapter 5: Learning to Live with Parkinson's and an 'Unpredictable Body' as an Aging Man: An Investigation into Age, Masculine Identity and Disability

Disability is not only a medical tragedy but a socially oppressed position. The author investigates this claim through examination of one man's struggle with Parkinson's disease. The actual variability of the condition allows the participant to question the masculinity myths of inhabiting a supposedly stable, unified body.

After setting this man's life history into the wider context of contemporary ideas about disability, three main discourses are examined. They are the biomedical, the discourse of embracing bodily vulnerability, and the contradictory discourse of rational control and leadership. The conflicts between these three discourses are investigated and assessed.

Chapter 6: The Challenges and Opportunities of Aging Men's Spousal Caregiving

One of the most startling revelations of this study is that aging men's experiences as caregivers, rather than care receivers, have been largely ignored. Roughly similar proportions of men and women in the UK give informal care to their partners who have chronic physical or mental disabilities.

In challenging this marginalisation, the chapter interrogates two aging men's caregiving experiences, one heterosexual and the other a gay man caring for a partner with AIDS. A key part of this questioning is considering how much aging men's caregiving is instrumental rather than an emotionally nurturing caring.

Chapter 7: Learning the Hidden Skills of Staying Alive: How Do Some Aging, Working-Class Men Survive the Processes of Aging?

The author contests the view that aging men are a problem group and a burden on the community. He suggests the possibility, largely neglected in the field, of alternative insights to be gained from a study of working-class men's survival strategies.

Through an analysis of the life stories of three aging, working-class men, the author reveals a number of resilient resources: the contemplative life and body of a Pakistani Muslim, locally and globally; how early health issues and becoming labelled as a 'delicate boy' helped develop a subject's self-awareness about bodily identity and well-being; and how a position of defiant, class energy led another man to value 'purposeful discontentment' and helped him to thrive.

Chapter 8: Exploring Aging Men's Embodied and Social Agency in a Free Market Economy Context

The author focuses on aging men's ways of retaining independence in later life through the use of bodily and social action to initiate change. Examples of this are set within the context of a free market economy and the erosion of the welfare state.

The research critiques the impact of the free market on the socially vulnerable (including aging and disabled men) and their need for care. In contrast, he describes the caring activities of a virtual, mutual-help group giving collective support through shared emails.

Finally the author cites the example of aging men's defiance through questioning the need for bodily strength and suggesting the advantages of possessing a 'weak', non-aggressive body.

Chapter 9: Conclusion

Key themes are acknowledged and examined. These include the unique features of change in aging men's lives; the distinctive research methodology which captures the emotional realities of the participants; the central importance of aging men's bodies and their contradictory relationship to patriarchy and power,

A major section of the conclusion investigates aging men's complex relationship to standpoint theory and the importance of marginalised knowledges and experiences, especially the different positioning of 'subordinated masculinities' (Connell, 1995). It ends by looking at the inadequate theorisation of aging men and suggests alternative forms of enquiry into their lives.

The Logic of the Chapters

The underlying structure and logic behind the unfolding of the chapters in this book are based on the connecting concepts of 'Subordinated Masculinities' (Connell, 1995) and 'less-normative bodies' (Gerschick, 2005) However, my personal motivation comes first. During this research project I have aged from a man of 65 in 2005 (the start of the project), to becoming a man of 76 in 2016. As a result, I identified myself as a retired man of lesser power living in an impaired body with heart and vascular problems, being closely dependent on pills, having had a cataract operation, a pacemaker fitted and, lately, a hearing aid. So early on in this project I was personally focused on aging men's lived and embodied experiences and the possibly shared common ground between myself as a researcher and the researched.

Therefore, initially in this project, I followed the direction of the interpreted data. Perhaps I unconsciously selected some chapters and subject matters that seemed to have a key relevance to aging men's viewpoints, situations, knowledge and experience. It was only much later that I began to recognise more fully the possible links between my experiences as an aging man and other forms of 'subordinated masculinities' like some ethnically diverse masculinities, working-class, gay, disabled, caring and mentally challenged masculinities. (See 'Change and Situated Differences in Aging Men's Everyday Lives' in this Introduction and 'A Short History of Critical, Men and Masculinities' Studies and Practices' in the Preface.)

Within this broader theoretical context, I began to see that the introduction needed to explain the main purposes of the book – to challenge the deficit narratives associated with old age in the UK and to find alternative narratives (Segal, 2013) of change and difference. The second chapter on the research methodology makes clear that an unusually extended interview process can produce a 'slow research' that is appropriate to the daily rhythm and age of the research participants. The deteriorating, often fragmentary bodies of aging men form the central focus of Chapters 3, 4 and 5. The frequent bodily losses and disruptions of aging men's lives can lead to self-critical, reflexive change, as it does in the lives of Ray, Roy and Dennis. As well as the theoretical connection with 'less-normative bodies', these chapters also engage with the problems of aging men's sexual impotence as in the example of a Jamaican man's struggle in Chapter 4. Again in the same chapter, two aging gay men's different sexualities are also examined at some length as well as those of two, heterosexual men. Chapter 5 moves the reader on to look closely at the disabled challenges faced by one aging man with Parkinson's disease and the demands of an 'unpredictable body.'

At first glance, Chapter 6 on, 'The Challenges and Opportunities of Aging Men's Spousal Caregiving' seems oddly out of place in this context. However, the more the reader considers the marginalisation of certain groups of men from the central principles of dominant masculinities (e.g. tough, aggressive, self-aggrandising and in a dominant position over women), the more likely the reader can see that the caring features of some aging men (e.g. empathetic, nurturing and compassionate) are often relegated as aspects of 'subordinated masculinities', and therefore fit in to the general organising logic of these chapters. It also makes clear how the role of caring for aging men has to work very hard to confront severe cultural barriers in order to be effective.

In Chapters 7 and 8 there is more emphasis on the social lives of aging men, although a concern with aging men's bodies reappears in the latter. Chapter 7 deals with another hidden group of 'subordinated masculinities', in this case, aging, working-class men. This chapter demonstrates how class-based resilience, in some cases, helps aging, working-class men to survive through the rigours of the aging process. These last two chapters also introduce the reader to the different life stories of an aging Pakistan Muslim.

Chapter 8 looks closely at some aging men's autonomous, bodily and social actions to initiate changes in their lives. This discussion is set firmly within the contemporary social context of a free market economy and the erosion of the welfare state. There is a critique of the impact of the free market on the lives of the socially vulnerable (including aging and disabled men.)

A major section of the Conclusion investigates aging men's complex relationship with standpoint theory and the importance of marginalised knowledge and experience, especially the changing viewpoints and positioning of 'subordinated masculinities.'

2
Research Methodology

One of the most unusual and distinctive features of this book is the original set of primary data on a diverse selection of aging men's lived and embodied experiences. This has been achieved through a five-fold interview process, each interview lasting one and a half-two hours. I call this process 'intimate conversations' between the research participants and the researcher. This research method is also exceptional in terms of the length of time these conversations took. As such, this might be referred to as a research method of 'slow research' that often fits the occasional slowing down and more careful scrutiny associated with the changing ages and bodily experiences of the research participants.

I have chosen a qualitative research methodology for this study within a biographical, narrative approach (Chamberlayne, Bornat and Wengraf, 2000; Roberts, 2002) Biographical research is part of a wider practice of qualitative enquiry and methods. Biographical research has developed from an earlier cultural and linguistic turn, including the rise of cultural studies in the social sciences (Chamberlayne, Bornat and Wengraf, 2000), and is now being followed by a narrative, biographical or auto/biographical turn.

First some points about 'narrative' and 'biography'. Narrative is the 'primary form by which human experience is made meaningful' (Polkinghorne, 1988). It does this through organising random flux, actions and experiences into time-based, structured episodes. Biographical-narrative research makes informed use of the narrations of individuals in order to analyse and interpret the complexities of aging men's lives and the social contexts within which these lives are situated. Some of these important contexts are gender, men and masculinities, disability and old age.

Some of my research methods are influenced by Hollway and Jefferson's account of the biographical-narrative-interpretive method

(Hollway and Jefferson, 2000; Rosenthal, 1993; Schutze, 1992). Their emphasis on eliciting stories rather than asking why questions have directed some of my interview questions such as, 'Can you tell me what work has meant to you during your lifetime?' However, I have also had to adapt my methodology to fit into the concrete, actual events of some of these aging men's lives.

So in this research I use spoken language to socially interact with research participants and to stimulate stories, often informed by the culturally ascendant identities of that time and moment. (Often research participants are caught, transitionally, between hanging on to stable, familiar identities and the newly emerging ones.) Through sharing their stories both researcher and participant interpret what has happened and, slowly, there is the production of a narrative text within a database.

My biographical research method, using oral history interviewing methods, seeks to understand the changing experiences and outlooks of aging men in their daily lives set within a social and historical context. The strength of qualitative methods is seen in the way that it allows the researcher to delve deeper into masculine identities and subjective complexities (Emslie, Hunt and O'Brien, 2004). Also, qualitative methods reveal unsuspected disruptions and complex motivations in individual biographies due to physical injury, illness, depression, hospitalisation, loss, grief and so on, that often provoked research participants into re-assessing taken for granted attitudes to gender identities and other intersections with class, race, age, sexual orientation and disability.

Understanding narrative, together, is a crucial part of interpreting the data in this study. In contrast to the positivist, research paradigm that emphasises issues like validity, credibility and reliability, the idea of narrative is 'firmly grounded in qualitative traditions, and stresses the 'lived experience' of individuals, the importance of multiple perspectives, the existence of context-bound, constructed social realities, and the impact of the collaborative processes of researcher and participant working on the research process' (Muller, 1999).

One of the main emphases in understanding narrative is on how the story is formed and how the meanings of the story are mutually constructed between the researcher and the research participant. As Josselson comments:

> ...narratives are not records of facts, of how things actually were, but of a meaning-making system that makes sense out of the chaotic mass of perception and experiences of a life. (Josselson, 1995)

And that 'meaning-making' system' is produced through a mutual process of researcher and participant engaging in the reciprocal processes of making sense of a life.

This leads us on to investigate methodological alternatives to quantitative criteria. The work of Atkinson (1998) and Bornat (1994) help to clarify some of these alternative possibilities. For Bornat, an 'obsessive concern with validity has changed into a more 'relaxed attitude' which has allowed a focus on interpretation by both researched and researcher to surface. This is why I have concentrated my own research focus on opportunities for conversational interaction and shared meaning-making in my study. (See 'Practical research strategies' below where my research participants are invited to take part in five interviews of 1 and a half to two hours each, where they are encouraged to look more closely at gaps, omissions and silences in the fourth interview, and to negotiate joint interpretations of data with the researcher in the final interview.)

The negotiated, dynamic interaction between the researcher and the research participant is at the centre of this approach to an alternative methodology that I have decided to use in my own study. Atkinson reflects that:

> ...quantitative criteria are not required for the interpretation of life story interviews.

Instead the interview is influenced more by the social interaction between the researcher and the researched than theoretical frameworks.(Roberts, 2002)

Atkinson argues that the accuracy of the record of a person's life is not the issue-it is whether the story is 'trustworthy'. He goes on to say:

> ...internal consistency is a primary quality check that can be used by both the interviewer and the storyteller to square or clarify early comments with recent insights, if they appear to be different. (Atkinson, 1998)

Roberts' account of the life story interview makes clearer the context and the interactive nature of the interview:

> ...there is the context of the interview-the prior expectations of the participants, the dialogical or conversational character of the interaction and subsequent (post-interview) interaction between researcher and researched. The questions, cues, prompts,

clarifications, examples, anecdotes. Self-editing and reassurances and other aspects of the interacting 'frame' what is remembered, but it is not a one-way process: the researcher brings a life experience and memories which inform the relationship and may well be alluded to. (Roberts, 2002)

Reflexivity

The reflexive monitoring of my own involvement in this study of aging men's lives is an important part of the research process. As biographical researchers we make sense of our own lives as we try to make sense of the lives of others. So during the research process our own biographical experiences and feelings are involved. For example, my treatment of the life stories of Brian and Roy in my study of aging men as spousal carers is directly influenced by my own emotional preferences, unconscious biases and desires to present myself in the study as a particular kind of pro-feminist man in the gender relations' field. In this context I wanted to confirm my progressive credentials as an anti-sexist, older man by over-identifying with the principles of emotional nurturing against instrumentality, and setting up a far too rigid, binary opposition between Brian/instrumentality/negative quality on one side and Roy/nurturing/positive quality on the other. Learning from my mistakes, I want to dissolve the oppositional structure that I have forced these two life stories into and re-frame my dealings with these two life stories by re-integrating both Brian and Roy within a more fluid continuum that illustrates the complex interrelationship of doing practical things, feeling affection and occasional nurturing.

Another area of problematic difficulty in my research was sticking to my chosen approach of grounded theory (Glaser and Strauss, 1967). I was already alert to the danger of imposing a pre-existing, theoretical framework on the data I had collected. Instead, I wanted ideas, concepts and key questions to slowly emerge from close, detailed reading of the data and sharing interpretations with research participants. Although I closely followed these principles in dealing with Brian's and Roy's life stories, my prior reading of theoretical articles on gender and caring influenced me in my selection of one of my key, research questions:

Are aging men as caregivers to be seen as mainly instrumental and managerial in their styles of caring and how much are they engaged in emotional and nurturing caring?

Before my analysis of the data, I had been reading an article on, 'Masculinities and care work in old age' (Calasanti, 2003) where she discusses Russell's comment that:

> ... thus men can often separate and detach 'caring for' from 'caring about', and this assumed ability to detach and separate emotional from functional aspects of care is thought to provide a buffer to stress. (Thompson, 2000; Russell, 2001)

I now regret my decision to allow pre-existing, theoretical questioning to partly dictate my formulation of the research question above. The other research question on relationship dynamics evolved more gradually from a careful pondering of the collected data.

Conversational Interaction and Shared Meaning-Making

Probably the most distinctive feature of this research process is the focus on intimate conversations between the research participants and the researcher. The richness of the resulting data comes directly from these intimate conversations. This quality of intimacy between aging men and a male researcher instead of defensive wariness has been produced through a combination of different factors: first the length and engagement of the interviewing process; the quality of the relationship between the research participants and the researcher, and the prioritising of internal complexity and contradiction in the interviewing process of aging, masculine subjects (Connell and Messerschmidt, 2005).

The extended length and engagement of the interviewing process was a key part of this research project. I felt that aging men needed time and space to thaw out their initial suspicion and distrust. Some of the most emotionally honest interactions between the researcher and the researched came in the fourth or fifth interviews after a slow building up of mutual trust and relative openness.

The growing quality of the relationship between the research participants and the researcher was closely connected to their shared physical vulnerability and the researcher's 'insider' knowledge of confronting similar problems (e.g. glaucoma, heart problems, blood pressure anxiety etc.) in his own life. In the 'Preliminary interview' and elsewhere during the interviews, short, autobiographical incidents were occasionally shared by the researcher if the context was appropriate. The intimacy of the conversations between the researcher and the research participant often depends on the emotional depth of the studies. 'Most studies of old age focus on the outer self,' (Hazan, 1994) but what I was prioritising in these five, research interviews were explorations of aging men's inner selves. By this I mean creating a talking space for the research participant, with the support of the researcher, to investigate his own 'motives, emotions, desires' (Jefferson, 2002). This is what I mean by internal complexity.

At the end of the research project all of the eight participants were asked about their impressions of the interviewing and shared meaning-making process. What came through generally was an atmosphere of growing mutuality and trust. Hanif commented that:

> I think we are talking like two friends. We are just going through a life history. One friend wants to know about the other friend.

Brian remarked that:

> I think that older people probably would benefit from being able to sit back and have a look at their life.

This note of self-reflexiveness was expanded by Dennis into a more collective, collaborative form. He said:

> ...what we have gathered may be able to help somebody when they look back at the book and they say, 'Oh, I'm suffering from this.'

And again:

> ...we are interdependent upon each other. And I believe in that one: that we should share our knowledge.

But two other research participants, Robert and Ray, were more focused on what they learnt from the process of being interviewed. Robert said:

> I've learnt a lot about myself. It's made me think about how I think about things.

And Ray added a more social action version of what he had learned:

> I've also learnt that older people should be more active and shouldn't just sit back and let things happen to them.

Practical Research Strategies

My research strategies cover five main areas:

1. The 'insider' quality of the interviews; I have opted for greater emotional intimacy and a psychologically in-depth approach (5 interviews of roughly one and a half hours/2 hours each but recording only interviews 2–4) of a selectively focused, small scale kind rather than aiming for a wider representativeness.
2. Preliminary interview: an introductory, unrecorded meeting between the researcher and the researched that explains the project, offers reassurance about the confidentiality of the project and gives a chance, in an informal setting, to develop empathy and trust between the researcher and the research participant. Adequate time was given to the research participants to start talking about their own life histories.
3. Creating independent space in the processes of the research for the participant's selection and elaboration of life narratives through the sharing of his individual biography.
4. The importance of the fourth interview: this interview offered a more reflexive, pondering time to mutually explore the research participant's own words, narratives, key images, contradictions, gaps and significant silences arising from a shared interpretation of the first three interviews.
5. Preliminary findings: the research participants were invited to an exploratory meeting where the researcher shared his first perceptions of the emerging patterns of interpretation and invited questions and suggestions for revision. The meeting offered a more democratic space to negotiate joint interpretations of data with the participants. This meeting ended up being an individual encounter between the research participant and the researcher rather than a collective coming together of the whole group.

The Diversity of the Research Participants

Saint-Aubin (2004) in a critical review of books on aging men draws the readers' attention to a narrow, limited focus on white, middle-class and heterosexual men in these books. For these studies to become more fully representative of the wider populations of aging men, a broader diversity of aging men needs to be carefully selected for their investigations.

Bearing this wider perspective in mind, eight research participants were recruited in my own research from the local web of social networks, community organisations and activist groups (mainly focusing on men's health, a local Parkinson's group and a pensioners' action group). I made a conscious effort to ensure that there was a wide range of class-based, ethnic, racial, gay and heterosexual etc. participants. These groups were located in a part of the North and East Midlands in the UK.

Concentrating my focus on 'activist' groups and community-minded research participants does give a socially and politically engaged bias to my selection of aging men. I am aware of this trend but hope that the bias does not give a lop-sided viewpoint to the research.

A purposeful sampling strategy was selected to ensure inclusion of a diverse range of older, disabled men. They included: different ages and partnership arrangements (living alone or living with a partner or spouse); diverse losses (loss of partner, different levels of impairment or disability); varied minority ethnic groups (African-Caribbean, Pakistani Muslim); different sexual orientation (two gay men of very different ages were interviewed): two men looked after their ill spouses or partners. Many of the men were affected by chronic illness or physical impairment, which included long-term asthma, glaucoma, bad backs, colon cancer, Parkinson's disease, and many minor ailments.

Class relations were an important aspect of the research, especially the focus on working-class, older masculinities, although there was also a connected interest in middle-class masculinities. Working-class masculinities were closely interrogated because of their subordinated and marginalised position (Emslie, Hunt and O'Brien, 2004) in relation to more dominant masculinities.

Having made a close, detailed reading of the research data, I approached the interview transcripts purposefully on the lookout for emerging themes. In this I was guided by my reviews of the relevant literature, and I was able to identify the following thematic emphases: health, age, bodies, disability, sexualities, work, family relations, housing and economic position, friendship, social isolation, loneliness and political engagement.

Alternative Forms of Enquiry into Aging Masculinities

Over the last twenty years I have searched for alternative forms of exploration and analysis that would begin to capture, more adequately, the everyday, fragmentary realities of my own, embodied life from my early fifties to my present age of a 75-year-old, disabled, aging man, and the lived experiences of other aging men. This I have done through critical autobiography, (Jackson, 1990; 2001;, 2003) and through biographical research (Jackson, 2016).

Critical autobiography is a mode of social enquiry that explores the dynamic interaction between social forces, contexts and personal narratives. It is not intended to be individualistic or narcissistic (see Church, 1995; Jackson, 1990). As Hearn comments about my use of critical autobiography:

> ... [he] uses his own life as a resource to theorise his male selfhood and gendered construction of boys and men more generally. (Hearn, 2007)

In this book about, 'Aging Masculinities', I only include, sparingly, five traces of critical autobiography because I do not want to divert attention from the complex lives of the eight, research participants. They are:

- The personal roots of my project
- The first interview with Peter
- An oppositional example of social agency: the collective interaction of a virtual, mutual help group of aging men
- A short history of critical, men and masculinity studies and practices in the UK
- Aging men as researchers

I feel that these autobiographical fragments are included here because they are more closely integrated into the main themes of the book.

Learning to Become a Social Researcher

This piece is included here to illustrate the difficulties and contradictions I, as a person learning to become a social researcher, encountered in the process of interviewing aging men like Peter, who was struggling to come to terms with Parkinson's disease.

'There was a clenched, edgy feel to my body as I arrived at Peter's house for the first, recorded interview in September, 2007. The last year had been an extremely frustrating time for me as an independent researcher desperate to locate a disabled, aging man who was prepared to talk to me openly and honestly about his disability as well as his life history.

My anxious and frustrated body was weighed down by the year-long search that I had just lived through. In my busy body I felt a pressing need to rush on and get this interview recorded and in the bag. I was driven by a research agenda which was targeted on finished product and outcome. However, when I entered Peter's house I found out from his partner that he was sleeping after taking his mid-day pills. I was shown into their front room and given a cup of tea. After the tea I decided to close my eyes and have a short rest myself.

About twenty minutes later, Peter appeared in the doorway but I had calmed down enough to recognise that I was tired out and I needed to slow down. It was as if Peter's body had dictated an entirely different pacing of the session for both of us, not just him. I started to acknowledge the unfamiliar realities of his daily routine. I think I was learning that to communicate with him during the research process I needed to start respecting his uncertain bodily realities and stop trying to force him into the task-orientated frame that I had imagined him fitting into.

About half way through the first interview, Peter interrupted the sharing of his life story and said that he was becoming too tense and stressed in his body and he needed to switch to doing things that made him relax more. So I stopped the digital voice recorder and then we walked slowly around Peter's garden and went on into his kitchen and had a glass of water each.

At first I was a bit surprised and put out by Peter's intervention. But later I began to understand that what Peter had done was a constructive challenge that provoked me into learning a bit more about myself as a researcher and about the fragmented world Peter was inhabiting. By interrupting the recording he shifted the unequal power dynamic operating between us and re-defined the terms of our future pattern of communication within the interview.

After his interruption I became more aware of his emotional, mental and physical boundaries and started to re-think my expectations of what Peter could manage. I wondered whether an hour and a half was too long for him and began to re-arrange a much shorter interview in my head. Perhaps the usual recorded interviews needed to be split into four, five, even six?

Peter's noticing of problematic bodily signs challenged us, and particularly me, into a re-pacing of the interview. I was being challenged to slow down enough in order to recognise the emotional, mental and physical demands I was making of Peter during the interview. Through his assertive behaviour Peter helped to create a more democratic and equal space between us.

Peter indirectly persuaded me to modify my rigidly, pre-determined agenda and then invited me into experiencing something of the confusions and irregularities that he was having to face in his everyday living. Through interrupting my semi-structured agenda he motivated me to edge closer, in my own terms, to the unpredictable and erratic, daily rhythms of his embodied self.

In the shortened, second half of the first interview; we took turns to reflect on what the interruption had meant to both of us. Peter commented that he needed a change in activity because of the build-up in mental and bodily tension:

> I mean this is not exactly relaxed sitting down – it's comfortable but it's not relaxed because I am having to think about things which are, of themselves, requiring some attention and some tension.

Later in the interview I stopped being the facilitator of the interview and I'm recorded on the tape as saying:

> I wanted to make a comment about the pace of this interview with you at the moment which seems to have been changed according to the actual, different pace of what you can manage...

Peter responds to this by saying:

> Yes, I think that's true.

I then finish the reflection by saying:

> And that in a way helps us to communicate.

Perhaps both Peter and myself could meet each other more fully and vulnerably in a slowed down and disrupted form of the interview?

The other key result of the interruption was the rupturing of my taken for granted assumptions about the usual length and style of the interviews. Peter jolted me into a self-critical reflection on my inappropriate expectations about how the first interview should have gone.

By the end of the interview I, as a social researcher, had been shaken awake into relating to Peter as a more fully rounded, complex human being rather than viewing him, exclusively, as a Parkinson's victim.

3
Aging Men's Embodied Selves: Rethinking Aging Men's Relationships with their Changing Bodies

Previous research on men and masculinities as well as the field of aging studies has largely ignored aging men and aging men's bodies in particular (Calasanti, 2004; Fennel and Davidson, 2003; Fleming, 1999; Hearn, 1995; Thompson, 2004). Accordingly, this chapter draws on data from a three-year study in the East Midlands' area of the UK that explores aging men's lived and embodied experiences.

Specifically, an analysis of the life stories of three of the research participants from the study revealed the following discourses of aging in action: the biomedical, the positive aging, and the alternative discourse of creative discontinuities and disruptions. Each of these discourses will be examined and critiqued in relation to the ways in which they shape the masculine subjectivities of these aging men.

I hope to illustrate that the processes of aging and bodily adaptations in aging men's later lives bring about changes in the meanings of masculinity. As a result, the chapter ends with a discussion of how studies have the potential to radically destabilise and enrich our conventional practices and theories of masculinity.

Prior to investigating the tangled complexity of these aging men's lives, a number of conceptual frames that inform my analysis will be outlined. These conceptual frames are: embodiment, gender, and embodied and narrative-based selfhood.[1]

Embodiment

Bodies are of central importance in the exploration of aging men's lives, both their intimate experiences and sensations of their lived in bodies and their social or discursive bodies. However aging men's bodies have been largely absent (Fleming, 1999; Oberg, 1996) from gerontological and sociological literature (Tulle-Winton, 2000). Therefore in this chapter I want to bring aging men's embodied selves into greater, critical visibility. Also I want to draw attention to the way that frequent bodily interruptions in old age disrupt normative bodily habits and rhythms and often lead to destabilisation and life review re-assessment.

Gender

Many aging men are still privileged (especially heterosexual, white, middle-class, able-bodied, aging men) by a complex web of gender relations that often subordinate women and other marginalised men of lesser power. Gender can be seen as a dynamic set of power relations within a specific culture and society at a particular historical moment.

In many aging men's lives there is a contradictory mixture of some legacies of gender privilege interacting with the threat of loss, bodily fragility and defeat. Aging men's greater access to occupational pension schemes and the relatively low number of women over 65 who have financially adequate state pensions produces considerable gender inequality between many older women and aging men. Add to these injustices the unacknowledged legacies, for many older women, of unpaid domestic labour, unpaid informal caring and childcare, and one can get a sense of the largely hidden social injustices here.

However it is not as simple as that. Although some aging men's inherited privileges through a life course is still very significant, 'Not all men have access to the patriarchal dividend' (Hatchell, 2007). Some working-class, black, disabled and other aging men are having to confront forms of inequality in a much more nuanced and complex way.

Embodied and Narrative-Based Selfhood

A sense of self is not something we are born with, innate and essentialised, but something socially produced through the narratives people use to make sense of and understand their lives. We all keep on telling stories about our embodied experiences, both to ourselves and to others (Lawler, 2008). Through these processes of re-ordering, selecting and re-assembling the random flux of our lives, we constitute a sense of self as we shape a narrative account of how we got to be the way that we are (Steedman 1996). This narrative of self cannot stand alone but must partly depend on wider, cultural narratives (Lawler, 2008) like the narrative of inevitable, bodily decline in aging studies. Also there is not a single, unified, coherent narrative of self but a diverse multiplicity of possible narrative selves often competing with each other for dominant representation.

An Exploration of Three Aging Men's Embodied Selves

I want to investigate how three diverse, aging men (snapshots of their life histories can be found on pages 12–15 of the 'Introduction') bodily engage with the dominant conceptions of aging and a gender-focused examination of men and masculinities, and question how these different men negotiate these processes.

Drawing upon the evidence of my study on the lived experiences of aging men, I want to use three life stories to question how these men related to their bodies as they age. In doing this I also want to emphasise the point that aging men's embodied selves are contradictory, contested sites where multiple meanings are in dynamic conflict with each other.

Ray

On the surface, Ray seems to fit in to one of the central conceptions of aging – that of the biomedical discourse and a linked discourse of failed or diminished masculinities. Having struggled with asthma from the early age of 7 or 8 and having had severe respiratory problems for some of that time, Ray's life history seems to conform to the biomedical perspective that represents men's aging bodies as associated with inevitable physical and mental decline, illness and decay. Viewed from this angle, aging men like Ray would be seen as a health and social care problem and dependent on younger people to provide the support and care he needs and therefore adding to the overall burden on society.

These negative images of aging are also intensified by a society and culture that projects distorting and inaccurate cultural representations onto aging men. As a result, aging men are surrounded by, 'Invasive and negative images that associate old age with ill-health, mental decline, disability and passivity' (Townsend et al., 2006).

A life course focus on Ray's 70 years of lived experiences certainly seems to support this initial impression of bodily weakness and fragility. During the interviews he admitted that, 'Asthma has probably shaped my life quite a bit'. He also says that, 'bearing in mind that I had a chest problem, I wasn't always capable of doing games.' From an early age, when he was officially diagnosed with asthma, he was side-lined from the dominant norms of masculinity and opportunities to identify as masculine (particularly through constructing a combative, physically active, gendered self through an engagement in regular, sporting activities.)

Through his early life Ray acknowledges that he has 'never been particularly physical' and that he 'kept on the periphery of things.' This meant that he 'didn't quite feel that I fitted in' with the dominant culture of young, working-class masculinities' involvement in 'fighting, fucking and football' (Mac an Ghaill, 1994). Instead, he was negatively labelled as a 'delicate boy' (notice the effeminising threat of 'delicate') and bullied through being talked about 'as though I wasn't there.'

Although Ray tried to defend himself from the pain and emotional distress of being bullied ('I suppose there was a bit of bullying but it was nothing too serious.') by deliberately minimising the emotional effects, his personal hurt comes through obliquely in his account of an asthma attack. Perhaps it is plausible to suggest that some unconscious aspects of his buried hurt were linked to the emergence and continuing struggle to overcome asthma? Ray describes a bad, asthma attack like this:

> You stop breathing and you feel the restriction and it's not particularly breathing in that's the problem it's breathing out. That's what I found anyway. And you can hyperventilate can't you? You can breathe in okay but then you can't get rid of it and that causes a lot of panic.

This stifling and constriction of his embodied, masculine selves also seem linked to his bodily sensation of panic and distress at not being able to breathe out properly. It is almost as if his physical incapacity is an integral part of not being recognised (talked about 'as if I wasn't there') and not being allowed to express himself, adequately, in a bully boy culture.

This restrictive narrowing of his emotional and expressive abilities led Ray to searching for something different in his life as a young man. Although he was still being bullied in his early days of his electrician apprenticeship, he joined a theatre group in the East Midlands region. This allowed him to take acting parts that 'portrayed a different class of person' and, in a way, also allowed him to loosen and release his expressive voice. Later, Ray wondered whether that was a way of 'moving up a class via the drama.'

During his adult, working life, Ray worked for a variety of different companies as an electrician. But it was during the 1980s and early 1990s in the UK that most affected working-class men like Ray:

> Millions of men in the advanced economies lost their jobs and economic authority in the succession of recessions throughout the 1980s and early 1990s. (Beynon, 2002)

The Thatcherite deregulation of the economy, the dominance of market-led policies within the overall decline of manufacturing and heavy industry led to Ray losing his job because of a corporate down-sizing (Wagner, 1997). At that time he was working for a company that produced equipment for the mining industry. Ray's experience of that time went like this:

> We were doing the electronics for massive coal-cutting machinery, and of course when the cuts came in the mining industry [1984–85] I suppose they had to cut down and reassess the business and, consequently, the branch [where Ray worked] was the first to go.

These economic and social set-backs had marked emotional and bodily implications for aging men like Ray. After a period of unemployment in his late fifties (the poorest time of his life), he moved into the service sector from the manufacturing sector to work for a security firm. The wages were very low and Ray felt guilty about not providing for his family. He also felt that his carefully acquired skills were drastically undervalued.

All this undermining at work directly affected Ray's health and his asthma/respiratory condition. As Ray comments about that time:

> It did affect my health and I started getting chest infections and, whether it was the stress of the job or the actual environment I'm not quite sure. Obviously it was in a closed environment and there were no windows to look out of and it could feel a bit claustrophobic as well.

Again, a stifling context where he felt emotionally and physically confined has directly affected his breathing and chest condition. Ray was working in the 'cash' part of the security firm:

> What the company used to do, [...] was to bring cash from companies who didn't have the facilities to count their own money so they'd send it to us and we'd count it and bank it for them.

Ray's description of his last working experience focuses on the imprisoning suffocation of the job. He comments:

> It was enclosed. There were no windows and to get out you had to go through two security doors and you had to get permission to go out...

His personal and bodily alienation is accurately caught here. Lacking money himself he is paid a pittance for counting other companies' profits and in an airless context where his every movement is regulated and controlled. After five years of working under these conditions he retired at 63 because of ill-health recognising that, '...in another five years I wouldn't be alive to enjoy my retirement.'

However, Ray refused to be totally, negatively defined by the biomedical and 'failed masculinity' discourses. Despite what Ray called the 'obvious deterioration' of physical aging with the everyday, 'aches and pains of aging', Ray had developed a more mature acknowledgement of the physical realities of aging. He still had to take his inhaler every day but without the work stress and the stifling context of the job he could 'walk for miles.' He also felt that he was able to pace himself more shrewdly: 'You had to be aware of your limitations, I think, and not to try and do too much.' This development also went hand in hand with an awareness that masculine myths of self-sufficiency and a tendency to force yourself beyond your bodily capacity need to be broken and re-constructed. Ray commented that:

> If you've got something to lift and you know you can't do it then you get someone to help you rather than try it by yourself. I do sometimes think: 'Shall I do it or shall I not?' and I think: 'No, don't be silly. Ask for help.'

Some of the alternative, unexpected advantages of being diagnosed as a 'delicate', asthmatic boy began to surface through the interviews. The odd, isolating experiences of his younger years of not fitting in with the taken for granted norms of a dominant, masculine culture, seemed to produce in Ray a different way of being as an older man. His sense of early marginalisation assisted him, in later life, to develop a more thoughtful awareness of his embodied selfhood.

At the age of 70 Ray talked about living through, 'One of the healthiest times of my life.' He explained this by linking it to the gradual growth of an embodied self-awareness about, 'thinking about breathing slowly in and out', as a way of improving his asthma. He maintained that this self-reflexive process, initiated by a lifelong experience of asthma, gave him more of an understanding, 'of my own and other people's situations.'

There are some tentative hints in the data that Ray is in the process of making the transition from the discourse of 'failed masculinity' towards an emerging discourse of sociable masculinity and communal well-being and interdependence (Townsend et al., 2006). Edward Thompson also makes the point that, 'Later life masculinities seem to be defined by norms of sociability,' and reveal more vividly, 'men seeking connection with others' and less, 'by the triumphs they used to define themselves as younger men' (Thompson, 2006).

At 70, Ray seems to position himself as a practiser of 'norms of sociability.' He is very involved in social activism and other groups where there is a great deal of social interaction. He takes an active part in the Pensioners' Action Group and the Elders' Forum and is on the committee of his local allotment group. He says:

> I don't miss work now, no. But I probably would miss something if I wasn't so involved in other things now and that takes the place of work.

When I asked Ray, 'What do these groups and networks mean to you?' he answered:

> Well there is the social aspect of meeting people and we have guest speakers and we can get a lot of information usually about older people and it keeps you in touch with what's happening.

This emphasis on communal well-being rather than competitive individualism in Ray's later life is seen clearly in his response to my question on religion and spirituality:

> Spirituality is not quite the same thing as religion, is it? It's more a feeling of empathy for other people around you. And I think my feeling about religion is what it should be: a concern and consideration for other people rather than someone persuading you to be like that.

Brian

Here I will investigate the embodied, masculine, life story of Brian through looking more closely at how he negotiates the subject positions offered by the 'positive aging' discourse and the complex intersections within that discourse of neo-liberal ideology and the ways it addresses the 'desired modern retiree' (Sandberg, 2007; Laliberte-Rudman, 2006); dominant forms of embodied masculinities related to sport and the military and the historical influences of an English, imperialist discourse mainly encountered in Brian's life during the preparations for the Suez invasion in 1956.

The 'positive aging' discourse is very seductive in that it seems to offer an immediate escape from the restricted narrative of decay and inevitable decline found within the biomedical discourse. The 'positive aging' narrative doesn't see aging as a disease and substitutes instead an heroic 'image of agelessness' (Townsend et al., 2006) within an anti-aging culture heavily marketed and targeted towards the grey consumer. Such a culture offers new, constructive emphases on physical activity, leisure sports in order to promote satisfaction and health. Involved here are fantasies of prolonging youth and mid-life styles and a focus on what are termed 'adaptation-skills that reduce dependency on public healthcare systems' (Katz and Laliberte-Rudman, 2004).

At 70, Brian does not want to be primarily defined by the conventional limitations and constraints associated with old age. He says:

> I think in some respects I am weary of this old age label and I am reluctant to be old aged.

And again:

> ... there is no connection between what your age is and how you are.

Brian defines himself as a 'fitness fanatic'. He is very proud of his extremely fit body and physical capacity, running full marathons and climbing mountains in Scotland. He comments in a very brisk and assertive manner:

> I can walk ten or fifteen miles without any significant problem. I can climb all of the British mountains and enjoy doing so.

Taking a life course perspective on Brian's gradual construction of his masculine embodiment and selves, it is possible to see how his present, embodied selves at 70 have been partly shaped by gendered, sporting experiences over a lifetime.

His first reference, in the interviews, to his body is to a ruthless and competent, fighting and warrior body at nine and a half when, according to Brian, he 'kicked all manner of shit out of these boys', referring to three older boys at his recently entered public school who were trying to bully him.

At 16 he joined the army and quickly developed a fiercely competitive, strong body. Perhaps under the strictly disciplined, bodily regime of regimented, military training Brian became 'a good, middle-distance runner' and in the 'top two or three in the gymnastic, display team.'

From about his late teens, playing rugby initiated him into the more savage sporting world of embodying force and violence. Brian comments that playing rugby in the army 'was a matter of kicking, pulling, pushing and punching.'

In all of this bodily shaping and disciplining there was a dominant streak of competitive individualism. For example, during his army training Brian describes a key incident for him of racing the bus from Chepstow back to camp:

> It is a very steep climb out of Chepstow and there is a path which goes up the cliff-side which is very much a short cut and it takes about a mile off the journey. We could actually race the bus back to camp on foot because the bus used to stop, of course, and we didn't.

Here, Brian sems to be relishing the risky edge to the challenges he is setting for himself and others. He appears to be thriving on pushing himself to his limits while tackling the 'very steep climb' and the dangerous 'cliff-side' path. It is almost as if he can't experience himself fully without driving himself to take on these risky challenges and edges.

However, later in his life, Brian went through a key, transitional moment that changed his customary dialogue with his body. During his work in the Middle East he was working so hard he stopped all normal forms of exercise and drank a lot to relieve the pressure. One day he understood, more clearly, how relatively unfit he was when he attempted to run upstairs to 'get to the showers first', and then Brian realised, 'I could hardly see and my heart was pounding away and then I thought, "Christ, what a state you've got yourself in!"'

This revelatory moment in Brian's life introduces a tone of finger-wagging, self-disgust and moralistic admonition into his life narrative. This new, self-critical note of, 'regarding myself as a slob,' shows Brian entering a world of bodily self-regulation and self-policing. He begins to reflect on the condition of his embodied self:

> I first became aware that my body would go off if I let it.

Between about 30–35 Brian internalised this self-regulatory, embodied regime. He moved into a strict exercise routine and he took up jogging and running. That has continued to the present day. His body was turned from a 'slobbish' one into a much more tightly disciplined body with specific goals, targets and challenges. His body has become the object of a self-critical and occasionally self-punishing review. For example, Brian organises a very carefully worked out bodily preparation for running the marathon in his recent life as an older man in retirement. Brian says:

> I still set myself goals. I walk around Bestwood Country Park so from my house and then back to my house is a nice twelve mile walk. There is a short cut through the park where there is a short but very steep hill and I always manage to walk that hill non-stop and keep walking at the top.

This, almost obsessive, self-policing of his embodied self produces just the kind of modern retiree that neoliberal ideology is predicated upon.

In Brian's case it is possible to recognise how much he has been shaped by the 'positive aging' discourse and neoliberal perspectives to become 'independent, autonomous and responsible' (Sandberg, 2007). Also, as Lynne Segal suggests, Brian's masculine fears of dependency (perhaps viewing it as a form of 'weakness') have shaped an over-valuing of autonomy and independence in his life history (Segal, 2013) instead of learning to recognise the social importance of mutual interdependence. As a result, Brian is comfortable in being a 'solitary individual', extremely self-reliant and without friends. These discourses maximise individual responsibility for health, welfare, and well-being rather than seeing them as also the collective responsibility of the state. The political goals behind these emphases on independence and autonomy are clear to see; governments want to minimise dependency and universal entitlements and also want to decrease public sector expenditure (Laliberte-Rudman, 2006).

At the heart of the 'positive aging' discourse is the attempt to capture the desires and longings of a relatively affluent, middle-class, older man like Brian who wishes to prolong his youth and fitness. It also recommends clinging on to the enticing promises of an anti-aging, market-led culture that doesn't listen to the limitations of age or decay.

When I asked Brian the question: 'Are you ageless?' he replied:

> ...in most respects I am, so far, although I'm apprehensive about getting old and infirm. Physically I'm virtually as good as I was at 40, in terms of stamina and ability to do physical things.

The historical legacies of an English, imperialist discourse are also still very much with Brian at 70. Although Brian at 20 was closely involved in the preparations for the Suez crisis – 'refurbishing tanks for three tank regiments' – the wider, social context was very much about the decline of the empire and the final death throes of English supremacy. However the imprint of imperial manliness still left their marks on Brian.

The origins of empire in Victorian and Edwardian Britain (Beynon, 2002) still left some questionable but powerful expectations about English men being supposed to be 'strong, authoritative, decisive, disciplined and resourceful' (Beynon, 2002). Assumptions about the, supposedly, innate superiority of English masculinities to other races still guided Brian's dealings with 'foreigners.' Brian admitted that:

> I have a great regard for the ability and the competence and the general good that the British empire did.

In his dealings with other races in the Middle East in 1956–59, a nationalistic arrogance emerges:

> Brian: I had complete confidence that they (Arabs, Cypriots and Libyans) would listen to what I had to say and would respect what I had to say and they would probably do what I asked them to do.
>
> DJ: Was that a kind of imperial deference?
>
> Brian: Yes. It was definitely there. Even with the very able Arab and various Asian nation technicians, they would listen to what I had to say. Because I was white and because I was English this still mattered. I didn't need to milk it but I was able to get them to listen to me because of who I was and what I was. I hadn't done anything to achieve this. It had been done donkey's years earlier.

The complex coming together of historical influences in Brian's life, along with dominant forms of masculinity very much shaped through sporting activities and military training, meshed into the seductive discourses of 'positive aging' and the neoliberal project have forged Brian into a very proud, fit and self-reliant older man.

But the darker shadows of what Brian is keeping hidden in his life are partly discernible in the significant emotional resonances that co-exist alongside his pride and fitness. When I asked him about what he feared most as an aging man, he answered:

> ...disability... at the moment I remain dextrous; I remain quite strong; I remain fit and these things enable me to do a whole host

of things that perhaps if I was disabled I would not be able to enjoy. Inability as well as disability, I think, are the two things that concern me with regards to advancing old age.

It seems plausible to suggest that Brian's heroic, self-aggrandising, embodied, masculine selves have been constructed through a systematic othering and expulsion of what he fears most – physical inadequacy, disability and loss of a fiercely competitive, bodily mastery and control. In assembling himself as a marathon runner and imperial, 'fortress' man, it seems possible that he is simultaneously defending himself from his anxieties about aging and the pain and hurt associated with a disrupted childhood in the second world war and the divorce of his parents. Brian comments about his disrupted childhood in this way:

> From being a young child – six or seven – my life was in turmoil, so having to come to terms with relying on myself I then almost became dismissive of other people's assistance because I thought that I could do it anyway so why bother to let other people do it.

Instead of confronting the 'turmoil' of his early life, Brian has built a self-protective myth of independence and self-sufficiency around himself and, in doing so, has possibly attempted to conquer his pain through the construction of an heroic, performance, embodied self.

Dennis

Many aging men are stuck within the binary construction of an either/or approach to old age. Ray's and Brian's life stories (even though with contradiction and an occasional refusal to conform) have revealed the ways that aging men are sandwiched between the cultural ideals of staying young and fit within the 'positive aging' discourse and the bleak equation between old age and bodily decline in the biomedical discourse.

What is now urgently needed is more sustained, investigative research, searching for possible alternative discourses that are capable of breaking out of these binary traps. Or as Emmanuelle Tulle has commented: 'what we need now are ways of imagining old bodies that aren't predicated on their disappearance' (Tulle, 2004).

Dennis's life story offers some possible glimpses of what these alternative perspectives might look like. At this stage these are tentative hints and suggestions only but perhaps a start for future research. Here, I'm going to explore an alternative suggestion of a different kind of discourse built upon the idea of creative discontinuity and radical disruption in the lives of some aging men like Dennis. My selective focus here is on two main aspects of Dennis's life history; his experience at 69 of a major stomach cancer operation and his connected experiences of sexual impotence.

Dennis is a 72-year-old, Afro-Caribbean, older man. He came to Britain in 1959 as a part of the main period of migration from the West Indies to Britain from 1955–62 (Blakemore and Boneham, 1994). He came from a rural background of farming and fishing in Jamaica responding both to a demand for labour in the industrial world and also as a reaction to a decline in rural work opportunities in Jamaica.

In Britain, Dennis worked in many unskilled jobs as a labourer and more semi-skilled jobs as a mason. His memories and experiences are tinged with having to confront continuous racism and feelings of being unwanted in Britain. In family terms he also had to face up to and care for his wife who has mental health problems (from 1966 onwards) and, more recently, his son's.

Dennis's early experiences of his young man's body in Jamaica are filled with a joyful, physical exuberance and pleasure of just moving around in his body:

> My body was, I would say, a healthy body. I was able to run and I liked running. I was very fast and agile. I liked walks. In those days we don't (sic) have any transport other than riding the donkey. But I like running and I like walking. And that was my delightful pleasure – to walk.

Later, in Britain, he was proud of his labouring competence:

> I was strong and I was able to shovel and concrete and there would be no problem.

When stomach cancer was diagnosed in 2004, Dennis was confronted by the abrupt shock of not having a physically robust and healthy body any more. The taken for granted continuity of his embodied self was suddenly disrupted and the illusion of possessing a permanently strong and well-defended, body-self was invaded. As Dennis says:

> ... as human (sic) it's something really frightening.

It is as if the precarious physicality of his existence is brutally re-introduced into his life and he has to pay attention to those bodily conditions. The everyday illusion of his bodily stability, solidity and coherence, as well as the protected integrity of his embodied selves suddenly collapse, and fear and anxiety, that he has been defending himself from over all those years, flood back into his life. What Dennis was forced into encountering was the excessive pain and hurt of the physical reality of his operated on body:

I've been through a lot. The pain was atrocious. It came from the operation to remove all of the bowels. There is still pain until now.

Disorientating life events like Dennis's stomach operation, force embodied self adjustments in later life. Although some aging men attempt to cling on to their safer and more secure pasts sometimes avoiding having to confront traumatic events, many aging men are stripped of their denials and evasions and are provoked into gradual reassessments of who they think they are as aging men.

As a regular church-goer, Dennis often uses a philosophical and religious style in addressing these transformations. It is his way of trying to come to terms with these abrupt changes in his life. So, at times, he comes up with religious aphorisms to talk about his operation:

...for a living dog is better than a dead lion.

Although his approach to physical change is stoically and philosophically accepting, he is also struggling to make sense of his new, bodily conditions:

...having that operation it made me a stronger person [...] it helped me to see life in a different light. It helped me to know that I am mortal.

Slowly, through the interviews, Dennis began to view himself in a different way and a major part of those new perceptions was to articulate an emerging mode of masculine being that was starting to come into his life. First he became aware of the fragmentariness and fluidity of existence as an older, physically impaired man:

...the physical change, the biological change. It's inevitable.

And then:

...stop fooling our self [sic] and face up to the inevitable.

Learning to tolerate and embrace his vulnerable, embodied selves was an integral part of learning 'to live life in a different way.'

In terms of Dennis's contradictory struggle to accept his sexual impotence (a result of his stomach cancer operation), he vacillates between stoic acceptance and some emotional confusion about really believing that, 'Sex is not everything. I have life.'

Early in his life he was very much a self-defined, heterosexual 'top boy' luxuriating over his sexual conquests and predatory behaviour. He comes across as sexually triumphant and is very proud of his virile reputation. As Annie Potts (Potts et al., 2006) comments in her study of 'counter-stories' on 'erectile dysfunction' the movement from 'selfish', penis-focused sex to a more mindful, partner-oriented sex is a difficult but achievable journey. Dennis recalls a difficult time in his life when, in a context of despair and some depression at home, he took a holiday in Jamaica and had an affair with a young woman that he met there. I asked him:

DJ: Were you sexually proud as a man?

Dennis: Of course it is (sic). I'm 51-years-old and I can satisfy an 18-year-old. I know she enjoyed it because I've got staying power. I've got a good erection and many girls told me that.

Here Dennis's focus is not on mutual pleasure and human reciprocity but on reassuring himself about his performance anxieties as an older man. 'Can I still get it up?' as a concern seems to take precedence over questions of intimacy and communication. As Toni Calasanti comments, 'staying hard' is one of the chief concerns of aging men (Calasanti, 2005).

However, Dennis was much more bewildered and puzzled about the sexual changes that were going on around him. On one hand he was asserting that:

I lose my sex drive but I gain life. I lost it to save my life.

While on the other he was still trying to preserve his 'top boy' sexual reputation by being insecure about revealing his impotence to a woman friend in Jamaica. When I questioned him about this he replied:

But I don't have the courage to tell her that I'm not like I used to be.

First, it takes a great deal of emotional courage as an older man to talk openly about impotence and performance anxieties so I have considerable respect for Dennis's position but I also sense his unspoken pain and loss beneath his avoidance of the word, 'impotence' and his defensive circumlocution in referring to impotence as, 'I'm not like I used to be.'

The processes of re-assessing his gendered selfhood are also apparent in the emerging shifts in his sexual selves. Towards the end of the last interview Dennis began to consider more other-related, empathetic, sexual identities. He said:

> I'm alive differently. I don't let it revolve around sex any more. It can revolve around listening and caring for people in a different way. Listening to people's needs instead of being self-centred about sex.

In reading this closely I can sense the amount of self-disciplined effort ('I don't let it revolve around sex anymore') that Dennis is using to force himself away from an adolescent, predatory model of sexual behaviour. He is still caught in the middle of these different models of aging men's sexualities but he is beginning to be aware that it is possible to move towards a different way of masculine being in the world. It is through the physical shocks and dislocations in aging men's lives that the dominant ideals of masculinity and gendered, sexualised expectations begin to become destabilised and unsettled and more open to possible changes.

Discussion

Aging men are not passive, static, embodied subjects. Although from a distance aging men's lives seem hardly moving, in fact their lives are characterised by rapid changes mainly experienced in their bodies and a restless confrontation with changing, ambivalent and emerging selves. Frequent life events, like severe illness, breakdown, hospitalisation, loss of job security and status, and the death of a spouse, force adjustments in later life. Alongside these uneven processes of aging and bodily adaptations go changes in the meanings and experiences of masculinity.

The evidence of my research study and the three masculine life stories reveal the ambiguities, uncertainties and diversity of some aging men's lives. Ray's embodied selves were tightly constrained and undermined by a biomedical discourse on one hand, but on the other his experiences of being a 'delicate', asthmatic boy and young man helped him to use his marginality and later integrate his anxious and panicky bodily sensations with a more self-reflexive process of understanding.

Alternatively, Brian seemed to be dominated by the cultural ideals of young, middle-aged men, especially in the social context of the UK where generational differences are in the process of being eroded (Phillipson, 2006). His constant pursuit of staying fit, active and young was built upon his sustained denial of the physical realities of aging, saying that, 'There is no connection between what your age is and how you are.'

Dennis is suspended between stoical acceptance and emotional confusion of living with the abrupt changes of stomach cancer and sexual impotence. He is in the middle of a traumatic, gendered reassessment of his embodied selves. He is partly giving up his dreams of his old, forceful, competitive body and moving, hesitantly, in the direction of more fragmentary, embodied selves that are more relational and other-centred.

In some ways both Ray (although much more poised between decline and growth) and Brian are still trapped within the dualistic structure of either defining themselves within the biomedical discourse or the 'positive aging' discourse. The possibility of change in the embodied, masculine selves of aging men comes from the breaking down of these binary and normative structures and discourses often provoked by what I call creative discontinuity.

Threat and opportunity are strangely linked in the changing processes of aging men. The threatening loss of socio-economic productivity, social status, fears of sexual impotence and the disorientating shocks of physical disruptions and discontinuities in aging men's experiences often create a destabilising, social context where dominant ideals of masculinity and gendered expectations are weakened. These shifts and shocks, very much experienced in bodies, can sometimes construct the new opportunities and conditions for modifying embodied, masculine selves. In Dennis's case, there are emerging hints of his gender modifications. We see him in the process of dealing with the collapse of his defended, masculine, embodied selves (Hollway and Jefferson, 2000) and being provoked into a critical re-assessment of who he might be as an older man.

Of course, not all men respond in the same way to these bodily disruptions. Some aging men like Brian prefer to hang on to the illusions of the past and the relative security of repeating familiar, defensive routines and keeping the myths of total self-sufficiency intact.

However, if we pay closer attention to the bodily dimensions of aging men, and particularly the physical realities and sensations of living in aging bodies, it is possible to discern different ways of masculine being in their lives. At the moment, these different ways of being are only glimpses of becoming selves, fearful but excited, often in pain but emerging. Nevertheless, future studies of aging men, if appreciated and interrogated in their own valued terms, have the potential to make an important contribution to rethinking and re-practising our current models of men and masculinities.

4
An Historical and Cultural Analysis of Aging Men's Sexualities in the UK

Conventionally, aging men as sexual beings are seen as past it, unobtrusively stable, or even asexual (Gott and Hinchliff, 2003; Serrant-Green and McCluskey, 2008). Sexuality is popularly viewed as the exclusive domain of the young and mainly as youth-focused activity (Schiavi, 1999) and so the assumption is that aging men and women do not have the right to enter the privileged space of the young and certainly not with their perceived undesirable and unattractive bodies. Viewed through such an ageist prism, aging men who display a sexual interest are liable to be seen as inappropriate or even 'dirty old men'.

Academic research has not helped to improve this negative situation. Generally, scholarly work has not challenged age-related sexual stereotyping. With only a few exceptions, (Sandberg, 2011; Calasanti and King, 2005; Gott and Hinchliff, 2003) the dominant research paradigm has been quantitative analysis through large surveys but this mode of research has shed little light on the actual dynamic, sexual fluctuations and adaptations met within the complex, emotional lives of aging men within the last sixty years in the UK.

Primarily what is not heard in the quantitative work is the actual living voices of aging men. The main limitations of statistical analysis are that it leaves little space for the understandings, experiences and attitudes of aging men to emerge, understandings which are sometimes confused, sometimes pondering and teasing out the meanings of their own sexualities (Gott and Hinchliff, 2003). Instead of being the distant objects of quantitative research, aging men can be active agents and actors who are capable of disturbing interpretive orthodoxies through the force and inventiveness of their own stories (Plummer, 2005).

Ageist myths, normative assumptions and some narrow forms of quantitative research obscure our understandings of aging men's sexualities. I question these cultural myths and assumptions by choosing a qualitative, life history, story work mode of research. However, aging men's life stories cannot just be accepted at face value as literal truth. Their life experiences, and their attempts to share them, are always culturally mediated. It does this through shaping and re-ordering the random flux of their life experiences into purposeful and crafted narratives.

As Jacqui Gabb suggests: '...the narrativisation of experience does not simply tell a story, it constructs an account within the language, conventions and social milieu that translates experience. Life stories do not mirror experience; they re-present them in particular contexts in culturally intelligible formats' (Gabb, 2008).

Also, this narrative re-assembling of experience socially produces embodied identities through the narratives people use to make sense of and understand their lives (Jackson, 2008). Through the twists and turns of narrative re-ordering, they construct a version of narrative-based identities, although these narratives of identity do not stand alone in aging men's lives but partly depend on wider, cultural or key narratives such as the main tensions between the sexual drive narrative and the sexual retirement narrative. Furthermore, there is no single, unified narrative of identity for aging men but a diverse multiplicity of possible narrative selves often competing with each other for dominance.

In order to try and capture something of the intimate contradictoriness and ambiguity of aging men's sexualities I have deliberately attempted to employ what Geertz (1973) and Plummer (2005) refer to as 'thick description' – the deep, extended stories people use to make sense of their sexual lives if the relationship between research participant and researcher is trusting and relaxed enough. As Plummer suggests, these stories are not only ways of understanding sexualities but also ways of 'bringing about political change' (Plummer, 1995, 2001). In this specific context these sexual stories of aging men in the UK have the potential to challenge and change these ageist myths and narrow normative assumptions. Four of these aging men's (two gay, two heterosexual) sexual life histories will be considered in detail in order to identify, illuminate and critique aging men's sexual narratives and narrative identities over the personal and cultural shifts and changes of their life courses.

Prior to examining the tangled complexity of these aging men's sexual histories, a number of conceptual frames that inform my analysis will be outlined.

The Relations of Gender and Sexualities in Aging Men's Lives

Here, I shall examine aging men as gendered and sexualised beings and the ways that they change over a life course. In doing so I shall use a critical studies on men and masculinities perspective (Hearn and Sandberg, 2008) in order to examine how these gendering and sexualising processes intersect with other social relations such as class and race. Here, gender can be seen as a dynamic set of power relations within a specific culture and society at a particular, historical moment.

Aging men's perceptions of their masculine selves regularly shape their sexual selves, their sexual activities and their sexual identities and these in turn also help shape their masculine identities. As Fracher and Kimmel comment:

> Gender informs sexuality; sexuality confirms gender. (Fracher and Kimmel, 1987)

It is therefore not practically feasible to talk about gender and sexuality as separate items because gender and sexualities are so closely interwoven that it only makes sense to focus on the nuanced and complex relations existing between them.

Heterosexual masculinity in aging men is often dependent on a sexual display of competence and adequate performance to shore itself up. Certainly some aging men use sexual activities to build, confirm and consolidate an occasional shaky grip on their masculine selves. Generally, aging men find sex or the lack of it more significant in their lives than older women (Gott and Hinchliff, 2003). More seemed to be at stake in their processes of negotiating sex for aging men than for older women. Perhaps what is at stake here for aging men is the possible loss of masculine identity, pride and self-respect. The aging process is challenging and threatening enough for aging men, but it also brings with it the frequent encounter with shame and sexual humiliation (Gott and Hinchliff, 2003). According to Feldman et al. (1994), 'by the age of 70, 67% of men will experience some degree of erectile dysfunction', and this may present an anxiety-making threat to aging men's masculine, gendered and sexual, normative stability although some men might experience impotence as a release from exacting sexual demands.

Recently, gay and heterosexual aging men's sexual identities have become more unsettled, fluidly diverse and more open to flux and change in a society that is rapidly shifting in terms of economic and social circumstances (Plummer, 2005). This has led to greater ambiguity and variety in heterosexual and gay men's sexualities. On one hand, some older gay men still display their enduring interest in phallocentric performance, even though there can be also an ironic playfulness that seems to debunk and parody the traditional hegemonic sex script for men. On the other hand some older, gay men seem to be tired of the fickle gay scene and are more interested in exploring the connectedness and relational sexual scripts which endorse 'obligation, fidelity and romance between sexual partners' (Levine, 1995).

Along with the social and cultural changes of the last twenty years we have also seen some blurring of the tightly controlled gendered and sexual binaries (masculine/feminine, gay/straight etc.) As a result of which there has been a playing with the traditionally gendered and heterosexualised roles of masculine/on top and feminine/passive bottom so that now some gentle subversion of those predictable roles can happen (Graham, 2007).

The Sexual Life Histories of Four Aging Men Set Within Public Histories of the Last Sixty Years in the UK

As a general background to this section it might be useful to read, 'The importance of history in biographical research' on pages 15–16 of the 'Introduction.' In this section I focus on the sexual life histories of two, older, gay men. But first a background of the public history of gay men's lives:

Gay Histories

1950s/Early 1960s

In the 1950s homosexual, sexual activities were illegal in the UK. Homophobic culture defined homosexuality as a disease or an illness within a dominant, 'medical model' (Weeks, 1977). Homosexual men were talked about derogatively as 'queers, poofs or nancy-boys'. This savagely negative backcloth bred an atmosphere of secrecy, furtiveness and self-doubt. 'Homosexuals were isolated in positions of self-hatred,' commented one of the research participants.

Although most homosexuals, at that time, were met with discrimination and harassment, some cities in the UK had bars where homosexuals were tolerated. Also there were some 'pockets of resistance' to the invasive, homophobic culture to be found in the larger cities of the UK as well as within certain avant-garde sectors such as the acting community.

1967-1979

The sexual offences act of 1967 partly decriminalised homosexual activities in private for adults over the age of 21, though the really important loosening up of the atmosphere of sexual repression was produced by the emergence of the gay liberation movement in the US (Stonewall) and Europe in 1969-70. Thus homosexuals gradually moved from being 'nancy-boys' to being 'gay men'.

The gay liberation movement affirmed gay men's sexualities, as 'every bit as good and valid as heterosexuality' (Shiers, 1988). The seventies in the UK shook apart the restrictive and repressive sexual climate that most gay men inhabited in the 1950s and early 1960s. According to John Shiers: 'We no longer had to live in the closet, furtively meeting in the shadows. Our sexuality could be expressed openly' (Shiers, 1988).

1979-1990

As a part of a wider attack upon the supposed, 'permissive society' of the late 1960s/1970s, Thatcherism (1979-90) set out to reverse the perceived decline in traditional family values and morality. This moral conservatism was explicitly anti-gay and anti-lesbian and deliberately attempted to regulate non-heterosexual sexualities through Section 28 of the local government act which banned the 'promotion of homosexuality' by local councils.

The spread of AIDS marked a setback in the 1980s, initially destabilising the growing confidence of gay sexual identities, especially through the media's 'gay plague' attacks in 1985 and the overt linking of AIDS, in popular consciousness, with gay men. Although still precariously positioned, the gay movement in the UK fought back in the 1980s to become a much more coherently organised, community-based network with the expansion of friendships and support groups.

1990-Present Day

Although gay men's sexual activities are still opposed by the forces of moral conservatism, there has been an emergence of new forms of equality in relation to intimate life and sexual choice (Weeks, 2004). There are, admittedly, pockets of violent homophobia still existing but, generally, the UK population has become more tolerant in its attitudes to sexual diversity; 'There is plentiful evidence that the old taboos against homosexuality are beginning to fade away' (Weeks, 2004).

For example, in 2000 the sexual offences (amendment) act was passed, reducing the age of consent for gay men from 18 to 16. However there was also strong opposition to the equalising of gay men's consent with that of heterosexuality (Epstein, Johnson and Steinberg, 2004).

The growing liberalisation of public attitudes to homosexuality and other social rights is now seen in the vitality of gay pride celebrations and the introduction of civil partnerships for same sex couples. There is still confusion, conflict and ambiguity about these social shifts in a bitter arena of church-instigated moral outrage and other areas of society, such as compromised guest house landlords, but there is also considerable public support for these equality changes.

Michael's Sexual Life History

Brief snapshots of the research participants' life stories can be found on pages 12–15 of the 'Introduction.' When I first interviewed Michael he seemed very confident and self-assured about his gay identity, openly admitting that sex was centrally important to his sense of self at his present age of 60. Although he also expressed some concern about 'not being able to get it up any more' he was eager to demolish, even reverse the negative myth of inevitable, sexual decline in the lives of aging men, saying that 'the older I get the more sexually motivated I become' and that, 'my sexual appetite is still very strong'.

However, as we began to dig deeper into his life history over the course of the research interviews, he begins to recognise the 'long political struggle' that he had been a part of. In personal history terms, he particularly emphasised the confusing and bewildering period of his adolescence when he was anxiously concerned about his sexual identities.

In the late 1950s and early 1960s in the UK Michael remembered 'the days when there were no clubs, networks, support groups, when gays were isolated in positions of self-hatred'. Living in a stigmatised, social context where homosexual, sexual activities were officially criminalised, Michael was coerced into policing and censoring his nascent, gay sexual desires:

> And that period where, I guess, I found myself attracted to the male species more than the female species. But I was wondering whether that was okay or not; whether that was normal or not and you know it wasn't. I don't think even the word 'gay' was used in those days and reference to homosexuality was about terms of abuse and ridicule and of a derogatory nature. So I thought, 'Oh, I'd better keep that side of me a bit quiet.'

The power and coercive force of heteronormativity at that historical moment is shown clearly in Michael's uncertain wondering about whether fancying boys and men 'was normal or not'. His considerable self-doubt about his sexual identities is produced through the exclusive, heterosexual culture pressurising him through, fear of bullying ridicule, into an act of secrecy and self-policing. As he says: 'I'd better keep that side of me a bit quiet'.

These self-doubts were exacerbated while still a young man, age 17–21, by the disintegration of his immediate family circle when his only brother, his mother and father died in quick succession leaving Michael in sole charge of the family house. Confusing as this was, it was compounded by his sense of personal shame about his (as he perceived it) 'gangly' and tall body, not to mention his ambivalence and confusion about his sexuality.

During his adolescence there was a cultural, social and religious tension and confusion in his life. His mother was a devout Christian and, with her approval, he became an altar boy. He also experimented by going out with girls and, later on, even got engaged to an older woman as a way of seeking cultural acceptance. In this double life he went out in a group of young men, socially, and everybody seemed to have a girlfriend and most of them were getting engaged so Michael did not want to be left out. But at the same time as his engagement, Michael was also trying out his gay sexualities in secret, being fucked by a signalman, an event that he described as, 'sordidly wonderful' and 'painful but enjoyable'. He was also exploring 'exciting horseplay in the showers' at school and enjoying, 'wank off parties with friends'.

The contradictions and confusions in Michael's sexual identities came to a head when, in a depressed moment, he began to think of suicide as a way out of his problems. But helped by a sympathetic psychiatrist, who gave him social permission to respect the validity of his gay, sexual desires, he started to believe in his gay, sexual identity and quickly became a part of the local gay scene. This acceptance of his homosexuality coincided, historically, with the relative loosening up of an earlier climate of sexual repression, stimulated, to some degree, by the 1967 Sexual Offences' Act in the UK and the emergence of the gay liberation movement in the US and Europe from 1969–70. Thus, at the age of 20, Michael was able to describe himself as 'much more of a whole person'.

The Erotic Adventure Narrative

For most of Michael's life as a gay man, three narratives summarise his shifting, sexual identities and passage through the life course. The first sexual narrative is the erotic adventure narrative suggested by Matt Mutchler (Mutchler, 2000). These erotic adventure narratives are characterised by often opportunistic, spontaneous, sexual encounters referred to by Michael as his 'crazy days' of 'casual sex'. Michael defines this as a 'strange sort of liberation and release' through cottaging, going to gay pubs, and finding pleasure in unexpected encounters. Particular episodes in Michael's sexual life history give something of the flavour of these surprising, erotic adventures. The first one took place while Michael was still at school, possibly 15 or 16 when he is talking about sexy, visual images:

> Sometimes somebody would bring 'Health and Efficiency' to school but I actually wasn't looking at the women... I found out that what I could do was go to the local public library and look at magazines of tribes of Africa or South America... and I found out that some of the books had been withdrawn from the shelves but were available to be seen or borrowed on special request. So I took the bull by the horns and specially requested these books and was shown in to the office where the senior librarian was and he locked the door behind me and invited me to go down on him. Which I duly did and he returned the compliment.

This early adventurous seeking out of sexual skirmishes is portrayed as virile daring ('took the bull by the horns'), almost like a sexual initiation ritual in Crete. There is an element of extraordinary risk-taking (senior librarian inviting 15/16 year old boy to 'go down on him') that also creates the unexpectedness of the erotic adventure. However, the half-mocking, slightly archaic, playful tone of the telling ('Which I duly did and he returned the compliment') tends to cushion the shockingly irreverent details.

The second episode comes from a much later period in his life, from 1982–83, when Michael lived with another gay man in a monogamous relationship for seven years. After a long, loving relationship with this man, Michael began to 'stray a bit' and picked up another man from a local cottaging venue for casual sex. His explanation of why he did this reveals a guilt-free, hedonistic, sexual pleasure in what he did (Plummer, 2005). He says matter-of-factly, 'I fancied a shag with somebody else'. Here he seems to be openly admitting that he needs to keep on separating out his need for the sexual intensity of wild flings, on the one hand, from the long-term intimacy of a committed relationship on the other.

The Hypersexual, Sex Drive Narrative

The next sexual narrative in Michael's sexual history is the hypersexual, sex drive narrative (Hollway, 1998). This narrative comes across as very orgasm-centred as Michael confirms, 'the ultimate for me is achieving orgasm'. Here, the aging men's sexuality in inevitable decline is not for Michael. As he declares, 'I've found that the older I get the more sexually motivated I become and the more often I want sex of one sort or another and if I don't have an orgasm every day I'm not a happy bunny really'.

It seems plausible that this constant sexual need to pleasure his penis and his self – i.e. an orgasm-centred focus rather than an other-centred orientation – might contain some aspects of defensiveness against the early pain and hurt that Michael experienced when all his close family died in the space of four years (Blake, 2009). During the interviews, for example, Michael was reluctant to investigate what he termed the 'serious depression' that he lived in between the ages of 17–21, when he was forced to come face to face with considerable grief and loss.

Carol Staudacher (1991) also suggests that 'excessive sexual activity' might be a way of 'avoiding feeling the pain of loss, the deep, wrenching emotions that follow the death of loved ones'. She goes on to say that some men may seek to lose themselves by 'submerging (themselves) in obsessive sexual activity', and that perhaps men like Michael might want to believe that he will remain less susceptible to these difficult emotions if 'they concern themselves with physical release and performance'.

The 'Gentleman Callers' Sexual Narrative

The final sexual narrative that I want to draw attention to in Michael's sexual life story is what he calls the multiple 'gentleman callers' sexual narrative. After three seven-year-monogamous relationships with gay partners sharing his house and life together, Michael decides that 'he doesn't believe in long-term, monogamous relationships'. In later life, Michael rejects 'the norms of the nuclear family' and now believes that:

> Friends are more important than sexual partners actually. Always have been. Because, if you like, sexual partners come and go but friends stay with you.

He now recognises that, although his relationships with his three monogamous partners were important to him, and still are, he's got to a point in his life when he's had enough of serial monogamy. He seems to have become more aware of the fact that sharing a house with a partner entails compromise, complex negotiation and constant consultation. Now, at 60, Michael has found a 'new freedom of doing what I wanted to do when I wanted to do it'. Thus he feels released to live alone in, with relative financial stability and surrounded by friends and his 'gentleman callers', a support network that he has built up over the years.

Michael has a regular understanding with these 'gentleman callers' – some gay men and some married male friends, – on Thursday evenings for a sexual encounter that he describes as, 'not just about lust or love but in-between'. Playfully and semi-ironically again, Michael refers to having sexual relations with married men as 'providing a social service' in the community. When talking about his 'gentleman callers' Michael seems very relaxed and easy about this Thursday evening rendezvous. This new kind of improvised living arrangement has something of the living apart together (lat)innovatoritiness but it also has a much more specific, sexual function connected to it. Crucially, this new arrangement does not take away his autonomy and independent material space. He does not need complicated consultations. Instead, he arranges these sexual encounters through a mutual and trusting agreement. Michael says that: 'if I'm horny I wait for Thursday evening'. As a result, Michael defines his 'gentleman caller' arrangement as 'satisfying, trusting and fun'.

Roy's Sexual Life Story

Unlike the three other research participants, Roy maintains that, 'I've never placed sex highly', and that, 'Affection is more important to me than coming'. In his interviews he comes across as a man of sustained caring but also of a determined, independent character who, although accepting that he was gay from the age of 14, also knew that he did not fit into the fashionable, gay scene. He comments:

> From an emotional point of view I discovered that, when I was 14, that I was gay but perhaps somewhere out there was the possibility of some sort of relationship. And when I looked into it I discovered not the gay world I felt I wanted because I couldn't fit into it because I didn't really perhaps have it – and that was good looks, a beautiful body and a big dick.

The stress here on an 'emotional point of view' and on seeking relationships rather than casual sex contrasts with what Heaphy et al. (2004) have suggested makes up the dominant features of the gay scene – its 'great emphasis on youth and physical appearance' reflecting a culture where you have to stay young and daren't get old. Roy never saw himself as physically attractive and instead made it clear that 'I thought my mind was desirable'.

This emphasis on the importance of mind and personality probably has its roots in Roy's working-class childhood in South Wales. As a boy he experienced significant poverty and a lack of material resources ('I can never remember wearing underpants'). He grew up in a community where his father was a local miner, stating that: 'it was just rows of houses owned by the coal mine and, you know, we lived in a cottage which belonged to them'. These early experiences of working-class poverty and the two years he spent after he left school at 15 working as a general labourer in a small building company, possibly helped him to see through what he saw as the world of fashionable pretence and appearance:

> I was never a person of fashion or anything else so I never thought a lot about all that or about my body per se. I ate food. I enjoyed myself and people accepted me as I was, you know. I was more interested in the things of the mind than the body.

The stark, economic reality of 'I ate food' rather than elaborating on other types of nutritious food, reveals the emphasis on basic, material survival at that time of his life that perhaps, later, gave him more of a critical perspective on the more decorative life styles of the later, fashionable, gay scene.

He was also influenced by the calm understanding of his father who enjoyed reading books and most likely contributed to shaping Roy's interest in books, music and 'things of the mind'.

Viewed from an historical perspective, Roy referred to 'a degree of innocence', both internally and externally, in the late 1940s/early 1950s when he was 16–19. He never heard of the criminalisation of homosexual, sexual activities at that time (though he had read about Lord Montagu)[1] and suggests that one reason for his relative lack of knowledge about what was going on might be related to his perception that 'the police weren't as active as they are now'.

His first gay sexual experiences mainly involved mutual masturbation but he 'preferred kissing and cuddling' to penetrative sex. He felt there was no chance of 'personal involvement in penetrative sex' and instead was 'looking for intellectual involvement' with another man. This was about the time of the Sexual Offences' Act of 1967 and the 1970s but, generally, he kept himself private and did not get involved in bar culture, being 'only interested in one person at a time'. He did not 'feel the need to come out' and did not associate himself with the gay liberation movement. He admired gay activists from a distance but the political movement seemed not to touch him personally.

However, the situation changed in the 1980s when his personal and political lives started to come together for the first time. Because Roy's long-term partner was dying of AIDS Roy nursed him for eight years. Perhaps because he was more emotionally engaged, he felt that he had something to give professionally and personally to combating AIDS in his own hospital and outside. He helped in 'setting up an AIDS information project,' retreats and benefits, and developed a keen interest in the treatment and care of people with AIDS. Outside his workplace he also gave his time as a telephone counsellor. Later he joined a gay bereavement group.

Relationship-Focused Sexual Narrative

The two main sexual narratives in Roy's life history are a relationship-focused (Levine, 1990), sexual narrative and a romantic love, sexual narrative (Mutchler, 2002). During the interviews, Roy reveals a sustained scepticism towards alienated, casual sex and the 'butterfly' culture of the gay scene. As we have already noticed, Roy feels that 'affection is more important to me than coming' and that he prefers, 'hugging, kissing and holding' to orgasm and penis-centred models of sex.

His strong belief that you cannot separate dick from mind and personality is frequently referred to. His criticism of gay saunas is that other gay men, in that situation, often do not appreciate the person behind the dick. He says:

> I mean you might be sitting in the sauna and someone admires your dick but I will always say, 'There is a person behind the dick.'

Elsewhere he comments on the fickleness of the 'butterfly' culture of the gay scene:

> Gay people are like butterflies. There is a chrysalis and they come out and that's it. As a gay man there is a period in your life from 18 or whatever, it is when you are the ticket to the ball or whatever. You can walk into a place and you have no difficulty in picking up someone and all these things come together. But there is a point when all those things drop away.

Roy's image of young, gay men as butterflies nicely captures that cultural obsession with glitzy youth, good looks, fashion and beautiful bodies. Roy believes that this obsession acts as a cultural barrier to the development of enduring relationships based on affectionate reciprocity. In contrast to these views, however, his own contradictory and promiscuous past comes to light when he talks about being picked up when he was a younger man working in New York:

> I remember very clearly in New York the first time I was in a bar and this chap was interested in me and I went out with him to his home which was unusual for me really. But the thing that has stuck in my mind – I don't know how well I performed in sex with this man – but what sticks in my mind was when we were sitting down having breakfast the following morning – there I was sitting down having breakfast with this stranger. I didn't know his name and I felt embarrassed and I felt I wanted to get out of the situation and I felt that was what, possibly, he felt. And that kind of situation, to me, is not what I want.

We can sense here that Roy has learned the hard way; his bleak account of waking up to the empty anonymity of 'stranger sex' provides a clear motivation towards a more relationship-focused model of sexual encounters.

Although he is trying to adopt a more relationship-focused basis to his sexual identities, Roy's actual experiences emerge as more turbulent and nuanced than I've been suggesting so far. For sixteen years he lived with his gay partner in a shared house in what seemed to be a mutually caring relationship. But for the last eight years of their twenty-four-year relationship Roy's partner was slowly dying of AIDS. This situation was made even more difficult for Roy because the reality of his illness was concealed both from his partner's workplace ('because if they'd have known they would have got rid of him') and also his partner's parents, who had no idea that their son was gay until the last two years of his life.

As his partner's health gradually deteriorated Roy seemed to be caught between a wounded sense of having been betrayed by his lover and, simultaneously, a very close intimacy ('deep down I still had feelings for him'). Roy had suspected for some time that his partner had been 'playing the field', even before the medical confirmation that he had AIDS, and comments that 'when I found out that [he] had AIDS, the trust had gone'.

Roy's emotions are painfully mixed; his mounting distrust mingles with a hurt but sustained commitment to his partner over many years. Through the interviews a contradictory tension develops in Roy's account of this difficult time; on one side there is a troubled but deeply concerned empathy for his partner, and on the other an angry sense of personal and bodily betrayal. Roy carried on looking after his dying partner for a very long time while still working in a demanding job. The strain of caring comes through in his account:

> We used to go down to London towards the end about three times a week – right into one of the hospitals in the centre.

Roy still slept with his partner during all this time and when his partner retired through ill health he 'took him off to China for two weeks' holiday'. Despite feeling partly abandoned, he also reveals a tender, empathetic awareness of his partner's otherness and different needs in the final phase of the illness:

> Well when you are lying next to someone and you know they are dying but you don't know when. I mean once he'd gone to sleep I'd come down here [the lounge] and put the TV on and watch something. But I couldn't stop down here because I would then start worrying about what was happening. Was he still alright?

Even on the edge of nervous exhaustion Roy still clings on to his responsibility for caring ('Was he still alright?'), attempting to recover some normative stability through watching television. On the other hand, he also reveals a bleak sense of being sexually abandoned by his lifelong lover, commenting that:

> Because he lied to me I didn't feel he belonged to me anymore

And then, even more poignantly:

> I know every inch of his body but so does somebody else now.

The pain of his close bodily intimacy with his partner being invaded and destroyed by a stranger's touch reverberates powerfully and his anger is palpable. Roy seems to be left with the desolation of the broken trust between them now that somebody else knows 'every inch of his body.'

The Romantic Love, Sexual Narrative

Roy was very clear about what he wanted in any emotional relationship with another man:

I want love and romance in my life ... I want love in my life not dick.

It is no longer the physical sex that is most important to him and he seems to have come to terms with his past sexual life: 'I had it and that's that'. What he values now is the possibility of going 'to bed and holding hands' with his lover. Also important is the capacity for cultural and intellectual sharing within an intimate relationship: 'to be with a person you should be able to read a poem to them and talk about music'.

At the point when I interviewed Roy he had recently entered into a new, loving relationship with a much younger, gay man of 33:

I am living by myself although I've now got a partner who I see four times a week. He's 33 and I'm 72 so there is quite a difference. But he's a very loving person. He came into my life four to five years after my partner of 20 odd years died.

In this extended account there's an emerging awareness of 'learning to live within the confines and restrictions or whatever of that age' and this awareness seems to have informed the setting up of a series of innovatory living arrangements with his new partner (3 days by himself and 4 with his new partner). Roy wishes to give his new partner more independent scope than perhaps he gave his first, major partner. He says: 'I really don't want to restrict him at 33 years of age and I know he genuinely loves me'. Perhaps Roy is now able to trust his new partner in a different way to his first partner. He seems to be reassured by the genuineness of his new partner's love and as a result he is able to respect his partner's different needs. However the background of these innovatory living arrangements is very tangled and complex. Roy comments about this in this particular way:

Well when [his old partner] died, for four years I was by myself and then I met [his new partner] and he had never had a relationship before. He met me. He fell in love. I think during that time I was gradually getting used to being by myself but the thing with [his new partner] is that he is not out to his parents. He is not out to his friends. He's not out to anybody and he's frightened of hurting his parents and he knows that one of his friends is homophobic and his friends don't take too kindly to gay people although he has now told one of his three friends. So I share him really – every Friday, Saturday and Sunday he has always spent with his mates and so we live with that. I see him Sunday during the day before he goes to his mates. Monday is his own day – we agreed that he would have a day to himself and then Tuesday, Wednesday, Thursday, I see him.

There is a marked difference in this account to Roy's responses to his dying lover: 'he met me. He fell in love'. It is almost as if Roy allows somebody else to love him at a time when he had become accustomed to being by himself. At first glance there does not seem to be a more active, loving reciprocity in his relationship with his new partner. But with a more careful analysis, Roy comes across as somebody who is more prepared to live within the parameters of his new partner's routines and weekend meetings with his friends, even though some of them are homophobic. Now he says that he is open to sharing him with his heterosexual friends. And perhaps there is also a new willingness in Roy to negotiate with his new partner about their differences ('we agreed that he would have a day to himself').

Roy's comments about relating to his new partner are significant:

> ... I enjoy initiating [his new partner] into the world out there ... and I really passed on some of my experiences in life and I've helped to calm him down a bit.

Although there are some issues of power and control here, there is also some evidence of Roy trying to view the world in a fresh way, of trying to see the world and the possible future of their relationship through his partner's eyes that might be close to loving him. From a wider, historical perspective Roy's fresh way of looking might be connected to the political emergence of new forms of equality in relation to intimate life between gay and lesbian people commented on in the public history section above.

Later on in the interviews, Roy admits he is anxious about sharing his own fears of mortality with his new partner, arguing that:

> If I tell him things [about his fears of mortality] he worries so it's better that he doesn't know.

Heterosexual Histories

A Brief, Sexual History of Older, Heterosexual Men in the UK from the 1950s to the Present Day

1950s to Early 1960s

In the 1950s in the UK the system of gender relations was generally far more polarised than today. As a result, there was a rigid segregation of male wage-workers operating exclusively in the public sphere and female, unpaid domestic and childcare workers in the separated and unequal domestic sphere.

In terms of sexual relations, from a woman's perspective, sex was often conceived of as a marital duty. Some women still thought of sex as 'dirty', something that had to be endured. Sexual expectations (if not the actual reality) were very disciplined: no sex before marriage; the stigmatisation of sex outside marriage; many young women were scared of getting pregnant; the threat of back-street abortionists regulated many young women's sex lives. Many men thought that sex was just about penis-focused, penetrative sex. There seemed to be a large number of frustrated, sex-hungry men obsessed with sexual performance and conquest.

Mid-1960s to 1979

This was a contradictory and contested historical period (King, 2010), although on the surface a more liberal and permissive, gendered and sexual culture was emerging during this period, 'permissiveness was more talked and gossiped about than indulged in' (Holdsworth, 1988). Furthermore, Sandbrook (2006) has commented that: 'for millions of people the sexual revolution of the sixties was little more than an illusion.' However, attitudes limiting sexual relations to reproduction within marriage were beginning to loosen, allowing for greater sexual openness, pleasure and fun. Gradually, the contraceptive pill became more easily available, and in 1967 the abortion act made abortion far easier in the UK as social grounds for abortion were acknowledged in addition to medical grounds.

Young men seemed to go along with these sexual changes in a generally unquestioning and sometimes manipulative manner. Young women were being seen as 'dolly birds' and sex objects and instead of pleasing themselves, at times ended up just pleasing men. However, the second wave of the women's movement, coming in the late 60s and early 1970s, had begun seriously to question whether sexual permissiveness also implied submissiveness for women (Holdsworth, 1988). Importantly, gender equality legislation emerged in the 1970s with the Equal Pay Act of 1970 and the Sex Discrimination Act of 1975 leading to the setting up of the equal opportunities' commission in the late 1970s. If there could be equality in the workplace, then why not in the bedroom as well?

1980s to the Late 1990s

There were some strange contradictions during this period. On one hand, Thatcherism dissociated itself strenuously from the supposed, 'permissive society' of the late 60s and 1970s, stressing moral conservatism and traditional family values and attempting to regulate sexualities through Section 28 of the Local Government Act. But, on the other hand, some women appeared as more actively desiring and assertive in sexual terms. It was during this period that women began to 'appear at least as sexual as men' (Plummer, 2005). This re-positioning of women as active desirers and active pursuers of men has also probably, to some extent, helped destabilise men's certainty and stability as dominant, heterosexual, sexual beings. Consequently there is a growing awareness on the part of men of the problematic nature of their sexualities. Indeed, some pro-feminist men's groups, set up in the 80s and 90s, began to challenge men and their association with rape and sexual violence. On the other hand, many men still conformed (and still do) to the male, hegemonic model of sexuality with all of its implications.

Late 1990s to the Present Day

Profound changes to the socio-economic structure have led to a general loosening up of traditional gender relations in the twenty-first century, and with significant implications for men's sexual lives. A rigid, binary system that separated and polarised men and women, gay and straight in the 1950s, is now in the process of being challenged, further eroding the linked breadwinner/homemaker dichotomy as more women enter employment, and do so at a much faster rate than men (Mac an Ghaill and Haywood, 2007).

Sexual identities for men are now being disrupted by postmodern queer theory (Plummer, 2005) and starting to break down. Although many men are still focusing on a penetrative, penis-centred model of sex, male, sexual identities have now become much more unsettled, fluidly diverse and more open to flux and change (Plummer, 2005).

Male, sexual identities now include a wider spread of possibilities from fetishism, hypersexuality, sex retirement and withdrawal, living apart together, romantic love, being queer and other forms of non-heterosexual sexualities. New information and communication technologies (ICTs) are also starting to modify sexual practices from physical to more virtual encounters, relations, activities and experiments. Hearn comments: 'There are daily reports of how ICTs are changing how sexuality is done and experienced – in chat lines, internet dating, email sex, cybersex, cyber affairs, falling in love on the net' (Hearn, 2006).

Robert's Sexual Life Story

The main feature of Robert's sexual life story is a contradictory, unresolved tension between the sex drive narrative (Hollway, 1998) and the sexual retirement narrative (Marsiglio and Greer, 1995; Gott and Hinchliff, 2003). When I interviewed him, age 60, he was living alone (never having married) in a council flat on the east side of a city in the East Midlands.

Robert seemed trapped in the middle of a fading, sexual desire as an older man but still keeping an eye open for what he describes as, 'talent'. On one hand he suggests that he would be happier '... if you've got no sexual feelings... that's why it's probably natural, when you get older, your sexual instincts die'. On the other hand, when I pressed Robert about this and asked him, 'Have your sexual instincts died?' he answered immediately, saying:

> No, I wish it had. But obviously it's not as strong as what it was and I no longer think to myself that I've got to go out tonight and pick up a piece of talent.

The Sex Drive Narrative

In order to make sense of this emotional confusion in Robert's life, I propose to take a life course perspective on Robert's investment in the sex drive narrative. At about 13 or 14, in the late 1950s in the UK, he thought he was too thin and felt insecure about his body as a growing, white, working-class boy. He comments:

> I suppose I thought I was too thin because I used to go to the pictures – the kids' matinee – and watch people like John Wayne[2] and thinking that everybody should be like him, you know.

Although later on in his life Robert politically rejected what John Wayne represented:

> Well I think he was one of those sort of men who believed that a woman was a woman and a man was a man and she should stop at home and the man should earn all the money which I don't agree with.

While in his adolescence Robert very much wanted to model himself on Wayne's rugged, frontier masculinity (Kimmel, 1996) and become, in a real and imagined way, larger, tougher and sexually successful in his own embodied self, measuring himself against the culturally idealised masculine norms represented by John Wayne, Robert saw himself as personally inadequate and so wanted to be physically bigger to impress the girls:

> But you see in those days all the pin ups for the girls were all sort of bigger guys.

Robert's desire to become a 'big guy', or a 'he-man' – as he later defined his manly aspirations, was a part of a pervasive post-second world war culture in the UK that '... didn't have time for weaklings'. Influenced by working-class, peer group expectations at an historical moment that polarised and subordinated women's relations with men, he was persuaded into believing that '... you had to be strong or you wouldn't survive', and later notes that '... all my mates were tall, big guys'.

So from about 18 to 19, in the early 1960s in the UK, Robert took a friend's advice to 'build himself up' through using a Bullworker[3] and 'going to a karate class'. Through a regime of exercise, of working as a manual labourer 'lifting and shovelling', and then going to the gym after his accident at work, Robert developed a heavier, fitter, more muscular body over the years. He has also been able to maintain a consistent weight up to the present day: 'I've been twelve stone for about twenty-five or thirty years'.

Along with these adolescent cultural pressures to be a 'He-man' like John Wayne, Robert also developed adolescent, heterosexual, male sex attitudes:

> I mean when you were young, you think: 'I've got to have sex'... I went to dances and if you see this woman walking down the road when... not when you are 20 but when you are 15 and you think 'I've got to chat her up'.

Robert admits that when he was young he pursued sex in a very driven and compulsive way:

> ... at one time, daft as it sounds, I used to walk up and down the train to see if there was talent.

Referring to women repeatedly as 'talent' says a great deal; thus the full, human vitality of women is diminished, dehumanising them as 'other', an object to chase and pursue, not as full and equal human beings to get to know, respectfully and reciprocally.

The ideology of heteronormativity, shaped in Robert's adolescence, is clearly visible in his sex drive, sexual narratives. Here Robert's everyday practices of pursuing and objectifying 'talent' privilege masculine heterosexuality as the unspoken and 'naturalised' norm that he has to follow if he wants to prove that he is a 'real' man (Robinson, 2007). Likewise the male, heterosexual assumption that men should be virile, potent and strong, especially in their associations with women, and that they should function as dominating conquerors, is also clearly apparent (Johansson, 2007).

The Avoidance of Intimacy and Commitment

As a working-class, older man living in a council flat by himself, Robert lives close to the edge of economic poverty ('I could do with more money but, then again, I'm not bothered'). He says that he would like a relationship with a woman but not at the expense of losing his independence or (especially) of losing the security of his home. When asked what he feared as an older man, he answers, 'but growing old I think, my main fear is that there is going to be nobody I can relate to'. Robert clearly desires closer intimacy – living alone and never having married – but does not know how to get it and fears what might be at risk. Growing up in a culture and an historical moment in the UK that prohibited greater intimacy and closeness (Johansson, 2007), Robert is still ambivalent about expressing emotional tenderness. He explicitly denies that there was any need in his family circle for any outward show of affection:

> If we had an argument we didn't go round kissing one another and putting our arms around each other. No! People don't do that.

Again, in Robert's relationship with his brother, we pick up on a homophobic fear about crossing the cultural barriers of his gender:

> ...say when my brother walks in the house. I wouldn't go round hugging him. If I did they would think I'd gone funny or whatever.

'Funny', in this coded context, does not just mean 'crazy' of course, but homosexual or 'queer'.

At a more personal level, Robert is also anxious about a possible emotional commitment to a woman at his age of 60. The idea of holding on to a sense of emotional control is very important for an older, working-class man like Robert, who needs to survive alone and with dignity in the pinched, material conditions of a council flat. In effect, his avoidance of any emotional commitment defends him against any perceived risk that a relationship might endanger. Robert feels threatened by the possibility of losing his security in the future and jeopardising his ability to hang on to his home. But although later he admits that, 'I don't suppose I wanted any commitment', he nonetheless strenuously denies any emotional need on his part to overcome his apparent loneliness and isolation, asserting that he's glad to live alone and that he needs his own independent space above everything else:

> But I thought that I'm glad I'm on my own this Christmas so I can wake up in peace. It's a load of bunkum saying, 'this is sad-people living on their own'. That's a load of bloody nonsense. I should hate for anybody to come and live with me now. I couldn't put up with it.

There is an admirable robustness here; however, there is something in the fierceness of his declaration that he would 'hate' it and 'couldn't put up with it' that suggests an over-defensiveness that might conceal an unfulfilled longing.

However, it is also important to recognise that preserving the quality and continuity of the material conditions of his life are just as significant for Robert as an emotional, sexual engagement with a woman. Both age and economic/social class have the capacity to vary his sexual being as an older man. At 60, Robert's fear of homelessness appears to be just as important as his fear of emotional commitment.

Now, Robert sounds more careful and calculating about the outcomes of sexual relationships. He gives the impression that he has more to lose than just the possibility of sensual intimacy, namely his council flat. Symbolically his flat seems to protect Robert from losing his safety, security and means of future survival. Objects like Robert's flat become heavily invested with unconscious longings (Blake, 2009) and here the longing appears to be about his flat becoming a protective, comfortable nest that keeps him defended from the threatening volatility of a relationship with a fantasised woman who might take away his home if the relationship abruptly collapsed. This is what Robert says about his home:

> I mean I'd be a bloody fool now if I went to live with anybody because I'm quite happy living where I am. I live in a nice place and I can look out my window and I've got a nice view and decent neighbours so I'd be a bloody fool. I could go and live with somebody and five years down the line you don't like each other so what do you do then?

The Sexual Retirement Narrative

What is fascinating about the sexual retirement narrative are the hidden motivations of some aging men contemplating sexual retirement (Marsiglio and Greer, 1995; Gott and Hinchliff, 2003) as well as those who are reassessing the role of sexual activities in later life. Many aging men are ambivalent about sexual retirement. Some of them seem to sense that sexual retirement is a tricky business where they have to be careful about negotiating a potential loss of manly heterosexuality in a cultural context of possible shame and humiliation. Consider for one moment the cultural aura of potential dishonour, failure and loss of masculine power surrounding the term, 'impotence'. As a result, some aging men look for face-saving rationales for their sexual abstinence that include reasons such as 'boredom, systemic physical illness, medication and fatigue' (Marsiglio and Greer, 1995).

Other aging men appear to want to explore the relief and the release of no longer feeling pressurised into having to live up to the exacting demands of a continuous expectation to perform and measure up to the normative standards of being a heterosexual man. Certainly more psycho-cultural work needs to be done in investigating this extremely murky area of aging men's lives.

In Robert's case, unresolved tensions remain between the sexual drive and the sexual retirement narratives. Although he still seems to be caught between these conflicting narratives, he tries to rationalise his sexual abstinence by buying into the discourse of biological, 'natural' aging (Sandberg, 2011). Robert is struggling to achieve a philosophical acceptance that, sexually speaking, he's had his time. But his attempts to persuade himself and others that 'it's no good trying to be a daffodil in the middle of September,' only rings partly true.

It seems plausible to suggest that Robert uses the 'natural' aging argument to defend himself from the possibility of shame and being labelled a failure while also expressing some kind of muddled relief. Thus he states:

> That's why it's probably natural, when you get older, your sexual instincts die...Your hormones aren't so high so [sexual desire] doesn't play a major part like it did when you were younger.

He goes on to suggest that these sexual identity shifts through a life course are mainly determined by external, biological factors rather than shaped by a dynamic dialogue between biology, history and culture, commenting that:

Nature changes you... For nature, sex is not pleasurable. It's just for reproduction. The pleasure part comes with religion and love and all that type of thing but nature is just for reproduction.

It seems plausible to suggest here that Robert is partly searching for a way of letting himself off the hook. He is not only denying the sensual aspects of sexual identities (constructing a binary opposition between a spiritual form of sexual love and reproduction) but he also seems to be denying his own personal responsibility for his presently ambivalent state of sexual being. Again, he seems to be providing himself with a plausible, face-saving excuse for no longer being sexually vigorous. This includes some healthy movement away from a sexually obsessed and predatory mode of being but also an idealisation of younger sex and a clinging on to biological determinism as well.

... as you get older your face changes so you are not attractive to the opposite sex. This is just my belief. And that is nature telling you, 'come on it's time to move on to a different thing.'

As the interviewing process with Robert developed there emerged a different, more contradictory flavour. First, he admitted that his sexual instincts were still very much alive. I asked him what he liked about dancing. He answered in this way:

Robert: At the beginning of this interview I would say that I was going for the dancing but probably deep down I'm looking for something else.

DJ: Such as?

Robert: Well I'm probably looking for a bit of talent.

DJ: So you are.

Robert: No, I don't admit it. Not so much. I go for the dancing but probably, for all I know, deep down I'm looking around. That could be the reason but I like to think it's just for the dancing.[4]

The defensive alarm in Robert's refusal openly to 'admit it', suggests that he is concerned about loss of public face, an interpretation reinforced by the purposeful, self-deception of, 'but I like to think it's just for the dancing'. However, this is also a very open and exploratory attempt by Robert to come to terms with his own contradictory positioning, torn between the sex drive narrative and the sex retirement narrative. His search for 'talent' still goes on, beneath his protestations to the contrary, but in a milder, less intense form.

Dennis's Sexual Life Story

Dennis's sexual history is tangled and complicated by the social and cultural divisions between his earlier adolescent experiences of sex in a rural background of farming and occasional fishing in Jamaica ('I looked after the mules and cows and goats'), and the more urban and industrial setting of the UK after he came to Britain in 1959 as a young man of 24. In Jamaica he came from a working-class family that he describes as 'poor but surrounded by love'. In this case the love was provided by his mother, grandmother and great grandmother. He says that he was mainly brought up by his great grandmother.

Educationally, Dennis shared some of the same male academic under-performance experiences of boys growing up in Jamaica that Figueroa notes (Figueroa, 2004). Dennis talks bitterly of being beaten and humiliated by teachers during his schooling (from 7 to 15 from 1942 to 1950), reflecting that:

> If they [the teachers] asked me something and because I didn't answer quickly they would cane me. And they believed that by caning me they would make me learn – which is a fallacy.

He left school at 15 not being able to read and write. Figueroa understands experiences like this as linked to the differential, gendered, child-rearing practices in Jamaica that perceived boys as essentially restless, unruly and academically incompetent and perceived girls as quiet, conformist and confined to the domestic arena. Certainly, in Dennis's account of his early life, it sounds as if he was allowed to run up and down as he pleased and that he also possessed 'the right to roam the streets at will' (Figueroa, 2004). During his boyhood and adolescence in Jamaica he seems to delight in the privileged space of being a running and roaming boy, commenting that:

> I was able to run and I liked running. I was very fast and agile. I liked walks. In those days we don't have any transport other than riding the donkey. But I like running and I like walking. And that was my delightful pleasure to walk.

His labelling at school, however, ('I was told by the teacher that I'm a dunce') must have disturbed him. Confronted by his marginality and failure as a young but developing working-class man, Dennis was searching for another gendered and sexual identification that might give him more power and status. He found this through a strong investment in heterosexual masculinity and through an intensely sexualised assertion of his manhood. As Donna P. Hope suggests:

> ...a man with limited or no access to true power or resources, to define his maleness, his identity through the most available and accessible avenues legitimated under Jamaican patriarchy. These include sex, sexuality and male dominance of women. (Hope, 2003)

This heavily sexualised assertion and validation of manhood in Caribbean culture often worked through the securing and bolstering of a male sexual reputation (Nurse, 2004; Sampath, 1997).

The Male, Sexual Reputation Narrative

For women, the fear of a negative sexual reputation, of being labelled a 'slag' for example, can often regulate and curtail their sexual behaviour and experiences, but for men like Dennis the reverse is more likely to be true: 'for men, being known for sexual prowess represents a gain in reputation' (Holland et al., 1998).

Throughout the interviews, Dennis reflectively and retrospectively defines himself as 'top boy'. Referring here to his heterosexual, masculine experiences in Jamaica, he says:

> I used to call myself 'top boy' when I was very active and I see it that it was because of God's grace that give me that opportunity to be virile and women like my sexual play.

The very term, 'top boy' probably reassures Dennis now in his present position of impotence at age 72. He can now look back on what he perceives as his younger, superior, sexual prowess and take pride in his youthful virility, revelling in his past sexual conquests and his perception of being a very able lover. Here he is confirmed in his heterosexual, masculine identity through what he perceives as positive responses from women and through the social recognition of the dominant peer group:

> Because I can able [sic] to service women and they enjoy it. I know I was very popular and I made them comfortable.

His use of the phrase 'service women', however, says a great deal. It is a term usually associated with agricultural stock breeding (where the bull is brought in to 'service' the cow, for example) and thus, used in the current context, powerfully suggests a mechanical, detached, almost business-like sexual attitude that completely objectifies women and excludes any semblance of intimacy, reciprocity and commitment.

When he was in the UK Dennis continued to take regular holidays in Jamaica and one particular episode recurred in his stories. He recalls a difficult time in his life when, age 51 and in a state of despair and some depression at home, he took a holiday to Jamaica and had an affair with a young woman whom he met there. I asked him whether he was sexually proud as a man, to which he replied:

> Of course it is (sic). I'm 51-year-old and I can satisfy an 18-year-old. I know she enjoyed it because I've got staying power. I've got a good erection and many girls told me that.

Here, Dennis's focus, like his comment on 'servicing women' is not on mutual pleasure and human reciprocity but on reassuring himself about his performance anxieties as an older and impotent man. The pressing concern of 'Can I still get it up?' seems to take all precedence over questions of intimacy and communication, as Calasanti (2005) notes: 'staying hard' is one of the chief concerns of aging men. Perhaps his real anxiety is that his 'top boy' reputation might be crumbling.

The Sexual Retirement Narrative

When stomach cancer was diagnosed in 2004, Dennis was confronted by the abrupt shock of not having a physically robust and virile body any more. In terms of his contradictory struggle to face up to his sexual impotence (a result of his stomach cancer operation), he vacillates between his male, sexual reputation narrative and one of sexual retirement.

He partly takes refuge in the discourse of biological 'natural' aging (Sandberg, 2011) in attempting to persuade himself that his sexual impotence is an inevitable part of his illness and, as a result, his sexual incapacity cannot be viewed as a shameful, personal failure. He notes:

> What I'm saying is I don't see it [his sexual impotence] as a failure. I have to see it as a misfortune. I cannot control illness. I cannot stop the sun from shining and I cannot stop the rain from falling.

Dennis wants to accept his sexual impotence as biological misfortune but there are still unresolved tensions in his shifting attitudes. Again, he see-saws, on the one hand, between a stoic, philosophical acceptance of his condition – heavily influenced by a religious perspective and expressed in his comment that: 'I lose my sex drive but I gain life', and an emotional confusion on the other. He still seems puzzled about really believing that 'sex is not everything. I have life'. He is still wondering what kind of life it will be without sexual confirmation of his heterosexual, masculine identity, raising the awkward question as to: 'How can you live without sexual prestige and reputation?'

Dennis's bewilderment about his sexual changes becomes clear in his belated attempt to preserve something of his 'top boy' reputation in the eyes of a woman friend in Jamaica. He is anxious and insecure, for example, about telling her the truth about his sexual condition: 'But I don't have the courage to tell her that I'm not like I used to be'.

It takes a great deal of emotional courage as an older man to talk openly about one's own impotence so I have considerable respect for Dennis's position. However I also sense his unspoken pain and loss beneath his avoidance of the actual word, 'impotence' and his defensive circumlocution in referring to his condition as 'I'm not like I used to be'. In our final interview, Dennis reveals that he has spoken to his Jamaican friend and that he told her:

'I'm not "top boy" any more. I'm not like before'. And she says to me 'Do you still have feelings?' I said, 'Yes'. So she said there was no problem.

Although there is some ambiguity here as to whether she is referring to loving friendship feelings or sexual feelings, we can also see an emerging sense of a process of reconciliation and re-assessment starting to happen in Dennis. Towards the end of the final interview Dennis begins to consider more other-related, empathetic sexual identities:

I'm alive differently. I don't let it revolve around sex any more. It can revolve around listening and caring for people in a different way. Listening to people's needs instead of being self-centred about sex.

A close reading reveals the self-disciplined effort that Dennis is using to wean himself off an adolescent model of sexual behaviour. He is still caught in the middle of these different models of aging men's sexualities but he is beginning to be aware that it is possible to move towards a different way of male, sexual being in the world. It is perhaps through the physical shocks and dislocations in many aging men's lives that the dominant ideals of heterosexual masculinity and gendered expectations begin to become destabilised and unsettled and more open to possible changes.

Discussion

In a small research study as this, data needs to be approached as exploratory, and wide, sweeping generalisations avoided (Heaphy et al., 2004). Nevertheless, the data can also offer important insights into the sexual lives of aging men in the UK, both non-heterosexual and hetero-sexual. Or, as queer theory suggests, there also needs to be a questioning of the hierarchical, binary logic that keeps gay and heterosexual identi-ties so firmly separated from each other. Perhaps there are also hints in the data of blurring and a destabilising of these supposedly segregated, sexual identities?

In terms of non-heterosexual, aging men's sexualities, my research reveals how subtle and nuanced are the ways in which some gay men negotiate their sexual identities. Because gay men are subordinated in relation to the dominant forms of heterosexual masculinity, their sexualities are more hybrid and complicated. For example, although Michael partly came across as a gendered, 'manly' man in his obsessive sex drive, he was also capable of innovatory, 'gentleman callers' sexual strategies.

Michael also enjoyed being outside the normative, heterosexual framework. In later life he explicitly rejected the suffocating, couple-oriented culture of heterosexist ideology (Heaphy et al., 2004) and improvised in his own alternative terms to produce his more friendship influenced, sexual model of 'gentleman callers.'

In Roy's case, the stale stereotype of gay, male promiscuity (Mutchler, 2000) and assumptions about casual sex are effectively challenged. In his sexual life history, the prominence of a more relationship-focused, romantic love perspective suggests that he did not value wild sex with strangers very highly. Instead, he preferred 'hugging, kissing and holding' with a loving partner, commenting that, 'affection is more important than coming,' and, 'I want love in my life, not dick.'

Although my research offers some confirmatory hints that hegemonic, aging men's sexualities are still dominant in the UK (Plummer, 2005), there are increasing signs that aging men are broaden-ing their conventional, sexual range and starting to explore different sexual priorities, definitions, practices and ways of being. 'Real' sex for many older, heterosexual men is still narrowly linked to vaginal penetration but there are indications that the penis-centred and orgasm-centred model is beginning to lose ground (more of this below). Perhaps it is now more appropriate to consider a multi-layered model of aging men's more subtle, historical transitions and movements through a life course. Certainly, my research data unearths residual traces (Johnson, 2010, citing Raymond Williams' work) of earlier, hegemonic, male sex lingering in heterosexual, aging men's desires, fantasies and imaginings.

In the sexual histories of Dennis and Robert, for example, their adolescent historical investments in hegemonic male sexualities are still very much with them in later life, admittedly fading, but still ghostly presences giving shape to contradictory desires and unresolved sexual tensions within their present lives. Certainly, most of these aging men's sexual biographies reveal unresolved tensions as a major theme within my research. Instead of stability and certainty, there is much more of a dynamic see-sawing between a stoic, philosophical acceptance of a rapidly changing condition and emotional confusion and messiness.

In Dennis's case, his early experiences of working-class poverty, economic marginality and lack of power in Jamaica perhaps made him more susceptible to the construction of gendered and sexual identifications that might compensate for his lack of educational competence and self-worth. This is made possible through a strong investment in heterosexual masculinity and the construction of a 'top boy' sexual reputation, as seen through the eyes of his dominant peer group.

In older age, though, Dennis is confronted by the physical trauma and disruption of a stomach cancer operation that leaves him sexually impotent. In his ensuing struggles to re-negotiate his sexual identity, his initial reluctance to tell his Jamaican, woman friend the truth about his sexual impotence reveals a lasting attachment to his previous, 'top boy', sexual prowess, as though he cannot yet face up to losing his sexual swagger in her eyes.

Arguably, there are no entirely clear divisions or transformations possible in the sexual lives of aging men because the muddled traces of adolescent, heterosexual and homosexual, masculine investments and formations remain. These have their roots in particularly narrow and polarised, historical moments in late 1950s and early 60s and are still enduringly apparent in their later lives. This is not to say that no changes and developments are possible in aging men's sexual identities but that, sometimes, other older layers from earlier sexual formations occasionally overlap contemporary formations affecting the complex processes of sexual re-definition as they age. The enduring power of these earlier traces is also closely linked to the potential force and depth of adolescent investments in sexual identities. This defence of an often deeply insecure, emergent masculine identity is expressed through constantly seeking confirmation and approval from the 'real lads.'

Robert's sexual history with the contradictory tension between the sex drive and sexual retirement narratives, reveal elements of the same mixed collusion with hegemonic, masculine, sexual identities. Although Robert is trying to find a constructive way out of his fading, sexual desire as an older man, he catches himself still keeping an eye open for what he describes as 'talent'. Initially he attempts to explain his sexual abstinence and lack of sexual vigour through a face-saving justification, attributing it to the death of his sexual instincts.

Later, however, Robert admits that his sexual instincts were still very much alive, although different now from those of his adolescence and his desire to become a 'big guy'. Those predatory resonances of his early hectic pursuit of women (when he used to prowl up and down the train corridor looking for 'talent') are still dimly there in his later life. For example, when I asked him what he liked about dancing Robert said: 'I go for the dancing but probably, for all I know, deep down I'm looking around'. In spite of protestations to the contrary, his youthful search for 'talent' still goes on, if in a less-determined, more personally-reflexive form.

Another significant feature of my research evidence is the relative unsettling of ageist and stereotypical assumptions about the relationship between aging and sex. The aging men in my research present as neither asexual, 'past it', or passively withdrawn. Rather it seems that aging men may still be active sexually, if in a variety of different ways. They may no longer be tied down to a sex drive narrative but they show every sign of being able to improvise boldly and imaginatively as their bodies and their life conditions shift and change.

The research evidence also shows how much ambiguity and contradictoriness there is in aging men's sexual lives. There were extremely complex intersections of age, masculinities, class and race to be found in the four sexual life histories. For example, social class and the sex drive narrative intersect in highly ambivalent ways in Robert's sexual life history. Robert's need for a sense of personal security (especially his fear of becoming homeless) is at least as important to him as establishing an affectionate contact with a woman – perhaps more so given his current life of abstinence. Age, poverty and social class have the power to vary and modify his sexual being as well as gender.

Dennis's adolescent, sexual history in Jamaica is tangled and complicated by the complex intersections of working-class failure and marginality in the educational sphere, along with a powerful compensatory investment in heterosexual masculinity in his 'top boy' sexual identity. From the age of 24, in the UK, his experiences of institutional racism in the early 1960s further complicated and perhaps limited the range of his sexual identities.

The research data also suggests that the processes of aging often provoke a re-definition of aging men's sex drive narratives or taken for granted, heterosexual norms. Similarly, Gott and Hinchliff (2003) suggest physical disruption and changes in later life, might be linked to transitions in identities and sexual subjectivities. They also consider that this is particularly the case for aging men who are experiencing, 'barriers to engaging in penetrative sex' (Gott and Hinchliff, 2003).

Certainly the potential challenges which accompany the sexual retirement narrative, for example in terms of losing 'masculine face' and having to negotiate the possibility of shame and humiliation, have the capacity to encourage aging men towards a long and strenuous process of reassessment and contemplation of their changing sexual beings. As with Dennis's bodily and mental shifts after his stomach cancer operation:

> I'm alive differently. I don't let it revolve around sex anymore. It can revolve around listening and caring for people in a different way.

He is still partly trapped between these different narratives of aging men's sexualities but he is beginning to become aware that it is possible to move towards a different way of male, sexual being in the world.

As Potts et al. (2006) have commented, the purpose of sexuality and sex changes with age and experience. There appears to be less emphasis in aging men's sexual lives on penetrative sex and achieving orgasm at all costs, and greater importance given to, 'non-penile pleasures' and other bodily pleasures, along with a greater prioritisation of their partners' desires. In some aging men's lives this involved a deliberate turning away from self-centred sex, so often typical of their youth, and greater value given instead to more slowed-down, gentle and reciprocal sex. Sandberg (2011) in her detailed study of aging men's sexualities in Sweden, also goes beyond the over-emphases on erection and penetration. Instead she decentres genital penetration and, alternatively, draws attention to the evidence of aging men's:

> ... stress [on] cuddling, touch and other forms of closeness. (p. 28)

The historical dimension also proved to be a key feature of my research in highlighting the importance of making sense of personal, sexual biographies against changing cultural and social backgrounds in the UK. Thus it became clear that these aging men's present sexual practices and attitudes are directly influenced by the dominant, sexual standards of their youth. Although some are, of course, influenced more than others, generally speaking they are all touched, to some extent, by the shifting normative sexual assumptions of specific, historical periods in their lives. In terms of the two, older gay men, they had to live through and come to terms with the discrimination and social oppression of the 1950s and early 1960s, experiences which nearly silenced Michael ('I'd better keep that side of me a bit quiet'), and almost led to his self-destruction. But, remarkably, both men creatively worked out their eventual sexual positions with ingenious adaptation and improvisation.

If the inventive fluidity and diversity of these aging men's sexual experiences is anything to go by, then what is popularly understood as 'normal sex' for men needs to be re-assessed and re-evaluated. There is an urgent need to recognise what can be learnt from aging men's sexual experiences; their distinctive knowledges, their relationships, their awareness, in later life, and so on. Some of these new understandings and relations need to be put more at the centre of our debates around men and masculinity, especially emerging standpoints about sex as social reciprocity, if we are to stand a chance of altering conventional approaches to heterosexual masculinities.

A greater understanding of aging men's highly creative and adaptive sexualities has the potential to destabilise our conventional meanings and understandings about men, masculinity and sexuality, creating future possibilities for agency, development and change. Perhaps, through such destabilisations, there will even emerge a critical fracturing of the invisible, 'naturalised', heterosexual masculine norms that still keep many of us locked up like slaves to our own sexualities.

5
Learning to Live with Parkinson's and 'An Unpredictable Body' as an Aging Man: An Investigation into Age, Masculine Identity and Disability

The central focus of this chapter is to closely examine the embattled conflict between disability and men and masculinities in the life history of one man called Peter. The dynamic conflict between disability and masculinities consists of the opposing associations of disability-dependency, weakness and vulnerability-and masculinities that are usually perceived as strong, autonomous and powerful (Shuttleworth, Wedgwood and Wilson, 2012; Gershick and Miller, 1994). This leads me to ask the key, research question: How do disabled men like Peter negotiate the interaction between disability and masculinities in his aging life? Peter is a 64-year-old, white, heterosexual, disabled man. Parkinson's was diagnosed in his life six years ago as a late-onset, degenerative impairment. He is married with two children. He was born into a middle class family and he has followed his father in becoming a vicar in the Church of England. After working in the church he became the director of a large, voluntary organisation and then later worked for the local city council in education.

First, I need to make clear what Parkinson's disease is and what it does to our bodies and mental and emotional conditions:

> Parkinson's disease (P.d.) is a neurological disorder characterised by the presence of a resting tremor, bradykinesia (slower movement), and rigidity (overall stiffness). P.d.'s ultimate etiology is unknown, and it is incurable. However, P.d. patients can gain symptomatic relief through pharmacotherapy. Over time, patients' symptoms may require both higher dosages and polypharmacy, but patients obtain

less satisfactory relief with an ever-increasing range of side effects. A combination of disease progression and side effects contributes to sufferers' considerable physical and cognitive limitations, including freezing (momentary inability to move), impaired executive function, gait problems, chronic constipation, drooling, dyskinesia (uncontrollable spasm-like movements), the on/off syndrome (sudden loss of function between medication doses) and hallucinations. (Lees, 2002 [cited in Solimeo, S43, 2008])

The illusions of embodied coherence, physical competence and stability often experienced by the non-aged and non-disabled are sharply undermined by Peter's, disabled, bodily experiences of uncertainty and unpredictability associated with living with Parkinson's, like in this section of the interview where I asked Peter the question:

> D.J: What's particularly difficult for mainstream society to accept about Parkinson's?

> Peter: I think its variability probably. It [Parkinson's] could be very different at different times of the day and from one day to the next.

In the case of Parkinson's, the disabled bodies of men like Peter serve as a continual reminder of visible differences from normative, non-disabled men's bodies. They are often experiencing the sensations of living in shaking, stiff, rigid or frozen bodies. All these bodily irregularities and unpredictabilities threaten the cultural values of dominant masculinities, such as bodily strength, force and speed .From this perspective, it provides a thoughtful, analytical position to re-assess the contradictory relations between age, disability and masculinities. My intention in drawing attention to this one man's life story is not to individualise or pathologise him but to connect his lived experiences with broader social issues like gendered 'identity work' (Solimeo, 2008) and the multiply-contested discourses that surround disabled, aging men's lives.

I also want to bring cultural diversity and difference into my argument. It is important to recognise how age and disabled relations intersect with gender relations and other social forces like class, sexual orientation, ethnicity and race (Calasanti, 2004; Sandberg, 2007). In this chapter I selectively focus on masculinities as they intersect with disability and age. In order to grasp the tangled complexity of older, disabled men's lives, the subtle, nuanced interactions of age, disability and men and masculinities need to be carefully acknowledged and thought through. Age is brought into this research study as an explicit, critical emphasis, alongside disability and masculinity rather than a relatively neglected, marginal issue. Before I begin to interrogate Peter's complicated life history I want to pay attention to the conceptual background of disability studies framing Peter's lived experiences.

Theoretical Shifts in Disability Studies Over the Last Thirty Years

The dominance of the biomedical discourse in disability studies has come under sustained critical attack over the last thirty years (Oliver, 1983 and 1996; Barnes, 1990 and 1997; Finkelstein, 1993). Indeed the beginnings of a deconstructive approach to disability studies is centred on interrogating the biological determinism of the biomedical model.

These critical reassessments have provoked a major redefinition of disability as a social, relational construct (Thomas and Corker, 2002; Shakespeare, 1999; Bredenkamp, 2007) rather than a biologically defined phenomenon. As Shakespeare comments on the social model of disability:

> It explores disability as a form of social oppression, defining disabled people in terms of discrimination and prejudice, not in terms of medical tragedy: people with impairment are disabled by society, not by their bodies. (Shakespeare, 1999)

The social oppression of disabled people, or so the social model explains, is based on the hierarchical relationship between a socially constructed conception of 'normal' and 'natural' interacting with what is socially defined as inferior and 'abnormal' (Thomas, 2002). Moreover, as Corker and Shakespeare point out, 'normativism needs disability for its own definition' (Corker and Shakespeare, 2002). So that 'normality' is confirmed and empowered by defensively buttressing its own insecure condition against an 'othered' and feared 'abnormality' (Fawcett, 2000).

However, postmodern, theoretical interventions (Corker and Shakespeare, 2002) have recently brought in a fresh re-thinking of these debates about disability. It is now gradually being recognised that some of the more local, 'impairment effects' (Thomas, 2002)-emotional, psychological, embodied-have been excluded from these universalising theories.

A second, important, theoretical shift acknowledges the possibilities of new relations between impairment and embodiment. Aging men's disabled bodies, like Peter's, are contradictory, contested sites where multiple meanings, identities and discourses are in dynamic conflict with each other. The dominant, biological meanings of bodies within the biomedical discourse and the marginalising of bodies in the social modellers' approach(e.g. 'people with impairment are disabled by society, not by their bodies' –(Shakespeare, 1999) make no allowances for the complex, human resilience of actual disabled bodies nor for the dynamic interplay between disability and masculine expectations in disabled men's lives. There is now an urgent need to re-embody disability theory (Corker and Shakespeare, 2002) and to bring in disabled men's lived, embodied experiences along with the discursive clashes that can begin to make sense of Peter's life with Parkinson's.

Alongside these re-definitions concerning aging and disabled bodies, has emerged a closer awareness of impairment difference and specific, situational variety.(Shuttleworth, Wedgwood and Wilson, 2012) What this means is that disabled men differ from one another in embodying and experiencing masculine expectations differently, depending on the type and degree of their impairments and the social and cultural contexts that they exist within. What really matters here in understanding disabled men's lives is the ability to look closely at the specific particularity of impairments and how they intersect with other social forces such as gender, class, race, ethnicity and social status.

A major limitation of impairment-specific research, according to Shuttleworth, Wedgwood and Wilson, has been the tendency to 'focus on men with spinal cord injuries' and they suggest that there has been a bias in the field towards men with acquired injuries. Some of that research has been concerned with elitist sportsmen or 'real' men whose grip on masculine identities have collapsed, rather than widening the research field to include aging, disabled men of lesser power and bodily inadequacy like Peter who talked about his own body as 'fat and unfit' and 'as always (having) let me down a bit.' Perhaps Peter wanted to compensate for his body of lesser, masculine power through being able to activate an alternative, masculine competence from his past, social power and status as a middle-class Director of a large, city organisation?

There is also a disabled, re-definition of masculine identities available, particularly in later life, when some of the clashes between disability and masculinities take on a contradictory and sometimes confusing quality. For example, Peter at 64 displays strength and determination of inner character through attempting to embrace his bodily 'weakness' and occasional stuttering gait and physical movement as a Parkinson's survivor. In his case, the conventional, gendered expectations of bodily solidity and strength are converted into the ironic, masculine identity and new position of , 'Weakness is Peter's internal strength.'

Learning to Live with Parkinson's: An Investigation into the Lived Experiences of Peter's Aging and Disabled, Embodied Selves

(A) The Biomedical Discourse of Aging, Disabled Men Being Represented as Failed, Masculine Body-Selves

The dominant, biomedical discourse constructs older, disabled men's body-selves as sites of inevitable physical and mental decay and deterioration.

From a biomedical perspective, Parkinson's in aging men is seen as weakness and failed masculinity. Solimeo comments that many aging men feel emasculated by disability like Parkinson's (Solimeo, 2008). In his life course, Peter is very much aware of the implicit contrasts between his own present, disabled body and the idealised bodily, normative standards he encountered in his earlier life growing up. He does not want to see his body-self as a 'flop' but at school he was teased about his body being 'rather fat and unfit'. Also, later on, he says:

> ...at a sort of sixth form level I wasn't good enough to really be of distinction in any of the sports.

When I asked Peter whether he accepted his body or felt ashamed of it, he replied:

> I accepted it but I felt that other people probably didn't.

Any attempt on Peter's part to value his body on its own terms was undermined by his awareness of the 'other people' whom he internalised as making negative comments about the shape, size and appearance of his body.

Although Peter acknowledges the socially oppressive character of the dominant culture of his school days, he does not completely buy into the 'failed masculinity' discourse. Early on in his life, Peter distanced himself from the worst aspects of this erosion of body self-confidence through his rejection of the dominant forms of masculinity embodied by his father. This gradual rejection of ruling forms of masculine values worked on two levels.

First, Peter wanted to escape from his father's authority and power in the home by dissociating himself from his father's ways of doing things. He comments on his father:

> He was a classic example of somebody whose only interpretation of being male was to be right, to be in charge and to be making decisions.

In wanting to be different from his father Peter also began to interrogate the normative assumptions of gender and dominant versions of men and masculinities ascendant at that particular time (the 1950s). This challenging can be seen in a later part of the interviews. Peter begins to wonder about:

> ...men who have been brought up to think that their persona is based around doing and achievement and physical strength and leadership and these sorts of characteristics which fade as you get older. Now what is it that allows men to remain positive?

The second level in Peter's life (of rejecting ruling forms of masculine values) centres on the strangely positive dimensions of his less-normative body. He talks about his body as 'always (having) let me down a bit.' Over his life span he has recognised that he has 'never been a fit one, strong or athletic' so that over the years he has got more used to living with an untrustworthy body. As a result, Peter now reflects about the possibility that moving from an unreliable body to confronting Parkinson's is perhaps less of a difficult and disturbing transition than moving from a fitter, stronger body to having to live with Parkinson's. In a way, Peter had become habituated to a problematic, embodied identity that, 'always let me down a bit'. So perhaps, in terms of dominant masculinity expectations, Peter was used to accepting a less powerful, masculine body without the intense experiences of loss, bitterness and regret expressed by disabled men with spinal cord injuries or disabled men with acute, suddenly acquired injuries.

(B) Embracing Embodied Vulnerability and Fragmentariness

Instead of viewing a disability like Parkinson's as a 'medical tragedy', Peter's life history indicated that there are different, more constructive ways of living with Parkinson's that are also closely bound up with ways of radically disrupting and destabilising conventional notions and practices of masculinity.

The dominant, masculine myths of stable, coherent, unified embodied, masculine,selves are in the process of being sharply interrogated by Peter's experiences of his lived in, Parkinson's embodied identities.. When I asked Peter the question:

> DJ: What's particularly difficult for mainstream society to accept about Parkinson's?

Peter's answer was:

> I think it's variability probably. It [Parkinson's] could be very different at different times of the day and from one day to the next.

The erratic, unpredictable, bodily rhythms of living with Parkinson's seemed to invade the masculine illusion of solidity and rational control of many men's more ordered lives. Peter also defined Parkinson's as the 'uncontrollable disease'. In a relatively patriarchal society where many men invested a great deal of energy in retaining control of their bodies and social situations they found themselves within. Possessing a 'shaking, shuffling' body might seem transgressive and even subversive of a more taken for granted, gendered order.

When you consider that older, masculine body-selves reflect a lifelong engagement in a taken for granted, gender regime, and even a stable position in the male dominance hierarchy among men (Charmaz, 1995), you can begin to appreciate how potentially destabilising to traditional, gender relations the experiences of living with Parkinson's might be.

Although Peter was struggling with occasional, mild depression and an infrequent sense of 'aimlessness' in his life, he was determined to embrace his own, embodied vulnerability. On one level, he was openly critical of some Parkinson's men who were trying to hide their disabilities in public contexts. He thought that associating Parkinson's with secrecy and shame and trying to 'hide it from the bosses' only exacerbated the difficult realities of living with Parkinson's.

On another level, Peter openly recognised his embodied vulnerability. He said:

> I'm trying not to avoid it or mind it.

He had decided to be 'upfront' and positive about his disability. All through the interviews he spent time acknowledging his fallible and fragmentary embodied, masculine identities. He talked about having to walk more slowly and stumbling occasionally. He referred to the increases of tension and rigidity in his arms and legs (at one point he described his way of walking as the 'rigid steps of a wooden figure'.) Also he talked about his connected, occasional mental confusion and 'lassitude'. Parkinson's was not just a physical disease for Peter but a disease that affected him both mentally and physically. It also challenged his own grip on masculine identities.

In these various ways, Peter defied the 'tragic' connotation of the Parkinson's disease label. He said that, 'a healthy life needs gentle challenges' and he was very much doing that in his own life, challenging normative and restrictive assumptions about aging men's, disabled, masculine embodied identities. He was also countering what society expects aging men with Parkinson's to be like in their bodies.

However there were puzzling, internal tensions in Peter's life that I was aware of as an unresolved under current. To understand what these contradictory tensions might mean I now need to turn to the area in his life that I have called, 'the discourse of rational control and leadership.'

(C) Rational Control and Leadership

The shadow of the workplace in retirement was still very much influencing Peter's life at the present moment. He was still putting his considerable work and organisational skills to socially useful effect. Middle class men like Peter, unlike many working-class, manual workers, had experienced satisfying and mentally challenging work in community care as a progressive vicar and as the director of a large, voluntary organisation he had pioneered open and collaborative styles of working. Now in retirement, learning to grapple with Parkinson's, he was still excessively busy.

Peter had become the chairperson of the local Parkinson's group, had successfully bid for and was awarded a £9.000 research grant, was good at mobilising a social network linked to improving the social conditions surrounding Parkinson's and had also played a major part in creating a hospital exercise programme working with Parkinson's survivors.

However, Peter's position in relation to this discourse was more contradictory than I've been making out. For Peter to take a positive, pro-active approach to his Parkinson's was totally admirable. In one of the interviews he comments about his approach in the following way:

> ...seeing it as positive-well not really a positive in life but an aspect of life about which the only sensible recourse is to be positive. And

to say that it brings in another whole network of people. I'm back to being a secular vicar again.

The firm, matter-of-fact, unsentimental tone is courageous but it hides his underlying fears and anxieties. His need to preserve something of his past, working self ('I'm back to being a secular vicar...') and surround himself with a new social network hints at an unresolved, hidden area of his life.

Later, Peter talked openly and honestly about some of these personal needs, especially his need for public recognition:

> I need and am dependent upon public acclaim of doing a leadership job and getting it right.

And then again:

> I get an enormous kick out of doing things in public which brings me esteem.

Peter's need to do a very competent leadership job and 'get it right' carries with it uncomfortable echoes of his father needing to 'be right; to be in charge and to be making decisions.' Perhaps this points to internal tensions and contradictory desires in Peter's life?

In terms of a psychosocial explanation of what might be going on in Peter's life, I need to introduce other interpretations and theories at this stage of the argument. In looking at alternative forms of masculine subjectivity, Redman and Mac an Ghaill draw attention to middle class forms of doing masculinity that are organised around mental prowess, or what they call, ' muscular intellectualness' (Redman and Mac an Ghaill, 1997).

At a time in Peter's life of great uncertainty and threat, it seems plausible to suggest that his active buying in to the instrumental, rational control and leadership discourse could be partly read as a psychic and social defence against anxiety, about losing control and losing physical competence (Solimeo, 2008). Indeed it might suggest a compensatory trade-off between loss of bodily competence and his assertion of muscular intellectualness. So he fought back against his bodily destabilisation by engaging in the organisational, mental assertions and skills of leadership.

In Kathy Charmaz's chapter on 'Identity dilemmas of chronically ill men', she makes the point that middle class men seek to make illness and disability meaningful, to recast them into something through which positive identification could be made (Charmaz, 1995). Peter was very much in the process of doing just that, of converting a negative view of Parkinson's into something more constructive and meaningful for himself. This he did through the energy and commitment of his leadership role in improving the lives of Parkinson survivors in the local region of the East Midlands.

Although Peter was very engaged in important and socially useful work he was also, simultaneously, preserving and protecting his own threatened embodied, masculine identities.. His 'career in retirement' not only demonstrated Peter's considerable leadership and organisational skills in getting things done out there but it also gave him an opportunity to re-constitute himself as an honoured, caring person known and valued in the past and in the present in his local community. Perhaps this busy, leadership role helped Peter to retain a more stable and continuing link with a respected, past identity and with real, social status at a time of bewildering disruption?

Peter's anxieties and fears surrounding Parkinson's surfaced regularly through the interviews. He talked about the occasional bad times in his present life:

> ... when I have times ... It's probably associated with mild depression but it's a sense of aimlessness; listlessness; not knowing what to do; not getting anything done; not being able to rest and relax either.

His anxieties about instrumental efficiency and 'not getting anything done' are clearly present in his life but also co-existed with a deeper, existential threat and insecurity about body-self disintegration:

> ... I'm afraid that the Parkinson's will mean that actually I do degenerate into more of a vegetable than I want to be [...] I don't want to know what I'll be like in ten years' time.

So it seems possible that Peter's emotional investment in being an organiser and leader not only produced some strategies of stabilisation and survival for himself and some socially useful work but also formed a psychosocial defence against 'aimlessness' and fears of degenerating into a vegetable.

Discussion

From the research evidence above, it is clear that the dynamic conflict between disability and masculinities in Peter's life has not been fully reconciled and that he had not completely come to terms with his limitations as a disabled man. Even though Peter and other disabled men attempt to embrace the sources of their supposed 'weakness', they still value many masculine traits. The shaking foundations of Parkinson's and occasional forced passivity led Peter to emphasise his autonomy in other areas where he could display a more outward competence and independence.

His background of social class, partnership status and legacies of work as well as his specific impairment are central to Peter's life course. Peter is a man from a relatively stable, middle class background who has not had to struggle for economic survival. However he does not come across as self-indulgent or excessively privileged, partly I suppose because of the limited material conditions of being a clergyman. He acknowledges that he has experienced, 'a very comfortable and well looked after life'(referring to the NHS). About his material position in retirement, he comments: ' We are careful without being penny-pinching about it and we can have a very enjoyable life and I think that is an incredible privilege.'

Peter's use of 'we' rather than 'I' in the above quotation indicates just how important marital support and close companionship is to him in later life. Perhaps it also suggests how much he needs his wife's caring to survive in his present condition? As Kathy Charmaz comments, many married men, in roughly similar situations to Peter, 'received an outpouring of care, comfort and love from their wives and families' (Charmaz, 1995).

Certainly partnership status(and other conditions like non-married and non-heterosexual relations) is one of the key and often neglected aspects of aging men's lives that influenced quality of life, according to Arber, Davidson and Ginn in their work on the 'masculinity turn' in old age studies (Arber, Davidson and Ginn, 2003).

Class-related issues also have a direct bearing on Peter's relationship to work, his embodied sense of self and the legacies of work patterns in retirement. Middle class, aging men like Peter have a tendency to identify themselves very strongly through their prior investments in their paid work, whereas many working-class, aging men do not define themselves through their work (Emslie, Hunt and O'Brien, 2004). So Peter still identifies himself as a 'secular vicar', particularly one who is involved in constant community care and giving support to other members of his Parkinson's group.

Peter's disabled, masculine subjectivity remains a multiply contested site where different power relations and competing tensions are played out through the clash of different, dominant discourses, practices and identities. In Peter's case, for example, his strong refusal to be negatively labelled as a 'failed man' within the biomedical discourse has lured him in to actively taking up more contradictory, subject positions both within the 'embracing vulnerability' discourse and the instrumental leadership discourse.

This has led to a complex balance of different forces and rival discourses in Peter's and other men's lives. The movement within Peter's masculine subjectivity represents a fluid interplay between conformity to dominant forms of masculinity and contestation. Governing forms of embodied masculinity are problematised and destabilised through their conventional, bodily norms being confronted by the embodied unpredictability and vulnerability of less-normative body-selves. Sometimes this might lead to a questioning of cultural, supremacist ideals of complete and perfectly intact, dominating bodies or even the masculine fantasy of the invincible body. As a result some of the key, idealised features of dominant masculinities (like speed, agility, virility, strength and sustained stamina) are called into question by the 'embracing vulnerability' discourse.

These embodied disruptions and discontinuities are important and can lead to critical reappraisals of masculine, embodied, identities. Bodily breakdown and supposed 'failure' can provoke, 'reappraisals of productivity, achievement, relationships. All alter what these men defined as valuable. Their forced reappraisals led to setting priorities, making decisions, and also coming to terms with their pasts and presents' (Charmaz, 1995).

The evidence of my research project points to the contradictory and mixed nature of gendered subjectivities in disabled, old age. One noteworthy point is that there is little absolute rejection of dominant forms of masculinity. In Peter's case there are strands of male power, stoicism and authority and gender conformity (mainly in terms of rational, mental prowess) to be found in his deep investment in the rational control and leadership discourse. These strands intermingle with the embracing of vulnerability in his life. So that, in conclusion, Peter's life as a disabled ,aging man can be described as an example of modified masculine identities, clinging on to some strands of masculine authority while, simultaneously, destabilising and contesting dominant forms of embodied, masculine subjectivity.

Some aging, disabled men confront their position as a creative challenge not as a 'medical tragedy'. Sandberg (2007) brings up this related question of adventurous rebellion or what she calls 'norm-breaking' in aging, disabled men's lives. Peter did not want to be imprisoned by

Parkinson's. He certainly did not accept the passive victim label but kept on struggling to re-define who he was or who he might be in a society that fails to include disabled men. A large part of him did not want to conform to the standard norms of bodily shape, size, appearance, movement and performance.

His attitude to taking pills illustrates his independent scepticism about official authority. He says in relation to pill-taking:

> ...so you've got to be setting your own level really all the time and you have to balance out the needs of each part of the day...

Peter wanted to be able to 'move about and travel without too much pain'. In looking through the interviews again, I get the feeling that he was always looking for ways of moving beyond the charity/pity/tragedy model of disability. Indeed, he is becoming a critical norm-breaker in the putting together of his own life. In one of the interviews I discovered this interchange between Peter and myself:

> DJ: Do you accept your emotional and physical limitations?
>
> Peter: Yes and no. I think I do but I want to work beyond them. I see it as a challenge. There's no such thing as a hard and fast line-obviously I can't run a four minute mile. But if I'm going to have a healthy life I need to set myself some gentle challenges each day.

This active challenging of 'hard and fast' boundaries and normative structures is Peter's way of looking after his own well-being. Being prepared to go beyond familiar expectations and limitations, both mentally and physically, helps him to keep himself alive.

Aging, disabled men live active and fulfilling lives (Sandberg, 2007; Fleming, 1999) despite the threats (and to some extent the opportunities) of their disrupted embodied identities. Peter does embrace bodily fragmentariness in his own life with some energy and courage and he acknowledges the stumbling, shaking irregularities of his everyday living with Parkinson's. There's still a great deal to learn from supposedly 'marginal' men like Peter about the processes of living creatively with disability, aging and the conditions of being an aging man in 2016.

6
The Challenges and Opportunities of Aging Men's Spousal Caregiving

Although women carry out the major share of informal, family care work, (Arber, Davidson and Ginn, 2003), and, generally, there is a low level of men's caregiving (Hanlon, 2009), it is wrongly assumed that men are incapable of the caring role, (Applegate and Kaye, 1995) As Niall Hanlon (Hanlon, 2009) points out in an Irish context, there are specific groups of men who are much more likely to engage in caregiving, particularly aging men and gay men.

Therefore, my study focuses on these two groups of men. Certainly the social reality of aging men's lives in the UK tells a different story than the general point about low levels of men's caregiving. Contrary to popular belief, aging men, especially in their informal, spousal/partner relations, are heavily engaged in caregiving. Roughly similar proportions of men and women in the UK give sustained care to their partners and spouses who have chronic, physical or mental disabilities, (Arber, Davidson and Ginn, 2003).

Aging men's experiences as informal caregivers have been largely ignored or marginalised (Kramer, 2002; Russell, 2004). There is now a pressing need to delve deeper into aging men's caregiving experiences to understand more completely the subtlety of their caring relationships, circumstances and motivations. At the moment our understandings of the caregiving experiences remain underdeveloped as well as our need to challenge the social assumptions that men are unable to fill the caregiving role.

As Christine L. Williams comments: 'There is no question that men can do the work usually assigned to women' (Williams, 1993). The other important features of aging men as caregivers are the long-term commitment and frequent intensity of their caring (Kaye, 1997). Ducharme, (2006), have confirmed this long-term responsibility and commitment in their research study of aging men caring for their wives in Quebec, Canada. Out of a sample of 323 aging men, 'nearly 60% of them spent at least 84 hours a week caregiving,' (Ducharme et al., 2006).

I have also focused attention in my study on non-heterosexual aspects of informal, aging men's caregiving as well as heterosexual couples. Spousal care needs to be re-defined to include a wider, more diverse range of relationships and partnerships, particularly in the context of gay men, AIDS and caring (Sipes, 2005). My study will examine the experiences of a much older, gay caregiver in his seventies.

This chapter sets out to interrogate the subjective complexity of aging men's caregiving experiences within long-term partnerships and spousal care. It does this by drawing on data from my own three-year, small-scale, qualitative research study which explores the diverse experiences of aging men in the 60–75 age range, employing a life history, narrative, research method (Chamberlayne, Bornat and Wengraf, 2004). More specifically I will closely examine the informal caregiving experiences of two aging men, one heterosexual and the other a gay, older man who cared for his younger partner with AIDS, in the light of two key questions arising from the heart of my study. Firstly, are aging men as caregivers to be seen as mainly instrumental and managerial in their styles of caring, and how much are they engaged in emotional and nurturing caring? Secondly, is there a changing dynamic between the caregiver and care receiver and how much does it affect the quality of their relationship from the start of the relationship to the present moment or end of the contact?

Prior to interrogating my two case studies, a number of conceptual frames that inform my analysis will be outlined.

The Conceptual Frames

The Changing Meanings of Caring in the UK

In the 1950s in post-war Britain there was an extremely polarised, binary system of gender relations after settling down again after the shifts and disruptions of the Second World War (Segal, 1990). Despite a few partners who risked crossing the gendered divide, there was, generally, a rigid segregation of male wage-workers operating exclusively in the public sphere, (although some working-class women continued to work in factories), and female, unpaid, domestic workers in the private sphere. The legacies of that gendered, binary system still partly inform the changing meanings of caring over the last sixty years in the UK, although there have also been real changes in Western gender relations during that time (Annandale and Hunt, 2000). The traces of this binary system can be clearly seen in the essentialist framework (Stoller, 2005) surrounding the gendered division of labour to be found in family care. Thompson comments that, 'Caring is envisioned as the essence of womanhood' (Thompson, 2005) within a separate spheres' ideology where men are primarily seen as breadwinners (Hanlon, 2009) outside the house and women take on the majority of family caregiving inside the family home.

Underpinning this male breadwinner/woman caregiving division of labour was the nineteenth-century, gendered assumption that men and women are 'naturally' suited to their different and unequal spheres (Thompson, 2005; Kimmel, 1997). This gave rise to the distorted belief that it was 'natural' for women to be caregivers and 'unnatural' and possibly 'deviant' (Thompson, 2005) for men to be caregivers. Questioning this supposedly 'natural' and essentialised divide between men's and women's work became more sharply focused within second-wave feminism in the UK from the late 1960s and early 1970s onwards. With the gendered and sexual disruptions of gay liberation, feminism and the queering of gender relations came a wider destabilising of British men's conventional social status and positioning. Some men's traditional centre stage positions as main breadwinners, providers and heads of family households were in the process of being undermined. The rise of male unemployment, de-industrialisation and other changes in occupational structures, along with feminist challenges particularly around domestic violence and sexual abuse, were beginning to destabilise the habitual ways of being a man. Later in the 1980s, gay men working in the AIDS field developed an ethos of caring by men for men.

All these social and economic shifts have also gone along with a more political and detailed awareness of what caring means and might mean in the future. From the perspective of an emerging gender and sexual politics, more differentiated responses to caring have appeared, such as the 'distinction between caring about and caring for' (Hollway, 2006; Skeggs, 1997). Beverley Skeggs sums up the distinction in this way:

> Caring about which involves social dispositions that operate at a personal level and assume a relationship between the carer and cared for, and caring for which involves the actual practice of caring, involving specific tasks such as lifting, cleaning and cooking. (Skeggs, 1997)

Wendy Hollway also investigates the dualism in the caring literature between care that is, 'embodied, specific, relational,' and caring justice that is, 'abstract, rule-bound and intellectual' (Hollway, 2006). This commitment to the ethics of justice, as well as duty and obligation, is particularly significant in some men's definitions of caring.

Now as more women have moved into male-dominant work arenas, the challenge for many men is to learn how to cross over the masculine-feminine divide in caring and perhaps to explore the possibility of a more integrated approach that combines instrumentality and nurturing. But that crossover for men into family care presents many barriers and obstacles. Christine Williams writes about the fears of men who have recently crossed over into a female-dominated area or occupation:

> Almost immediately, he is suspected of not being a 'real man.' There must be something wrong with him ('Is he gay? Effeminate? Lazy?') for him to be interested in this kind of work. If these popular prejudices are not enough to push him out of his occupation, they will certainly affect how he manages his gender identity on a daily basis. (Williams, 1993)

There remains, in 2016, a contradictory tension between masculinity and caring (Calasanti, 2003). As Christine Williams points out above, there is a threat, in caregiving work for men, of losing their masculine identities. On the surface caregiving seems to conflict with the established and privileged norms of masculinity (Thompson, 2005). But if we dig deeper, beyond negative stereotyping, aging men's caregiving may be seen 'as providing men with an opportunity to reconceptualise the meaning of gender' (Kaye and Applegate, 1995), and a chance to move towards practices that are not only socially useful but also might be growth-enhancing for the caregiver. The enduring problems of this kind of caregiving remain the cultural assumptions and expectations associated with this caregiving work for men.

However, gender is only one aspect of a male caregiver's identity. There is greater variety to be engaged with in personal biographies and different social contexts than I've suggested so far. A great deal depends on other social features as well as gender, such as age, life stage, marital status, employment demands/retirement and a long history of interaction between givers and receivers, partners, and man and wife (Thompson, 2005). Also, the specific motivation to want to care for an incapacitated, older person may be influenced more intensely by a long-term partnership that entails living beside each other through frequent changes and challenges (Kaye, 1997) than by gender alone.

Research results on aging men as caregivers within the context of informal, spousal/partnership care are frequently contradictory and conflicted, particularly in their assessments of different gendered styles of caring. The traditional conception of aging men's caregiving is based on the notion that many men import their work and managerial skills into caregiving so that they are able, at times, to 'detach and separate emotional from functional aspects of care' (Calasanti, 2003). This suggestion that aging men's caregiving styles are mainly instrumental and managerial has been questioned by Kaye (1997) who, while acknowledging the occasional instrumental character of aging men's caregiving, has also commented that, 'there may be circumstances under which men are willing to accept the obligation of care and undertake a range of intimate personal care functions...'

The Caregiving Experiences of Two Aging Men

Brief snapshots of the two research participants' life histories can be found on pages 12–15 of the 'Introduction.'

The Informal, Spousal Caregiving Experiences of Brian

Brian had been caregiving to his wife, who had an MS-related illness, for 'ten or twelve years,' before I interviewed him at the age of 70. He describes his own economic condition as being, 'comfortably off.' During that time he had assumed primary responsibility for looking after his wife. So informal, spousal care for his wife was a long-term commitment without much external support from family, friends and community healthcare workers except for occasional sessions of physiotherapy and respite care from his four, adult children.

Brian's unique style of caring was showing affection for his wife through 'doing' and 'activity' rather than by talking (Femiano and Coonerty-Femiano, 2005). After a lifetime of military training and working as an international export manager it is not surprising that he approached caregiving as an extension of his work life. During his military training as an electronic engineer working on the refurbishment of tanks just before the Suez crisis he had the chance to build his confidence at twenty and take on extra responsibility:

DJ: So you'd come up in the world quite fast?

Brian: Yes, I was twenty at the time and also I had the benefit of taking these tanks right down to nothing and rebuilding them several times in the course of a year. So there was nothing about the tank that caused apprehension and I was totally au fait with the tank and I knew I was a good mechanic.

He also got used to the idea that setbacks were challenges that he later applied to the medical challenges of looking after his wife.

Brian: Yes in that I would regard any setbacks more in the nature of a challenge than as a setback. It was something to be overcome. So, from that point of view, if it were not for the confidence I couldn't have managed.

Brian learnt to thrive in his later work as an international export manager through developing an independent, competitive initiative and taking on extra responsibility for producing quality work. This is what he says about being an export sales manager:

Brian: My responsibility, as an export sales manager was, initially, to identify projects that we could sensibly go for. Damascus was a seven-thousand-year-old city and it was intending to replenish and replace its water supply system: new pumps; new valves and new treatment centres and, obviously, a very sophisticated control system to monitor and control it. We would be bidding for the control system for this.

DJ: What year was this?

Brian: 87/88. It was an eighteenth-month pre-qualification period and we finally produced a document over four inches thick explaining how we were going to do this. A colossal amount of work went into this and what then happened is, from sixteen international companies that were allowed to pre-bid, we came out top of the pile because these bids were marked for technical excellence.

However, in learning to look after his wife, Brian felt that it was both a technically demanding and an emotionally demanding job:

DJ: How did you get from being a very competitive and successful man at work through to a nurturing, caring man now?

Brian: By a fair amount of introspection, I think, in that it was necessary to do it. I had always had to think about what I did at work – it was a technically demanding job and it was an emotionally demanding job.

So, for Brian, doing things and emotional care went together although it is also true that aging men have a depth and breadth of caring and feeling that is not always immediately visible to the outside observer (Femiano and Coonerty-Femiano, 2005). In other ways, Brian gave the impression that he wanted to live up to his marital commitment in giving care to his wife. He seemed to approach the task as a dutiful obligation, driven as much by the 'rules, procedures and rights of the relationship' (Kaye and Applegate, 1994) as by love and affection. Viewed from this perspective, some men seem to be influenced by an ethic of justice in their processes of caring than by a more woman-centred approach that emphasises a relational, ethics of caring (Hollway, 2006; Gilligan, 1982).

Brian also came across as a 'solitary individual', his own description of himself. He acknowledged that he does not have friends, only acquaintances and tended to stress his autonomy, independence and commented that, 'I have been self-sufficient forever,' and, 'I'm reluctant to ask for favours. I'm reluctant to ask for somebody's help if I think I can do it.' In terms of his caring for his wife, Brian asserted that he did not need any form of social support or social recognition for his efforts. 'My own opinion of what I do is infinitely more important than anybody else's.' In focusing on the first key question: 'Are aging men as caregivers to be seen as mainly instrumental and managerial in their caring and how much are they engaged in emotional and nurturing caring?', Brian at first, seems to conform to the traditional conception of aging men's gendered styles of caring. But later he appears more ambivalent. He does seem to largely employ a number of work-related, task-oriented skills and problem-solving strategies (Vacha-Haase et al., 2011) in his caring that protect him from emotional disturbance.

He states that: 'At this moment I do a number of ordinary practical household tasks which previously [his wife] did...' These tasks also involve organisational and planning ahead skills that were probably acquired by Brian in his work roles as a technical sales' engineer and export sales' manager. He says, 'there is a need to consider in advance what you are going to do...' and also a need to, 'sort out menus.'

There is a strong, contradictory tension in Brian's interviews between masculine identities and caring. There is a stigmatising threat in caregiving work for aging men, of losing their embodied manliness through the emasculating association of femininity and care work. As a result, some aging men search for ways of keeping their masculinities intact and well protected.

However, this is not the whole story. There are also signs of half-hidden sensitivity and concealed affection for his wife to be found in Brian's account. Admittedly, these signs are often buried away and the reader has to scratch a bit deeper to interpret the signs but they are there. Brian is aware of his wife's pain, vulnerability and frustrated anger at her illness. Sometimes his description of his wife's illness is so painful and intense that the reader can sense a deep feeling of sadness for her predicament, '...but she [his wife] was so horribly hurt by what was happening to her and so horribly disappointed with what was happening to her...'

Occasionally, Brian and his wife went for a day out in their car and amongst the list of instrumental skills needed to get the car and his wife's wheelchair and scooter ready, the reader becomes aware of a softer thread of tenderness of loving care and concern for his wife:

> ...without necessarily having done anything particular but just being there to enable it to happen. Taking the car out; shifting the wheelchair; putting the scooter in or whatever – all these various bits and pieces. And also coming to terms with things that I previously probably would not have come to terms with in anything like as easy a frame of mind.

Without imposing his will on his wife but relaxing more into the situation 'just being there to enable it to happen', Brian is able to show affectionate care for his wife through being an 'enabler' rather than a dominating leader. He also seems more reconciled to the specific conditions of the outing in his remark that he was:

> coming to terms with things that I previously probably wouldn't have come to terms with...

Later on in the interview with Brian, he talked about how he needed to learn how to 'hover' and to be a bit more 'cautious' in his dealings with his wife. I asked him the following question:

> DJ: What does 'hover' and 'cautious' mean to you?

> Brian: By 'hover' it is being available and available to her quite quickly at times without necessarily being intrusive. So if she is getting out of the car then the walking frame or the wheelchair is parked

adjacent to the door. I've opened the door. I've put the brakes on either device and she'll swing herself round and get hold of the handle of the door and if she's a little too far back I may need then to steady the door so she doesn't pull it closed. So the 'hovering' turns into an 'action.' If she stands up then I can go to her and just catch her arm. But if, as she gets out of the car, I get hold of her arm and start pulling her out of the car then that's intrusion.

This quotation shows Brian's genuine respect for his wife's different needs and preferences. Here he is not focused on his own, individual self-interests but he is trying to arrange things so that he can meet the other's needs. As a result, the reader notices the way Brian parks the car 'adjacent to the door' so that his wife's exit from the car, close to the walking frame and wheelchair, is made easier for her. The manner in which Brian attempts to do this is also very important. He understands the difference between invasive 'pulling' that encroaches on her space and a more tactful 'hovering' that is more in tune with his wife's immediate needs. In this way Brian shows that he is capable of listening more carefully to her preferences and desires.

However, there is greater ambivalence in Brian's dealings with his wife than I've acknowledged so far. On the positive side there is evidence of Brian's affectionate caring and a respect for his wife's different priorities but shadows of his work life are still very much with him directly influencing his style of caring. He often recalls events in his life when he exercised power and control over other people and sometimes he seems blinded by these industrial ways of seeing to his wife's different perceptions and needs. As a result, Brian appears to construe her illness as a mechanical condition that he thinks he understands because of all the years he spent operating within a pattern of work relations and skills. At one point in the interview Brian accused me of 'failing to understand the nature of what I did at work' and he goes on to assert that:

There was no appreciable difference in understanding [his wife's] needs than appreciating the actual needs of somebody who wished to buy a control system . . .

When I questioned him on this he went on to define his wife as a potential 'customer' of his who needed the same kind of 'empathetic' approach as prospective business customers. Later, I pressed Brian to differentiate between caring for his wife and doing business with a work customer. He acknowledged there were contradictions in his approach and admitted there were real differences between business customers and his wife's needs. He said:

> The major difference – and it's not a slight difference, it's a big difference – is that you can dispense with your customer, but you can't do that with the wife.

But Brian stubbornly clung on to his convictions and was unable to see that he was on the way to ignoring the human, nuanced complexity of his ill wife and turning his treatment of her into a work-related project.

Turning to the second question of this study, ('How far is there a changing dynamic between the caregiver and the care receiver and how does it affect the quality of their relationship from the start of the relationship to the present moment or end of the contact?'), it is important to set caregiving within a relational context (Ducharme et al., 2006) that is, in part, a history of relations between the giver and the receiver over many years. The changes within Brian's relationship with his wife over the last ten or twelve years during her illness have centrally affected the quality of their interaction and Brian's caring. The shifts in their relationship are also closely tied in to a series of losses and dislocations for Brian and his wife, as well as a few gains.

For his wife, the early stages of her illness brought with them a loss of independent capability and the onset of severe, physical limitations. In Brian's account of their relationship, his wife is reported to be full of frustration and anger about the constraints of her illness. In the first stages of her illness, she found it difficult to accept her condition and did not come to terms with it. As a result, their relationship disintegrated into, 'a very, very bad eighteen months where she was coming to terms with this.' The exact causes for this conflict are only hinted at in Brian's account but they seem to revolve around the differences and contrasts in life styles and expectations between Brian and his wife. He was very proud of his physical prowess at 70 ('I'm a lot fitter than most people at 70'); he felt self-sufficient and self-reliant; he had achieved considerable, professional success at work; he was financially well-off and had gained some self-control over difficult emotions.

So perhaps Brian gave the impression to his wife that he was very confident and sure of his abilities. Their discussion of 'physical, sporting things' sometimes became a site of conflict between them. Brian acknowledged the widening gulf opening up between them over physical exercise:

...we have a vast difference of opinion over the efficacy of physiotherapy and physical exercise. I've always been a great believer in
that. So I have to be very, very aware that this will merely offend so
I shut up.

For Brian, his wife's illness has confronted him with several, deep
losses as well as an unacknowledged sorrow, the loss of his wife as he
knew her before the illness. This loss constituted 'relational deprivation'
(Ducharme et al., 2006). Over and over again in the interviews, Brian
refers to being deprived of a more rounded contact with a younger, more
independent, more able-bodied wife that he has increasingly lost contact with since the start of her illness. He contemplates the 'then' and
'now' contrast between the person who was: 'such an able person for so
many years', and also being, 'a very able nurse for many years,' who had
experienced, 'huge success as a mother.'

Brian is also faced by the loss of his industrial, masculine competence – his technical know-how and work-related skills – in his failure
at home to improve his wife's lot. He constantly returns to his 'inability
to put things right.' He's tried to sort things out and apply his problem-
solving techniques and work strategies to a domestic situation. But he is
very aware that he has failed to sort things out. In a way, he has failed to
control the uncontrollable (Vacha-Haase, 2011) in his fight to make his
wife's life healthier and better. This accumulation of losses and failures
in Brian's life had moved him on to a more thoughtful, self-reflexive
position and particularly in relation to his wife. He has learnt to self-
critically inspect his own behaviour and also learnt to adapt to shifts
and changes in his relationship with her. He comments that: '...then
you need to be far more cautious about what you say and what you do,'
and later when he recognises that he has made a mistake in his dealings with his wife, he decides to go for a walk and, 'gives himself a good
talking to.' These modifications in his own behaviour seemed to stimulate some positive changes in their relationship and a lessening of the
conflict between them: 'so she's looking at the positives. And in that
respect there is less conflict than there was.' From his wife's perspective,
perhaps she now seems capable of moderating her anger and frustration
and she appears to reveal an emerging tolerance for difference in her
relationship with Brian.

With these changes has come a greater acceptance of community
health support and her previous resistance to physiotherapy is now
beginning to melt:

...subsequently, she was persuaded by her consultant to try some
physiotherapy and this has worked very, very well. We are going there

tomorrow and that, I think, will be the fifth or sixth time she's been and she's enjoyed it immensely. The girls are wonderful and she likes them a lot. They have a good time. There's plenty of jollity and the rest of it.

Despite having to confront considerable pain and hurt in her life, Brian's wife reveals herself capable of opening herself up to enjoy social support and companionship with other people, improved interaction with her husband and 'jollity' through agreeing to attend the physiotherapy sessions much to the approval of Brian. It appears that he was also genuinely pleased that his wife could experience a 'good time' in an atmosphere of 'jollity.'

The Informal, Caregiving Experiences of Roy

In my interpretation of Brian's spousal caring, I comment that there was a strong, contradictory tension between his masculine identities and the processes of caring. But in Roy's case as a gay man caring for his dying partner who had AIDS there was no such visible contradiction. He did not seem threatened by being seen as a caring man in both a personal and public context. Rather, Roy viewed his caring as an integral part of being a human being. He remarked that:

> ...part of my personality has always been one of caring. And even now, late in life, it is still the same. I'm involved in neighbourhood watch and so on and I go and care for others.

This personal caring in Roy has also been consolidated by him being engaged in nursing as a caring professional. As he says:

> When I went into nursing it was necessary to have a caring attitude and I was always hard on people whose attitude towards patients was that they were a bit of a ruddy nuisance. I always used to say to people that this was someone's father, mother, brother or sister. It could be yours and so you shouldn't treat people – whether in hospital or the world outside – any differently than you'd expect to be treated yourself or you'd treat your own family.

He now feels that nursing has become more managerial and bureaucratic from the 1980s onwards and regrets the loss of that 'caring attitude' in young nurses. But some of the legacies of his nursing career have been constructive in that, 'I've got that backlog of care and information in my mind' that he has been able to use in looking after his dying partner for the last eight years of his partner's life. Roy's care for his partner was a part of a long-term commitment to the relationship between them that continued for twenty-four years. His partner died six years before the first interview took place between Roy and the researcher in 2005. Roy was still in a state of grief and loss about the death of his long-term partner, alleviated, to some extent, by the more recent relationship with a younger partner.

To provide a clearer understanding of the caregiving relationship between gay male caregivers and their infected partners, I need to challenge a few myths about gay men and also pay particular attention to the 'relational and community contexts in which non-heterosexual men' (Heaphy et al., 2004) have negotiated their caring relationships with their partners since the 1980s.

Most studies of aging men assume that all aging men are heterosexual (Kimmel, 1979) which does not help the reader to appreciate the diversity of sexualities and life styles to be found in later life. One of the other common myths is that older gay men are inevitably lonely and isolated, but this negative assumption has been exploded by recent research on gay communities (Shippy, Cantor and Brennan, 2004; Heaphy et al., 2004). This research has shown that gay men rely on friendship networks more often than on family contacts. Certainly in Roy's case he had frequent contact with partners and friends. Also, false assumptions in heterosexual cultures suggest that gay men are only interested in relationships of casual, erotic adventure and promiscuity (Mutchler, 2000) rather than caring relationships of long-term commitment.

Gay, male caregivers, like Roy, faced multiple problems and burdens because of the stigma, homophobia and discrimination to be found in the dominant, heteronormative culture and society of the UK (Sipes, 2005). Roy's partner worked in the same hospital as he did as a nurse administrator but their relationship had to be concealed in reclusive secrecy because of homophobic stigma amongst the work force and his partner's fears that he would lose his job if the hospital knew that he was HIV positive ('...because if they'd have known they would have got rid of him'). Roy respected his partner's position and the fact that his partner's parents had no idea that their son was gay until the last stages of his illness. But this situation increased the secret stresses and burdens of caregiving for Roy and kept him in a state of nervous apprehension: 'I was afraid that things would get out.'

Roy's caring response to his partner's illness was not only historically specific but also not just about an individual relationship with his partner. It is important to recognise here that Roy's caring response to his partner's AIDS condition was also more widely reflected in his social and community activism in his own hospital and in the local, gay community itself.

Martin Levine (1990) has already documented the altered, social climate of the 1980s in US gay communities. In the UK these changes came a bit later, perhaps around the late 1980s and early 1990s. Many gay men, threatened by AIDS and the loss of their loved ones, turned away from the erotic hedonism of the sauna towards a new commitment to connectedness and community service. In Roy's case, he not only looked after his dying partner but became actively involved in the late 1980s in AIDS organisations. As a result, Roy was practising a broader range of community, caring skills than just attending to the private needs of his partner. And both caregiver and care receiver benefitted from the shared insights, resources, information and support gained from their personal and public contexts in a wider, non-individualised model of caring.

In turning to focus on the question: 'Are aging men as caregivers to be seen as mainly instrumental and managerial in their caring and how much are they engaged in emotional and nurturing caring?' it is clear that Roy combined a 'caring for' his partner with a 'caring about' him (Hollway, 2006; Skeggs, 1997). So, in terms of gendered styles of caregiving, Roy took more of an integrated approach to looking after his partner, both giving him emotional support and also using his organisational and managerial skills probably learnt from acting as an assistant matron in a large hospital.

There was no local treatment for HIV/AIDS available so Roy spent a great deal of time transporting his partner to a London hospital. He says: 'We used to go down to London towards the end about three times a week – right into one of the hospitals in the centre.'

But he also gave his partner regular support that varied from holding and touching his partner in bed in the last stages of illness when Roy still slept with his partner, to giving him support in facing up to some of his problems. There was a point in their relationship, in the earlier stages of the illness, when his partner went for a job interview in the Middle East. During the linked medical assessment, a blood test had revealed that he was HIV positive and, as a result, he was rejected for the post. When he returned from the interview he began to recognise that he was trapped within the emotional and physical limitations of the disease, and he started to cry from frustration and despair. Roy's response to this partner's tears was immediate; Roy talked to him and held him until his partner felt calmer.

It is time to consider the second question of this study ('How far is there a changing dynamic between the caregiver and care receiver and how does it affect the quality of their relationship from the start of the relationship to the present moment or end of the contact?'). Although the reader only sees through the eyes of Roy, it is possible to discern the occasional turbulence of Roy's relationship with his partner as well as a caring attitude. As his partner's health gradually deteriorated, Roy seemed to be caught between a wounded sense of having been betrayed by his long-term lover and a very close understanding ('... deep down I still had feelings for him'). Roy had suspected for some time that his partner had been 'playing the field', even before the medical confirmation that he had AIDS, and he comments that: 'when I found out that [his partner] had AIDS, the trust had gone.'

Roy's emotions are painfully mixed; his mounting distrust mingles with a hurt but sustained commitment to his partner over many years. Through the interviews a tension develops in Roy's account of his changing relationship with his partner: on one side there is a troubled but deep affection for his dying partner, and on the other, there is an angry sense of personal and bodily loss of having been cheated. Much of this was experienced in the early stages of the illness when Roy carried on looking after his partner while still working in a demanding job at the hospital.

But the emotional dynamic within their relationship changed during the final phase of his partner's illness as he was approaching death. Although Roy was still very stressed by the strained and burdensome task of caring and the emotional burden of trying to keep everything hidden from his partner's work colleagues and his parents, ('... it was a tightrope all the time and it did affect me quite badly') the approaching terminal stage of the illness also brought with it a deeper closeness between them:

> ... but death, in a way, brought ... a better understanding between the two of us.

A community health worker regularly visited Roy's partner and Roy was able to express an affectionate awareness of his partner's otherness and different needs:

> ... well when you are lying next to someone and you know they are dying but you don't know when. I mean once he'd gone to sleep I'd come down here [the lounge] and put the TV on and watch

something. But I couldn't stop down here because I would then start worrying about what was happening. Was he still alright?

Even on the anxious edge of nervous exhaustion, Roy still clung on to his responsibility for caring ('Was he still alright?'), attempting to recover some normative stability through watching television. At the same time he also reveals a bleak sense of being abandoned by his life-long lover, commenting that: 'because he lied to me I did not feel he belonged to me anymore.' At the very end of his partner's illness, Roy supported him in learning to let go, as a preparatory way of accepting the reality of his own death and dying. As he remarks, 'In a sense I was giving him permission to go. I did not want to lose him but it was time.' So even in the last moments of dying, his partner was comforted by Roy's presence, 'He knew I would be there,' and his reassuring words of: 'The last thing I said to him when we were talking was that it was time for him to go on his last great adventure.' His partner's death left Roy with a great deal of sadness and loss. But, again, the wider community of caring in local gay men's groups supported him to voice and share his grieving over the loss of his partner through AIDS. He was not left as an isolated individual bottling up his lonely grief. He joined a gay bereavement group for 'older people whose partner or someone close to them had died' usually from an AIDS-related illness. The internal workings of the bereavement group are described by Roy in this way:

> We meet once a month and there is no agenda when we go in. We just sit down and we talk and, you know, if someone has just lost a partner we become a listening post or we talk through situations and we talk about our lives in general and how we are coping with bereavement.

When I asked Roy how that small group-sharing had helped him, he answered in the following way:

> It helped me by helping others. By talking through situations that one or two of us had already gone down that road and I suppose really it was very good that we could talk through those situations. It helped me to find it a bit easier to live with the loss.

In his phrase, 'It helped me by helping others,' Roy is caught in the process of converting his private grief into a more social and public form, where he could personally start to come to terms with his loss and emptiness and, at the same time, feel that he had made a small contribution to society, 'by helping others.'

Discussion

The pattern of gender relations in the UK has undergone considerable changes over the last thirty years. Women have made significant gains within the labour market (Office of National Statistics, 2012), however, while women are now more likely to be in paid work in the public sphere, they remain far more likely than men to be in low-paid, part-time jobs (TUC, 2012). Also, although the old gender divide between male breadwinners and women as homemakers has been gradually eroded and there are many more dual breadwinner households, 'egalitarian domestic practices' (Hanlon and Lynch, 2011), caring practices, in particular, have not kept up with these positive changes.

In some Western cultures and societies, the legacies of a gendered, binary system still inform their contemporary practices of caring. For example, in the Irish context, Hanlon and Lynch draw attention to the Irish, historical background of being a 'deeply conservative and patriarchal society' (Hanlon and Lynch, 2011) where men have the liberty of 'care-free masculinities unencumbered by primary care responsibilities' while, generally, women take on the everyday, unpaid labour of all those informal, caring relationships and tasks.

Although social features of these unequal, gender-segregated models of gender relations can be found in most Western societies, these rigid, hierarchical models also co-exist with specific groups of aging men and gay men, in particular, who are heavily engaged in informal, spousal/partner caregiving such as Brian and Roy. It seems to me that the contradictory and shifting realities of aging men's lives during their life courses are still being largely neglected in research on caring (Arber, Davidson and Ginn, 2003; Sandberg, 2011; Fennel and Davidson, 2003; Fleming, 1999).

The sociological picture of the last thirty years that depicted caregiving as solely 'a woman's issue' is gradually changing (Femiano and Coonerty-Femiano, 2005) as our awareness of aging men's diverse and growing contribution to caregiving deepens and becomes more publicly visible. As more and more women enter the paid work arena in the public sphere, some of these women may be increasingly unavailable for family caregiving because of 'competing responsibilities arising out of the workplace' (Kaye, 2005). Perhaps this will mean, in the future, an increasing expectation for more aging men to engage in family caregiving to fill in the gap left by working women.

To understand older male caregivers it is crucial to view them in relation to past work and gender. There's a wide range of possible styles of caregiving and, often, men will approach caregiving tasks differently according to past legacies of their work and the ways their understanding of caregiving is partly shaped by those everyday practices, habits and interactive patterns that they developed during their work, often over many years. It is also extremely important not to impose an ageist stereotype or traditional conceptions of gender onto aging men. As I've already indicated, aging men are also in the process of changing as Western culture and society shifts and changes. As Femiano and Coonerty-Femiano (2005) suggest:

> ...planners (of future programmes for older male caregivers) should be guided by a flexible view of mid-life and late-life that takes men's nurturant, expressive strivings into consideration.

In Brian's case he was powerfully shaped in his caring by his work as an international export manager for a global corporation. Within a global, gender order a new transnational business masculinity (Connell and Wood, 2005) was dominant and he was deeply influenced by the values prized by global capitalism and neo-liberalism. The values centred on independence, competition, aggression, individual responsibility and self-reliance (Hanlon and Lynch, 2011), so that in his caring for his wife, Brian took on medical challenges in much the same way as he had done in confronting challenges as an international export manager for a multi-national corporation. Davidson (2013) has commented that caregiving men:

> ...negotiated and realigned their masculinity within the feminised domain of caring. They combated the potentially negative connotations of loss of manhood by defining their care responsibilities in organizational, instrumental and functional terms.

In Roy's case, to explore the precise circumstances of his caregiving means to selectively focus on the broader, structural issues rather than on the details of a private, individual life. The reclusive secrecy and furtiveness of Roy's caregiving, within a background of a gay context of fears of social stigma, homophobia and discrimination (Sipes, 2005) added to the emotional stresses and burdens of being a caregiver. Roy had to face up to the constant tension of keeping his partner's AIDS condition and gay identity secret to his work colleagues and to his partner's parents. The precise character of Roy's caregiving introduces the reader to a non-individualised model of aging men caring for others. In this context, Roy was practising and using a broader range of community, caring skills, useful information, resources and contacts rather than just concentrating on the private needs of his dying partner. Roy combined 'caring about' with the practical skills of 'caring for'. He practised an integrated approach to emotional nurturing and managerial, instrumental organisation (probably gained from being an assistant matron in a large hospital).

In terms of the other key question about the relational dynamics between caregivers and care receivers, Roy had to confront the occasional turbulence of their interaction, particularly after the destruction of his trust. After being betrayed by his partner, Roy experienced a contradictory mixture of resentment, deep grief and tenderness as his partner's health deteriorated. The long history (twenty-four years) of their interaction and partnership probably intensified the depth of his sadness about the loss of his partner. In the later stages of their relationship Roy's sense of betrayal might have impaired the quality of their caring interaction.

Roy, despite his considerable sadness about losing his partner, also gained a great deal of inner growth and emotional benefit from caregiving to his partner and being a part of a wider, gay, bereavement group where members shared their grieving rather than being left as isolated individuals bottling up their lonely grief.

It is still largely women who provide the day to day care of the old and vulnerable but current health trends (Kramer, 2005) suggest that the physical and mental health demands placed on older husbands and partners are likely to increase in the future. Some aging men, like Brian and Roy, are certainly capable of adapting to new caregiving needs, although they lack public support. The limited evidence of my research project points to the contradictoriness and mixed nature of masculine subjectivities in aging men's caregiving experiences.

Clearly research on aging men and gay men as caregivers is in its infancy and much more future investigation is needed. Here are a few areas that need taking further:

- Further exploration is needed of specific sub-groups of older and gay men and their caregiving practices

- More detailed micro-studies are needed that tease out the subjective complexities of older and gay men as caregivers
- More research is needed on aging men's reasons for not wanting to use support groups and community services
- Further research is needed to investigate the differences and variety of male caregivers
- Certain research gaps in our knowledge need to be filled, especially the lack of work done on ethnic and racial diversity. (Kramer, 2005)

7
Learning the Hidden Skills of Staying Alive: How do Some Aging Working-Class Men Survive the Processes of Aging?

Introduction

Over the last twenty years or so, debates about men's health have been dominated by the thesis that masculinity is bad for men's health (Gough, 2010). Practical examples of this discursive tendency occur in a report, titled 'Man Made: Men, masculinities and equality in public policy' (Ruxton, 2009). The report comments, 'Boys and men are still socialised to be tough and strong, to appear in control and to take risks,' and later it goes on to masculine bodies:

> ... men expect their bodies to be capable of doing 'manly' things and not to be weak or vulnerable.

This repetitive emphasis on negative and often damaging features of men's practices and behaviours (Collier, 1998) does not do justice to the contradictory and shifting realities of aging, working-class, men's lives through their life courses. The dominant discourse in men's health discussions that masculinity is bad for men's health very often marginalises or even pathologises (Gough and Robertson, 2010) aging men's masculinities. It certainly does not allow for an acknowledgement of significant and varied changes in the meanings of men and masculinities over time.

Aging can facilitate a change in masculinity (Arber, Davidson and Ginn, 2003) particularly when biographical and physical disruptions are encountered (Emslie, Hunt and O'Brien, 2004). In terms of well-being over a life course much more detailed emphasis should be given to a wider spectrum of different, older masculinities, some ethnically and racially diverse (Saint-Aubin, 2004).

In this chapter I want to challenge the dominant discourse of men's health by introducing a selective focus on what some older, working-class men have been doing right in learning the difficult skills of staying alive and feeling alive and resilient instead of emphasising, yet again, men's negative features. I also intend to look closely at the weaker and less strong bodies of older, working-class men, or at least aging men like Robert who can recognise that

> ... as you get older, strength doesn't count, does it? Especially in this modern world it doesn't count so much. At one time –thirty or forty or fifty years ago – you had to be strong or you wouldn't survive but today you don't have to be but you still have to be agile and fit.

The assumptions in the earlier references in 'Man Made' to being tough and strong and the pressure to develop 'manly' bodies are questioned, here, from the perspective of an older, working man who inhabits a changing body and who can now see the difference between strong, muscular bodies and 'agile' and supple bodies.

David Morgan thinks that many sociological representations of male bodies as often hard and aggressive offer an 'over-phallusised picture of man' (Morgan, 2002). I want also to support his views by interrogating the life histories of aging men like Ray who experienced bodily weakness and fragility as an asthmatic boy from the age of 6 or 7. Also, I want to investigate the life history of Hanif, a Pakistani Muslim, who talks openly about his physical vulnerability and his 'weak body'. There are, he says 'unexpected advantages' of possessing a vulnerable body because it has kept him away from aggressive encounters with other boys and has helped him to learn to fight with mental power rather than with his fists.

I am intrigued by the question posed by Lee and Owens (2002) about how aging men become 'successful survivors of life's vicissitudes', (p. 101) and how far do they learn the hidden resourcefulness and skills of coping with some of the challenges that later-life throws at them. For Ray to get to the age of 70 and say about his life: 'I think it's probably one of the healthiest times of my life,' requires a careful teasing out of some of the key factors that have gone into his present feelings of whole-someness, and that is what I intend to do now in surveying the three life histories of older, working-class men. However, before I do that, I need to introduce a key, conceptual frame that informs my analysis.

The Conceptual Frame

Working-Class Masculinities

All three of the research participants' life stories that I am interrogating in this chapter have been influenced by working class masculinities but in one case, one of the participants reveals a more fluid and ambivalent relationship to working-class culture. Social class trajectories were significant in shaping these three men's attitudes to life chances, survival strategies and masculine identities.

My focus in looking closely at these aging men's lives is from a gendered viewpoint that approaches all three men as living examples of marginalised masculinities (Connell, 1995). That is, all are subordinated, working-class men and one is ethnically diverse very much straddling the intersections between race and class and between local, Western conditions in the UK and Pakistani, global influences. Here I am focusing on aging men's working-class lives because they are often neglected in the research literature or seen as archaic subjects slightly unfashionable now in a postmodern society. Also the subtle intricacies of their complex life stories are not given the detailed attention they deserve.

Recently, to talk about social class in the UK was often seen as unfashionable and politically elusive. There was a growing popular perception that class divisions were archaic and would be soon eroded in a more fluid, open, postmodern society (Morgan, 2005). However, my study, despite its small scale, has confirmed the importance of social class as a social division particularly viewed from a whole life perspective. The three men's struggles to keep open and alert in an aging context are closely tied in to residual traces of class relations and masculine identities usually forged in early childhoods and later periods of adolescence.

Social class in the UK is a 'system of social stratification' (Morgan, 2005) that privileges the lives of some people through the possession of economic and cultural capital and also reduces the lives of other people (like my three research participants) to that of an inferior class position in the social hierarchy (Collinson, 2007). Class works relationally, positioning people within the different levels of a social pyramid and the people at the bottom of the pyramid experience an unequal distribution of life chances as well as feelings of lowered confidence and self-worth. In the working lives of my three research participants – Robert, Ray and Hanif – none of them worked in heavy industry, on the shop floor, but one worked very much as a manual worker as a British Rail platelayer. (See 'Endnote' for a description.) Another participant worked as an electrician who had been trained as a part of an apprenticeship scheme, whose job was closely connected to the Nottinghamshire mining industry, and the final participant worked as a bus driver after migrating from Pakistan in 1962.

Robert, Ray and Hanif were all partly shaped by working-class culture or 'occupational culture' usually in an industrial context (Tolson, 1977). By that I mean that they all took on something of the working-class culture, or defined themselves in opposition to that culture, which surrounded young men in the late 1940s or 1950s in the UK, with the exception of Hanif who arrived later in 1962. This potentially subversive culture worked through jokes, parody, horseplay, mock fighting and ridicule, and frequent confrontation with authority or management. Tolson talks about this working-class culture acting as a 'vital, cultural defence of exploited working men against the bosses' (Tolson, 1977).

Some of this defiant, cussed, class energy comes through in Robert's life history in terms of a manual worker sticking up for his rights and also through collective group solidarity that he learnt through working in a small team of platelayers. Alternatively, Ray felt a marginalised 'outsider' in his everyday dealings with this masculine banter and dirty joke telling. He experienced bullying and ridicule from some of the lads at school and also in his apprentice training scheme where he learnt his job as an electrician. Hanif had to deal with working-class racism in his early work relations in the UK but, later, was able to channel some awareness of working-class political activism through his job as a bus driver and his union participation in the Transport and General Workers' meetings and his membership of the Labour party.

It is necessary to make certain historical distinctions clearer in the process of understanding working-class masculinities in the UK. From the 1950s to the 1980s there were relatively clear distinctions between home and work. An idealised image of 'home-centred leisure' was constructed, supposedly to compensate to the working man for his alienation at work (Tolson, 1977). Also, there were relatively stable occupations. The male breadwinner model was dominant within the gender relations' framework and heavy manufacturing industry continued to be important (Morgan, 2005).

After the 1980s and the early 1990s in the UK, working-class masculinities were significantly broken and changed. The break-up of a social-democratic consensus and the introduction of a neoliberal regime started in the 1980s Thatcherite deregulation of the economy, with her adoption of market-led policies and a refusal to offer any state support to halt the decline of heavy industry (Beynon, 2002). Economic and social change have undermined these pre-1980s patterns of employment: contracting out; downsizing; outsourcing of industrial work to countries where labour is less expensive; and a more docile, 'flexible' part-time way of working has brought the end to the UK as a major venue for heavy industry, such as coal mining. In the East Midlands where Robert, Ray and Hanif live, mining jobs that depended on physical strength and robust, bodily toughness rapidly disappeared after the collapse of the miners' strike in 1984–85. Many ex-manual workers are now confronted by a precarious form of living and working usually in the service economy. They are either unemployed, sometimes for very long periods, seriously injured, or working through short-term contracts, low pay and part-time work. These economic and social changes have effectively disrupted the force of organised labour protest in the UK and made it more difficult for community activism and group solidarity to take place. These unemployed and injured working-class men are also challenged by mental health and other health issues, such as excessive smoking and drinking, and poor dietary conditions, particularly if they are living alone and socially isolated.

The conventional position of social class in the UK has also been made more diverse and complicated by labour migration. Both global and local conditions have constructed Hanif's life story and his experience of social class in a more contradictory way. He is a 67-year-old, Pakistani Muslim with an ambivalent class position.

Hanif's subordinated position as an Asian migrant worker was both racialised and exploited within a British class hierarchy in a variety of low-paid, insecure, construction industry jobs. Later he found a long-term job working as a bus driver for the local bus company. In all these jobs, he felt that his actual resources and intellectual abilities were not fully recognised by the companies he worked for.

Robert

The residual traces of social class relations and the indirect influences of a working-class 'occupational culture' (Tolson, 1977) are visible in Robert's present attitudes to age and work. His interview comments on aging are characterised by a defiant, stubborn, class energy and cultural disobedience (Sandberg, 2008). In some ways Robert survived as a 60-year-old man living alone (never having married) in a council flat through his class refusal to conform and keep quiet about things he disapproved of.

He was very much against the tendency in residential and nursing homes for the nursing staff to treat old people as passive dummies. At one point Robert commented that:

> ... they think all elderly people are like tea cosies and they just want them to sit there.

The striking image of 'tea cosies' effectively suggests the submissive docility of some half-sedated pensioners. He is very much opposed to the practices in residential and nursing homes that make it easier to manage older people rather than work with their independent needs and desires. Instead of being stimulated and challenged many older people are institutionalised into a sleepy conformity or even treated like young children. Robert quotes approvingly the evidence of his working-class Aunt, Rose. She had to go into a nursing home when she was ninety and she remarked to one of the nursing sisters:

> I might be old, duck, but I ain't a fucking kid.

Robert's rebellious questioning of conventional attitudes to old age seemed to keep him mentally alert and fiercely alive during the five interviews I conducted with him over about a year and a half. What kept him dignified and full of self-respect was a passionate belief in old people's abilities to assert themselves and answer back to official authority:

> ... well you should stick up for your rights. Because you are old and senile it don't mean to say your brain's gone or that you are a kid!

His views are further backed up by the case of his 86-year-old father who, 'wasn't walking very well' at the time when he moved into a private nursing home:

> Robert: ... so I used to go and take him out in his wheelchair. They [the nursing home] said he couldn't walk but I said, 'I'll get you walking, Dad' because we were near Stoke lane in the countryside. I got him pushing his chair over and then I said, 'You go over there and come to me,' and then gradually he could walk a bit. But when I took him back to the nursing home they didn't like it.
>
> DJ: Why didn't they like it?

Robert: Because they wanted people to just sit down and not say anything because it's easier for them. They said that was because of aggression but my Dad was no way aggressive.

Later, Robert tried to explain his father's position:

My Dad was an outdoor man. I explained to them. He's not used to sitting down. He's worked outside all his life. How do you expect him to sit down in a chair all day, drinking cups of tea with the old ladies? That wouldn't have suited him.

There's a contradictory mixture in Robert's explanation with some strands of working-class family solidarity, sticking up for his misunderstood father and some other elements of misogyny. Robert may have a point about possibly distorted, official perceptions of 'aggression' pinned onto his father when he may well have been disorientated and physically restless living in an alien environment with his bodily frailty. However, the gendered stereotype of 'drinking tea with the old ladies' is demeaning and a reductive put-down that ignores older women's varied and often innovatory lives.

Robert was again partly influenced by working-class values in not primarily defining himself through paid work (Emslie, Hunt and O'Brien, 2004), whereas middle-class masculinities often kept in touch with work as a potentially fulfilling activity. Even after retirement, many working-class men like Robert were released emotionally and socially to go beyond the parameters of paid work and invent a new definition of community work or voluntary labour. This is how Robert puts it:

...when I finished that [his work as a British rail platelayer] I felt a sense of freedom...I could do what I wanted to do... as regards work I think you should work probably till you die. When I say that I don't necessarily mean paid work...I think work's important because it keeps you in touch with life and society.

For Robert, community work for the local Borough Council and participating in a local community forum has given him a new sense of meaning and purpose and seems to have increased his social well-being. As a measure of his own social connectedness and engagement, Robert contrasts himself with his next door neighbour. I asked him how his community work helped him to thrive as an older man:

Robert: I'm not really sure how it helps because if I didn't go to these groups I don't really know what would happen. But I've a rough idea what would happen: I'd probably be like my next door neighbour who does nothing apart from go to the pub at lunchtime and other various people I know who are just sitting there deteriorating and becoming unfit.

DJ: How do they deteriorate?

Robert: Well they seem to lose interest in life. I know one person in particular and I've known him for years and years. At one time he was a flash type of character who was a salesman and he had a car and a jag and all that type of thing but now, since he's turned mid-fifties, he's gone right down and that's because he don't take an interest in anything in life. When he can't do the things that he could when he was younger he's not progressed from that, you know.

Here, Robert is suggesting the importance for aging men of flexible adaptation in the difficult struggle to survive, of not clinging on to the old models of achievement and success but learning to: 'let things go that have happened in the past', and moving on. This present acceptance of constant change seems to keep Robert actively busy and engaged. I asked him:

DJ: Do you think there is a purpose in being active?

Robert: Oh yes. Because if you are not active – if you don't use a thing – you deteriorate. If you don't use your brain you deteriorate; if you don't use your muscles and your organs then you deteriorate. If you just sit at home you might get arthritis or rheumatics or whatever. They can't always be avoided but you can keep them away to a certain extent. The more active you are the happier you are, I believe.

Like his father, this principle of outdoor activity equals well-being informed Robert's everyday priorities, in walking every day, swimming, cycling and sometimes playing and having fun. He appeared to have a sense of being alive doing these activities and never paused to question his life balance between activity and relaxation.

Material conditions, like owning property that Robert felt comfortable in, was very important to a 60-year-old working-class man living alone without much money. In some ways, living independently in his council flat was more urgently necessary to him than a romantic attachment with a woman. The idea of holding on to a sense of emotional control was crucial to an older, working-class man like Robert, who needed to survive alone and with dignity in the pinched, material conditions of a council flat. In effect, his avoidance of any volatile, emotional commitment to a woman defended him against any perceived risk that a relationship might endanger his security in the future, especially in hanging on to his home. Robert is aware that he has got more to lose (the loss of his safety and security) than just the breaking up of a relationship with a woman. His fear of homelessness dictates his self-protective decisions and, possibly, makes him reluctant to confront his unresolved dilemmas around relating to women.

Finally, I asked Robert if he was content at the present moment. He answered by criticising the notion of contentment, 'because a cow is content with grazing in a field.' He wanted to live in a more purposefully discontented way in, 'trying to do too much and change the world too much.' He was not content to sit around and not try and improve the state of the world. He went on to say:

> ... if everybody is content then you don't get any progress.

Our discussion ended on a note of political dissatisfaction with the world, which I think Robert possibly considered a partly progressive position to be in.

Ray

I interviewed Ray at the age of 70 and this is what he said about his well-being as an aging, working-class man:

> I think it's probably one of the healthiest times of my life. Well at least for many years. The asthma is well under control and I can do a lot more physical things now than I could thirty and forty years ago.

When you consider that Ray experienced bodily weakness and fragility in his childhood, was bullied regularly and 'kept on the periphery of things' as a marginalised outsider, you probably would not have imagined that he would survive so successfully after those early set-backs. So how did he do it and what specific things was he doing right that allowed him to feel such a vigorous sense of well-being at 70?

To answer that question I propose to look closely at a combination of different factors in Ray's life that have helped him to thrive. Not in any hierarchical order, they are the marital support, companionship and advice of his wife; the growth in his life of a critical, self-reflexiveness that allowed him to see beyond dominant forms of working-class masculinities; the decision probably from mid-life to look after himself and his body; and the selective choice of engaging in varied community activities as a replacement for work that had caged him in and made him more susceptible to chest infections.

Ray's early experiences of handling a boisterous and mocking working-class culture (Tolson, 1977) were intertwined with grappling with asthma. During the interviews he admitted that, 'asthma has probably shaped my life quite a bit.' He also says that, '...bearing in mind that I had a chest problem, I wasn't always capable of doing games.' Therefore, from being 6 or 7, he was side-lined from the dominant norms of masculinity and opportunities to define himself as masculine. This was particularly so with regard to his inability to construct a combative, physically active, gendered self through an involvement in regular, sporting activities.

At school and through his apprenticeship as a learner electrician, Ray was hemmed in by the ridicule, horseplay, joshing and dirty jokes of a culture of dominant, working-class masculinities. These boys treated Ray, '...as though I wasn't there' and his personal hurt and pain come through in this comment:

> I did try and join in by playing football at lunch-time or cricket or whatever and I did join in most things but, somehow, even if I did score some runs or whatever it would never really be appreciated. They would say something like, 'it's about time' rather than, 'well done!'

Ray was now labelled as a 'delicate' boy who was 'never very muscular or physical' and he was associated with effeminacy and unmanliness in the eyes of the other working-class boys, and soon became the butt of bullying, laughter and mockery. At 16 Ray decided to join the local arts theatre, 'which was people of my own kind who I could relate to.' Looking back on that time, Ray commented that: 'it helped being able to play the part of somebody who is different. It might be a bit of an escape.' It certainly sounded to me like a conscious movement away from an oppressively narrow working-class culture to a more expressive culture that was more tolerant around difference and diversity. What Ray gained from this movement away from the familiar, cultural context of his home seemed to be a broadening of his social empathy and perhaps started a critical process that might have provoked an awareness of his dissatisfaction with dominant forms of masculine, working-class culture.

In the final interview with Ray, he began to address the possible links between being an asthmatic boy and the formation of a different kind of masculine being. Some of the alternative, contradictory advantages of being diagnosed as a 'delicate', asthmatic boy began to surface through the interviews. The isolating and 'outsider' experiences of his younger years, of not fitting in with the taken for granted norms of a dominant masculine culture produced in Ray a different, more explicitly articulated, way of being an older man. This more conscious articulation of a different gendered self also contributed to Ray's survival strategies.

I asked Ray the following questions about these matters:

> DJ: You've been an asthma sufferer for most of your life. Do you think that made you into a different kind of boy and man through your life?
>
> Ray: I think it probably has. As we've just been saying it has affected the physical side of things and, try as I might to overcome that, it is bound to have some effect.

I went on to ask him a related question:

> DJ: Do you think it's made you a better kind of man or a worse kind of man?
>
> Ray: I think it might have made me a better kind of a person. Who can say what would have happened if I wasn't asthmatic but it might well have been for the best.
>
> DJ: What do you think it gave you particularly?
>
> Ray: Probably more of an understanding of my own and other people's situation. Because everybody has their limitations.

This deeper understanding of his own experience and other people's seems to be about developing a more embodied, self-awareness about 'thinking about breathing slowly in and out' as a way of improving his asthma and surviving more adequately. Ray maintained that the critical, self-reflexive process, initiated by a lifelong experience of asthma, gave him a chance to develop a more thoughtful, self-awareness about his bodily well-being and others.

Gradually this led to Ray working out a more reflexive perspective on pacing his life and '...you had to be aware of your own limitations, I think, and not to try and do too much.' Ray also started to perceive contrasts between his father's life as an aging man and his own life:

I think I realised that I had to look after myself because my father didn't particularly look after himself. He was a smoker although I think he did cut down a lot in his last few years. He didn't drink very much so, from that point of view, I don't think he had an unhealthy life style but he also had a sedentary job – he was a bus driver – so he didn't get a lot of exercise as far as I can remember.

Along with these shifts and changes in embodied self-awareness went a simultaneous critical examination of damaging models of masculinity, probably based on his early experiences of being a 'delicate' boy outsider and being abused by his peer groups both at school and during his apprenticeship. I asked Ray the following question:

DJ: Do aging men need to be tough, hard and strong to survive after 65?

Ray: No, I don't think so. It's a preconceived idea that people have but I don't see it like that.

DJ: So what's got you through to 70? Not your hardness or your strength?

Ray: Being understanding; being able to relate to people and, as I said before, I think this macho male is a myth. Nobody needs to be, or to even seem to be tough and strong. I think there are quite a few men around who have this idea that that is what they have to do.

Ray, here, is arguing that a more compassionate, relational model of masculinity has helped him to survive to the age of 70. He does not believe that 'hardness' or 'strength' help you in the long struggle to stay alive, gain support and be open to other people. Later, Ray went on to expand his definition of damaging conceptions of masculinity. I was asking Ray about what made him feel excluded in his early years and he answered like this:

...well the general male thing of talking about sex and trying to be something that you are not really and having to prove yourself as a male all the time instead of being yourself.

In this comment, Ray contrasts a competitive, predatory model of being a man against just 'being yourself' and puzzling out, more independently, how to be a man in your own terms.

One of the other factors that kept Ray feeling alive and well was the 'importance of marital and partnership status' (Davidson and Meadows, 2010; Arber, Davidson and Ginn, 2003) in his life. As Davidson and Meadows put it:

> ...aging men who live without women are more likely to lack the health-protective support experienced by partnered men. (Davidson and Meadows, 2010)

The benefits of 'health-protective support' were certainly experienced by Ray in his marriage with a very active and caring woman, 'working as a carer in a care home'. His wife helped him to take responsibility for his 'diet and lifestyle' and as Ray says:

> ...we are much more aware now about how to keep healthy.

They also worked together on a neighbourhood allotment and shared intimate decisions and advice together. When Ray realised his health was deteriorating while working for a security firm, he negotiated his problem and possible solutions with his wife:

> ...yes, it was bad for my health to do this job because I felt that I had to get out because I couldn't stay there any longer. So my wife and I discussed it and we decided that we would sell the house in Bridgford. It was quite a big house and there was just the two of us and we didn't really need all that space so we decided to sell it and once we'd sold it I retired.

So they were able to work out, together, an alternative solution to a damaging job ruining Ray's health. This combined decision also had positive results in that part of the reasons for Ray's present sense of vigorous well-being was linked to him being able to retire and sever the connections with an oppressive environment in the security office.

Finally, Ray filled the vacuum created by his retirement and the absence of paid work by moving towards an emerging discourse of sociable masculinity and communal well-being. On this issue, Thompson (2006) suggests that later-life masculinities often seem to be defined more by 'norms of sociablity'. From this changed perspective, aging men seek greater connection with others and are led less and less by the successes and triumphs that used to define themselves as younger men. Thus, at 70, Ray seems to position himself as a practiser of norms of sociability. He takes an active part in the pensioners' action group and the elders' forum, and is also on the committee of his local allotment group. I asked him a question about his social activism:

DJ: You say that you are more socially active now at 70 than you have ever been in your life so how has that affected the quality of your life as an older man?

Ray: Very much and for the better as well. Being socially active you get to meet people and seeing their point of view and then forming your own opinions rather than just going to work and coming home and watching television. It's much more stimulating to be with people and listen to their views.

Hanif

Many aging men in the UK are tightly sandwiched between the cultural ideals of staying young and fit within the 'positive aging' discourse and the narrative of 'bodily decline' (Gullette, 2004) within the biomedical discourse. But an obsessive stress on remaining active in old age, like in Robert's life story, ignores the changes in aging bodies (Sandberg, 2011) that often provoke a new way of thinking about alternatives to the binary trap of 'positive aging' on one hand, and the discourse of inevitable decline on the other.

Here, in Hanif's life history account, I have tried to move beyond this binary trap in looking at an alternative discourse that might have contributed to Hanif's struggle to survive at 67. This alternative discourse I want to call the contemplative, self-reflexive discourse that includes considered choices about purposeful non-activity that might involve regular rest, periods of quiet, prayer, contemplation and perhaps meditation, existing alongside occasional engaged activity.

In Hanif's case he was a 'practising Muslim' in later life who felt that:

It was my faith activity that has (sic) kept me going.

He was now committed to a five times a day prayer and worship ritual within his own family and the local mosque. As a part of this spiritual contemplation, Hanif was also aware of trying to develop a more contemplative body. Now, at 67 he wanted to, 'give rest to my body', and he felt that he 'benefitted by being quiet.' He also regretted that, 'his young self should have been praying earlier.'

Hanif went on to contrast his earlier 'busy' life with his later movement towards shared prayer and life in the community:

> ...you know when you've spent a lot of your younger time in the midst of everything and you're busy, you know, and you are wanted here and there and your life is very active. And suddenly you come out of that and you're only limited to your family. That gives me a bit of time to work and to do something for the community. The religious part, in fact, has given me something to keep myself busy and be amongst the community where people congregate for four or five times a day and you share a lot of things and you learn more.

There is a contradictory tension in this account between turning away from his early, hectic activity and his later, contemplative life but which still contains a wish to 'keep myself busy.' However, the close association of activity with well-being in old age (Katz, 2000) has been partly challenged by Hanif's more balanced movement towards a mixture of contemplation and occasionally engaged activity.

Hanif's struggle to shape a more contemplative body for himself is also an important part of his survival strategies in old age. The historical legacies of the 'feminization of colonised men' (Connell, 2000; Sinha, 2007) in his early life in Pakistan seem to have partly combined with his present bodily fragility (e.g. glaucoma, diabetes, angina and a slipped disc in his back) in the UK to make him openly honest about his physical vulnerability. In my interviews with him, his personal owning up of possessing a 'weak body' keeps on coming up. He comments that:

> I'm not physically strong...there are a lot of physical problems with my body.

Also, earlier when he was about 9 or 10, Hanif acknowledges that,'

> I wasn't a very well-built lad...I was very young and weak.

This later life acceptance of his physical vulnerability has, according to Hanif, unexpected advantages. He does not pretend to be competitive and tough as a man. That would have attracted aggressive attention from other boys and men. Instead Hanif seems to have developed into a more thoughtful, self-reflexive, older man who knows his weaknesses and inner strength. He says:

> No. I've never been a physical fighter. I've always been a mental fighter.

So Hanif thrives not through using his fists but by using his mental power. Accepting his bodily vulnerability and perceived 'weakness' has helped him to turn this bodily feature into a positive advantage. Hanif reflects that:

> I think being weak has kept me out of a lot of trouble. Being weak has overwhelming benefits for me. Being weak you don't become too aggressive towards others.

Hanif's life as an aging man was significantly buttressed by his extended family network. He lived in a large Asian family house with joint family households mixed together with Hanif and his wife. It is important to recognise here that a, 'large proportion of older, Asian people continue to live with their relatives in large households' (Blakemore and Boneham, 1994). In Hanif's case, the care, support and financial assistance he received from his other relatives helped to keep him alive.

His family house was owned by one of his sons, and its inhabitants were Hanif, his wife, 'his elder son who is not married yet and my middle son who is married with one daughter and his daughter-in-law.' Hanif's wife is five years younger than he is and because of health problems she cannot do very much of the domestic labour that is expected of her. Hanif describes her health problem in this way:

> She's got mainly arthritis and knee problems and she also suffers from dizziness and she fell down and because she has a heavy body there is a danger that she will harm herself.

These domestic duties have now been passed on to Hanif's daughter-in-law. He says of her:

> ... we've got a very good daughter-in-law living with us and she looks after both of us [his wife and himself]. She is currently poorly herself.

On the surface, Hanif's family household arrangement looks like a patriarchal organisation with the main burden of work falling on women's shoulders, particularly the daughter-in-law's. But on closer scrutiny there are tentative signs that Hanif is learning to be more caring in the household, looking after grandchildren and giving more support to his wife. Also there is a sense that other members of his family are starting to move out of the extended family house and network and are creating their own independent space and living arrangements.

As an aging man, Hanif is aware that to survive he has to share things with other members of his family. He comments:

> ... if anybody who is relying on a state pension they will always be broke and they will always be in debt but, from my point of view, we are managing because we share a lot of things with my children now. One son will pay all the electric bills.

Hanif's extended family ties are also closely integrated with the local Pakistani community. He was 'known and valued in [his] community,', and he also felt a wider, community responsibility to others in his community. He puts it like this:

> I felt, you know, an awful lot of responsibility on me. Not only for my own family but my other relatives and the rest of the community.

This gave Hanif more of an active purpose in his later life, particularly at a time when Islamophobia was increasing in the UK after 9/11. He was a part of setting up a moderate Pakistani Muslim community group specialising in youth groups that explained the diversity of different Muslim organisations in Britain:

> We were getting flak from the local press on that [the after effects of 9/11] and we felt that it's not right that everybody is lumbered with the same image. So we thought that we need to prove ourselves and that everybody is not a crook and we can do things above board and with transparency and so that's how this organisation was set up.

Hanif experienced a combination of racial discrimination and social class ambivalence and put-down when he came to Britain in 1962. He encountered a savage, white racism that made jibes like:

> Why don't you get on your banana boat and get back to your own country?

He also struggled to accept migratory demotion (Jenkins, 2012). In Pakistan he had been trained to do an office job but in Britain he first became a manual labourer:

> I was thinking, at the time, that I'd left an office job and come to England and doing a labouring job with a shovel, cement and gravel.

Hanif was very aware of the social inequalities involved in this migratory demotion. He reflected further on these shifts:

> ...driving and conducting is a profession which, back in India and Pakistan, is not valued so much and it is considered as a third degree job.

And again:

> I saw people like university professors coming here and doing jobs – teachers coming and doing bus conductor's jobs – so we had people from India and Pakistan who were more educated than me so I thought: 'O.K. It's bad luck' but we've made the choice and I felt that the job was interesting. You meet highly educated people and you meet manual workers...

What probably saved Hanif from despairing and feeling depressed about this huge squandering of talent and abilities on the buses was a resilient commitment to defending the rights of Pakistani citizens at a time of white racism, cultural distortions and misunderstandings about the actual lives of Asian, Muslim families. Indeed, his growth of community and political engagement helped him to survive through troubled times.

In 1962 when Hanif arrived in Britain there was little cultural recognition of Asian people's needs. So he decided in the late 1960s to, 'set up a society – the Pakistan Friends' League – and we were meeting on a regular basis.' He started a form of community activism that tried to improve Asian people's everyday lives:

> We were helping people sort out their daily life problems like filling in forms for a passport; for social security benefit; for employment. We did an advice-giving role.

Later, his political engagement broadened out in the late 1970s and early 1980s when he joined the Labour party and participated in the Transport and General union issues. He was elected as a county councillor in 1985 and tried to defend people from cuts and 'economy measures.' A residential home for older people was in the process of being closed by the county council. But Hanif was against this decision. He argued that:

> We should stick up for these people and our group [labour group] should look elsewhere for savings.

Hanif began to formulate his political principles more clearly for himself and others. His main concern was about social justice and, particularly, to stick up for people from ethnic and racially diverse backgounds. He comments that:

> ... if you don't treat people equally and you don't accept that everybody is not accepting that this is a multi-cultural, multi-ethnic, multi-faith society ...

After Hanif retired as a bus driver through a slipped disc in his back in 1993, he still continued his community and political activism as the manager of a housing advice centre for Pakistani people. Reflecting back on this job, he comments that:

> Even to this time people still come to me for advice on matters relating to the housing.

He also feels that he represented a positive model for other Pakistanis in his community who needed some kind of inspirational encouragement to consider entering politics:

> In our community people never thought that going into local government as an elected member is an option for us but when I got elected in 85 it had suddenly given people something to think about: 'He's a bus driver so if he can be a councillor then so can we.'

Perhaps Hanif was able to channel some experience of union militancy and working-class political activism through his early manual jobs and his job as a bus driver into his community engagement and later work as a county councillor committed to social equality? Certainly his shared experience and varied social skills as a community and political activist helped Hanif to thrive in his neighbourhood. This is what he says:

There are a lot of skills which I believe I've gained and they are, in many ways, simple things like how to run an organisation; how to participate in major events; how to organise events; how to pass on the skills to the community.

Discussion

This chapter is not primarily concerned with illness and decline but with the most neglected questions and issues regarding how some older, working-class men like Robert, Ray and Hanif build a sense of informal well-being and resilient survival throughout a life-time. This resilience and well-being in aging men comes from their largely unrecognised hidden resources and unacknowledged survival skills, experiences, insights, knowledge and information that have kept them feeling alive, and offered direction and guidance through many years. However, it has to be admitted that older, married men lean heavily on their wives for everyday support, companionship, intimacy and emotional well-being (Scott and Wenger, 1995).

Professional health workers and organisations need to try and work alongside aging men's hidden skills of survival, activating and including these hidden skills and tacit knowledges in their medical treatments, rather than assuming that aging men know nothing about their own well-being or how to stay alive.

A life course perspective approaches aging men's well-being as being closely interwoven with the inventive adaptations and survival strategies used through a life to weather the frequent storms of contradictory and disruptive transitions and abrupt shifts of lived experiences. Some of these turbulent storms are the challenging times of hospitalisation, deaths of loved ones, physical injuries and changes, moving house, loss of work and family problems. What has happened before (particularly in childhood and adolescence) has a significant bearing on aging men's present states of well-being. An illuminating example of this is to be found in Ray's life story.

Although Ray survived his life-time of experience through marital support and community activism after his retirement, what he learned through being labelled as a 'delicate' asthmatic boy at the age of six, changed his whole relationship to being a man in later life. He talks of 'never being particularly physical' and not fitting in with the extremes of a dominant, masculinity culture. His sense of painful marginality seemed to produce in him a more self-reflexive awareness of his physical and emotional position and, accordingly, he sought a more caring and emotionally expressive way of being a man. This helped him to develop a more critical perspective on his masculine identities and bodily well-being. In a way, Ray survived his early experiences through the growth of a self-reflexive process, initiated by a lifelong experience of asthma, that later gave him, 'more of an understanding of my own and other people's situation.'

The three men's struggles to survive in an ageist, hierarchical context are closely tied in to the historical legacies of class relations in the UK (See 'Working-Class masculinities' above.) Robert was particularly shaped by those class-related experiences. His life history narratives revealed elements of rebelliousness, class defiance and cultural disobedience. Often this was expressed in terms of a breaking away from ageist norms of how one was expected to behave in old age (Sandberg, 2011).

To some extent, Robert survived the processes of aging through a class refusal to conform and give away his independent powers. He strongly believed that:

> ... you should stick up for your rights. Because you are old and senile, it doesn't mean to say your brain's gone.

He went on to say that distorting ageist stereotypes and constricting limitations imposed on older people should be challenged and fought against, like his prickly support for his father and aunt. He felt that old age needed a new vocabulary of rights, activism and empowerment. He was also convinced that constant activity kept you happy. This is how he put it in his own words:

> ... the more active you are, the happier you are, I believe.

Later, Robert expanded his views on the benefits of activity, saying that:

> ... if you don't use a thing you deteriorate. If you don't use your brain you deteriorate. If you don't use your muscles and your organs then you deteriorate.

However, Robert's praise of activity needs to be problematised. His prioritising of activity sometimes appeared to be motivated by his fear of sitting still and becoming passive. Passivity is a deeply gendered and feminised concept for men; in many respects it is regarded as a distinctly un-masculine quality and thus comes to constitute the demonised 'other' to a masculine preference for doing things outside and engaging in robust activity. It was common, therefore, in this study, that aging men, like Robert, constructed their masculine identities partly around a systematic denial and rejection of quiet, rest and imposed passivity in their lives, often with a correspondingly powerful reliance upon activity.

In contrast to Robert's commitment to activity, Hanif's entry, in later life, into a more contemplative discourse and subject position could be seen as potentially subversive. His regular rituals of prayer and worship as a practising Muslim allowed him space and time to, 'give rest to my body' and to benefit from 'being quiet'. This occasional preference for purposeful non-activity, especially in family or community contexts in the shared house or local mosque, represented a courageous alternative to the over-busy lives of other aging men, although, it also has to be acknowledged that Hanif also had bursts of engaged activity as well.

The other issue that gave Hanif the safety and security to survive was being a part of an extended family network, with close communal relations. His careful support for other people and his community and political activism kept him alert and alive. He also represented a positive role model after his election as a county councillor in 1985 onwards, for other people in his community to follow and to engage, politically, in the wider politics and social affairs of the country.

All three, older working-class men also illustrated the constructive benefits of recognising and acknowledging that they possessed, in different ways, fallible and vulnerable bodies. Instead of extolling the conventional masculine virtues of having tough, hard and aggressive bodies, they openly admitted that their bodies were weak, fragile and sometimes agile rather than muscular. Robert disowned the manly heroic possession of physical strength, commenting that: 'as you get older, strength doesn't count does it?'

Hanif does not pretend to have a manly body. He openly admits that he has a 'weak body':

I'm not physically strong ... I wasn't a very well-built lad.

His later life acceptance of his physical vulnerability has helped him to survive. This bodily recognition has supported him to turn these bodily features into a positive advantage for himself. He comments that:

I think being weak has kept me out of a lot of trouble. Being weak has overwhelming benefits for me. Being weak you don't become too aggressive to others.

Honestly acknowledging his own bodily fragility has helped Hanif to stand apart from competitive, aggressive masculinity and, independently, work out his own peaceful solutions based on mental capability and 'inner strength.'

Also, I have already commented on Ray's embracing of his own, asthmatic vulnerability, and 'never being particularly physical' in constructing a more critical awareness of his masculine identities and bodily well-being. All these acknowledgements of bodily frailty seem to have resulted in a deeper, human resilience in the lives of Robert, Ray and Hanif (Blakemore, 1994; Collier, 1998; Connell, 1995).

I want to finish by under-lining the insights that all three of these older, working-class men survived by not exclusively pursuing triumph, achievement and success in their later lives but moving towards, in many varied ways, a more relational and community-minded model of well-being.

Ray's perceptive remarks flesh out the specific details of this relational model of well-being and shows what survival might mean in gendered terms:

DJ: Do aging men need to be tough, hard and strong to survive after 65?

Ray: No, I don't think so. It's a preconceived idea that people have but I don't see it like that.

DJ: So what's got you through to 70? Not your hardness or your strength?

Ray: Being understanding; being able to relate to people and, as I said before, I think this macho male is a myth. Nobody needs to be, or to even seem, to be tough and strong.

8

Exploring Aging Men's Embodied and Social Agency in a Free Market Economy Context

Confronted by physical deterioration and reduction in bodily strength as a material reality, what can aging men do about this? Also, confusingly positioned between the dominant discourse of aging (the narrative of decline, [Gullette, 2004]) and the 'positive aging' discourse (Townsend, 2006) with its commercial exploitation of the old, how can aging men navigate their own routes in increasingly choppy seas?

Aging men are challenged by physical changes, biographical disruptions (Bury, 1982) and social issues about loneliness, intimacy, relationships and friendships. Some aging men find it difficult to share problems with other men and, generally, seem to avoid emotional disclosure. As a result, many aging men experience a lack of close, intimate friendship with other men and often face a diminishing social support network as they age. This often leaves aging men in a state of loneliness and social isolation.

These isolating circumstances are often exacerbated by heterosexual, aging men's tendency to 'take solace in seeking the primary, almost sole companionship of their wife or partner' (Drummond, 2007). This often leads to the problem, faced by many aging men who become widowed or divorced, that they lack a wider friendship and social support network when their wives or partners die or vanish from their lives (Scott and Wenger, 1995; Davidson, 2004).

As they age, older men are threatened and unsettled by their loss of physical and social capital (Bourdieu, 1980). The challenge for them is to find ways of using their own versions of physical and social agency (4) in their changing lives to recover social and cultural value (Tulle, 2008). Aging men's bodies are not just ruined bodies. They can also play a central role in initiating personal and social change.

However, the exercising of embodied agency in aging men can be blocked by social structures of regulation and control. In 2016 this investigation of social structures requires a wider interrogation of the prevailing culture and society aging men are living within in the UK, especially focusing on the free market economy with its promotion of individualisation and privatisation of everyday life (Tulle, 2004). The free market economy, over the last thirty years in the UK, has made important shifts and changes to the lives of aging men, particularly the erosion of the British welfare state and the loss of support for the idea that caring for older people should be a collective responsibility (Tulle, 2004).

But the exercising of 'self-actualised power' or agency in aging men's lives cannot be achieved without a critique of the free market economy in the UK. Before I start developing a critique, I would like to reflect a little more on the way agency can work through the rebellious or transgressive bodies (Tulle, 2008) of aging men. Aging men's bodies, despite physical deterioration, also carry with them the potential for social change and, in this case, they have the ability to challenge and refuse to conform to conventional, gendered norms of masculinised, aging bodies.

In this chapter, I want to explore two research participants' evidence of possessing rebellious, aging, masculinised bodies. One of the aging participants called Robert reveals a sceptical, probing response to one of the key, gendered norms associated with the dominant culture of men and masculinities, namely that of bodily strength. From his different standpoint of being an aging man, Robert partly disowns his habitual, industrial work connection to bodily strength, saying:

... as you get older, strength doesn't count does it?

A life course perspective will illustrate how Robert changes his relationship to his body from working as a platelayer (5) for British Rail (6) up to this present, transgressive, gendered position as an aging man.

The second participant reveals a contradictory attitude to his 'weak' body. Instead of regretting his 'weakness', Hanif praises his non-aggressive body and his mental strength and talks about 'the unexpected advantages' of possessing a gentler, peaceful, anti-warrior body.

After my critique of the free market economy social model, I include an oppositional work of social agency. In more detail, this is a piece of critical autobiographical work (7) where I explore the subject of collective support and mutuality through shared email contacts, made immediately after my collapse in Stockholm in August 2010.

A Critique of the Free Market Economy in the UK

It is important to set aging men in Britain within a wider social context, that of the free market economy and globalised agenda in public politics (Connell, 2004) which has eroded the foundations of the post-war welfare state in Britain (Jones, 2003). Viewed from a free market perspective, 'the welfare state is the enemy of freedom' (Hall, 2011). Aging men, used to a different, social-democratic society from early on in their lives, remember how that post-war social organisation tried to protect the socially vulnerable, remained committed to social justice and egalitarianism, attacked unemployment and wanted to redistribute wealth, but now, in 2016, they have to face up to a much bleaker future.

Instead, this neoliberal agenda focuses on the central idea of the 'free, possessive individual' (Hall, 2011), liberated from state intervention, involved in privatisation and an emphasis on individualisation, and encouraging open, competitive, unregulated markets. The destruction of the welfare state was also a way of doing away with what the free market economy perceived as passivity and dependency and, in its place, constructing an independent, autonomous, active psychological subject engaged in entrepreneurial and competitive activities (Steinberg and Johnson, 2004). Walkerdine and Jimenez summarise these new priorities in this way:

> ... within advanced liberalism, (or the free market economy), the 'social state' gave way to the 'enabling state', and was no longer responsible for providing all of society's needs for security, health, education and so on. Individuals, firms, organisations, schools, hospitals and parents must each and all take on a portion of the responsibility for their own well-being. The social and the economic were seen as antagonistic, which meant that economic governance was desocialised so as to maximise and facilitate the entrepreneurial conduct of an individual who should be responsible for their biography.

This was achieved through the restructuring, deregulation and privatisation of the economy and the labour market as well as the restructuring of welfare provisions that are seen as 'producing passivity and dependence...' (Walkerdine and Jimenez, 2012).

Some of my research participants have experienced major changes in their patterns of work influenced by the free market economy. Many jobs that depended on physical strength in heavy industrial contexts have disappeared, especially after the miners' strike in 1984–85. Now aging men are confronted by more precarious forms of living and working. Those who are still working are facing the casualisation of employment or they are either unemployed, seriously injured or working through short-term contracts, low pay and part-time work, like some of the work experiences of the research participants working in security firms, a laundry, or cleaning a large shopping mall.

These free market movements have alienated many aging men by severing the social ties and collective solidarity that some of them experienced in community and work networks. The rapid growth of technologically-based businesses, service industries and the rapidly rising communication and knowledge areas (Johnson and Walkerdine, 2004) have also disorientated some aging men, especially in their transitions from masculine, manufacturing industries to more feminine, service/communication ones.

Free market globalisation has generally subordinated aging, working-class men. There are still some manual labourers who participated through their early lives in manufacturing industries who are barely managing to keep afloat, economically, and who are faced by their own deteriorating physical conditions and the future necessity to keep on working. On the other hand, there are also some privileged, middle-class, aging men who have been able to take advantage of the neoliberal agenda who have immersed themselves in entrepreneurial activities, especially in the new service economy and communication and knowledge economies.

An Oppositional Example of Social Agency:[1] The Collective Interactions of a Virtual, Mutual Help Group of Aging Men

Within a free market economy context there is often an intensification of private isolation (e.g. 'old age has been reconstructed as a private problem' [Tulle, 2004]). In the everyday lives of aging men there is also an over-emphasis on the active, autonomous, responsible individual (Laliberte-Rudman, 2006) rather than improving the social ties and collective solidarity of aging men who are sometimes lost and extremely isolated.

Recent research by Independent age (2014) and the WRVS (Women's Royal Voluntary Service) published on 28 of July 2012 in the UK, has drawn attention to the amount of loneliness and social isolation rife among British, aging men. Their research indicates that over 190,000 British men, over 75, who live by themselves, are lonely. It also identified that 36% spend more than 12 hours of the day on their own. The research also found that aging men are more likely to be lonely than aging women as, 'they are less likely to confide in friends and family about their feelings' (WRVS, 2012).

In 1999, I formed an aging men's group in the East Midlands' area of the UK with the half-worked-out intention of cutting down on private isolation (including my own) and widening the friendship and social networks of other aging men. I am also focusing on my own personal participation in one particular incident, at the age of 70, in a virtual, mutual help group (Walters, 1999) where I will explore the subject of collective support and interaction through shared email contacts immediately after my collapse in Stockholm. This is a personal and political attempt to investigate possible ways of improving aging men's positions of social isolation in a virtual form that they might find non-invasive.

At that time I had been a member of this men's group for the last eleven years. The nine aging men, aged between 50 and mid-70s, met every two or three months either in Nottingham, Leicester or Leamington Spa, the three places where the aging men came from. This collection of emails represents a small selection from a mixture of various emails (from mainly aging men's group members and from a friend) received during that time. The emails also include one of my personal responses. I have kept the spelling mistakes as I found them in the emails.

THE EMAILS:

1. 16 August 2010: 23.26

Just a note that David is recovering from a nasty turn when we visited Stockholm last week. Their health services took good care of him after he collapsed. His heart condition is now being managed and he is on an ace inhibitor and beta blocker.

On the mend I think you may have heard but if not I am sure he would like your support.

2. 17 August 2010: 10.33

Dear David,

Sorry to hear about your turn in Sweden. Always nasty getting poorly away from home but what a dilemma-the old one- about how adventurous to be! I do hope the effects aren't lasting and this is 'only' another bloody unwelcome f***** lesson about 'not doing too much.' don't reply till you are better-then I want to come and see you.

Love

3. 17 August 2010: 19:07

Dear all,

I went to spend some time with David this pm.

He was ok, but tearful and concerned about how much of his activities such as writing, and political militancy he could do from now on, as it is so much a part of his identity.

He is most active in the morning, and sleeps after lunch, today 2 hours.

The ace inhibitor and the beta blocker are having the effect of really slowing him down and he has asked me to ask the group for any info on alternatives to these, or on which of these works best, or any useful information such as do the symptoms subside after some time?

He gets around 20 phone calls a day at the moment so would appreciate this info by email than by a phone call.

I found him generally well physically with a good skin complexion and no breathlessness whatsoever.

Love to all.

4. August 18 2010: 8:06

Some squiggles and loops
Here's like a very short stream of consciousness about what I'm living through.

The honeycombed man-the drifting, slurred man imprisoned in a small room. The doctor's voices tell me I shouldn't go round the block but I've been twice, turn right out of the house, right again and then right etc. Until I'm back at the house.

What purpose and meaning do I have now? What about my political activity with the pensioners? and my writing?

I'm feeling drowsy and giddy from taking these pills: betablockers and ace inhibitor and a 'water' tablet, a dieuretic.

This feels better to rescue a quarter of an hour from the drowsy slur of taking those pills and write in a disconnected, fragmentary way without all the fuss of making it coherent. Perhaps we can exchange some daft squiggles, occasionally?

All my love.
David

5. 18 August 2010: 19:15

Forget all about pensioners, writing, others, David, and even try to vaguely enjoy the wooziness(I remember when I had kidney stones many years back

I was given strong morphine and at last could see why the romantic poets enjoyed their drugs-but I wasn't tempted to follow in Coleridge's wandering footsteps.)Sleep and rest are good healers, so make the most of your Rip van Wrinkle stage, because it will not last long and there will be other options, other doors to prise open, other stones to peer under (I found a toad at the back of the garage and exchanged some ideas with him,mainly to encourage him in more helpings of slugs with the promise of more rubbish heaps for him to explore.)

Pill bashing isn't easy, but there was a man in the hospital when I was in who took 12 tablets a day, and he had a special pill tray which showed times and days. As he said he had a rattling good time! Yes, treasure those periods of clarity and then you may want to jot down some lines, words, squiggles, noodles, doodles, anything that comes to the surface.

We've been in the garden most of the day and I've been trying to rehearse sections of a letter I must write to Michael in Toronto but I don't want to sound like a prig, prat, goody two shoes, etc.

After what you've been through, mate, you're well and truly here,now, even if it's a different brand of Jackson. So keep to what your doc says, but keep one eye on the small print (side effects)

More tomorrow,
Love.

6. 19 August 2010: 11:04

Dear David,

Like so many others I am distressed to hear that you have had another health alert. No matter how well we try to prepare, these messages from our bodies are huge challenges. I have no advice to offer that you will not have thought of yourself. When I heard about your request for information on ace inhibitors and beta blockers, I asked Ann, my first port of call for advice of a non-specialist sort on matters medical. I readily pass on her comments. As far as she knows, side effects do diminish. She suggests, if you are concerned about the treatment that your doctors are giving, that you do a google search; if, for example, any of the possible side effects are happening to you talk it over with your doctors.

For my part, I offer my support and send you what Patrick called an electronic hug.

Do not feel under any pressure to reply to this. I look forward to seeing you when you are feeling better.

Love.

Commentary:

Aging men often have to confront loneliness and social isolation as they age, especially in contexts where their social networks collapse after the death of their wives or partners (Arber, Davidson and Ginn, 2003). Very often, women keep these social networks going and aging men sometimes experience a bewildering sense of isolation after their spouses die.

In 1999 I made a conscious effort to counter future loneliness and isolation in my rapidly aging life by setting up an aging men's group in the East Midlands of the UK. This group worked mainly through the shared, personal stories of our life histories with the mutual exploration of themes that were often important to aging men, like men's health, relationships with partners, relationships with our children, preparing for death and dying, aging men's sexualities and family issues. Instead of being individually isolated, the group often gave emotional and practical support to group members who were ill or sick or facing a particularly knotty problem in their changing lives. Much of that support was face to face in the group sessions but, occasionally, support, as when I collapsed through congestive heart disease, was through email contact.

Emails, as a form of electronic communication, are relatively fast and concise messages. They also allow varying degrees of detachment and intimacy for the sender that is clearly discernible in the selected emails above. I was also concerned about not being overwhelmed by the twenty phone calls a day I was receiving so I expressed a preference for email communication. Email number 1, for example, is crisp and to the point, factually describing what happened but also initiating some collective support and social solidarity within the group through suggesting, 'I am sure he would like your support.' Certainly when I received this email I felt more reassured that I was not alone in facing this dilemma. A roughly similar, practical support through factual information and advice from his wife can be found in email number 6. This email gives the impression that the writer is standing back, more philosophically and generally, from the experience and analysing what happened in a thoughtful manner:

> ... no matter how well we try and prepare, these messages from our bodies are huge challenges.

Email number 2 offers something different from factual information and advice. It is short but offers emotional warmth to the receiver. The eleven years of sharing our life stories in the aging men's group seems to have paid off in the sense of developing trust and mutual understanding implicit in the sender's response to my troubles. He fits his response into one of the group's familiar themes; the conflict between adventurous desire and 'not doing too much.' In the group we have often discussed this tension as a recurring conflict in our everyday lives and here it offers the emotional comfort to me of having been in this situation before with group members helping me to understand how I got here.

The central question here is how far the support offered by the email senders helps to restore in me a sense of being fully alive after my traumatic collapse. Did those varied messages help me to keep going at 70? There are two emails, numbers 3 and 5, which address, in totally different ways, my fear of self-annihilation and loss of masculine identity and give some answers to my questions. This deep, emotional fear is expressed in email number 4:

> ... what purpose and meaning do I have now? What about my political activity with pensioners? And my writing? [...] I'm feeling drowsy and giddy from taking these pills.

In the first month of taking the beta blockers and ace inhibitor, I felt constantly drowsy as if my clear-headed space that I needed to shape my masculine sense of self had been eroded for the rest of my life and all I could do was sleep.

Email number 3, in an empathetic way, directly enters my emotional space and fears in the first paragraph. Through a close, intimate connection, the writer is able to hear my muffled voice of fear and intense anxiety:

> ... he was ok, but tearful and concerned about how much of his activities such as writing, and political militancy he could do from now on, as it is so much a part of his identity.

The email is a mixture of emotional intimacy and medical information in the second paragraph.

In email number 5, a friend attempts to get me to let go of my fears through a jokey, playful irreverence. He does not want to give me a po-faced, moral lecture. So he lightens the tone of what he's saying through joshing ('Rip van Wrinkle' and the toad), puns ('a rattling good time') and reference to his own life. Underneath this jaunty, breezy surface there is a genuine affection. He wants to back me up. This is what he says:

... after what you've been through, mate, you're well and truly here, now, even if it's a different brand of Jackson.

Both these emails, numbers 3 and 5, helped to restore in me a sense of being more fully alive, and helped me to combat my terror of self-annihilation and my fears of becoming a passive dummy. In these two emails you can catch the flickering processes of re-awakening in me as I begin to understand what the problem is and what I can do about it.

In emails 2, 3 and 5, there are significant signs that a rigid, gendered dichotomy (women = emotion, and men = rationality and analysis) is being challenged in some of these emails. Aging men can give emotional warmth and empathetic understanding to other men struggling to survive. Not all of the time and often depending on the specific context but, occasionally, they can reverse the strict, gendered binary between rationality and emotion.

Also, these email interactions show something of the oppositional, social agency that is urgently needed to critique the free market economy context that we are living within in the UK. Some of these emails helped me to feel more socially connected and embedded in a wider group of aging men. However, there are still problems around aging men's patterns of men-men friendships. Cohen (1992) has pointed out the cultural barriers that prevent some aging men from trusting and confiding in others, such as:

> ... competitiveness and its inhibiting effect on self-disclosure; a lack of role models in intimacy; homophobia and a need to be in control, which also restricts men's willingness to be vulnerable.

That said, there are a few promising signs in this sharing of emails that suggests a possible way forward in countering private isolation and loneliness.

The Changing Bodies of Aging Men

The social definition of masculine identity is closely tied in to a man's physicality. As Connell tellingly suggests:

> ... true masculinity: is almost always thought to proceed from men's bodies. (Connell, 1995)

Therefore, body size, physical strength and musculature play a central role in the construction of masculine identities, particularly in young and middle-aged men's lives (Drummond, 2007). Indeed, through the turns and twists of complex lives, many men are haunted by the anxiety of not measuring up to a cultural ideal, within Western culture, of a muscular and strong body. As Lee and Owens comment:

> Even at an early age boys, like girls, frequently perceive their bodies as deviating from an internalised ideal. (Lee and Owens, 2002)

To understand more fully where this 'internalised ideal' comes from historically so that the reader can appreciate, more empathetically, what aging men are confronted by with the loss of muscle and physical strength in later life, I intend to offer a few comments about the construction of the muscular ideal.

A Brief History of the Muscular, Manly Ideal in Western Culture

Dutton (1995), in his massive study of the Western ideal of muscular bodies, traces the origin of such representations from the age of classical Greek sculpture to that of bodybuilding and Arnold Schwarzenegger. However, as Petersen points out, 'There is nothing inevitable about the association of muscularity with perfection or physical beauty. In many non-Western societies beauty is seen, or has been seen, to reside not so much in the body itself, but rather in body displays, body decoration or even mutilation' (Petersen, 1998). Dutton goes on to show how the West developed a symbolic language of muscularity which in most Eastern societies would have been meaningless.

Physical power in a male-dominant culture works as constructing specific male bodies as normal or natural and other bodies as pathological or unnatural (Petersen, 1998). Certainly, in my own case, that is true. In the late 1940s and early 1950s in Britain, the Charles Atlas adverts played on my anxieties and fears about bodily inadequacy and made a lasting impression. They usually centred on a contrast between a beefy hunk of a man scuffing sand in the eye of a 'seven-stone weakling'. I was desperately worried about having a 'weakling's' body so I was very susceptible to the dreams and fantasies of gaining He-Man muscles. One of the other adverts for Charles Atlas featured a comic-strip frame showing two weedy men saying to each other: 'Gee...I would like to have real He-Man muscles!' and the other replying, 'So would I but it takes a long while.' The feeble maunderings of the two weeds are broken into by the powerful physique of a real photograph of Charles Atlas, all bronzed and bulging with muscles. The banner headlines of the advert are shouting, 'Rot! – says

Charles Atlas. I'll prove in the first 7 days you can have a body like mine!'

Although definitions of masculinity and masculine bodies vary within different historical and cultural contexts, boys and men are privileged by the degree to which they approximate to this muscular, manly ideal (Gershick, 2005). Going alongside this is a significant gendered intolerance to non-normative bodies like disabled, injured, ugly, aged and so on. As Gershick comments:

> People with less normative bodies are vulnerable to being denied social recognition and validation. (Gerschick, 2005)

It is also important to recognise how sport (both for boys and young men) contributes to these robust, muscular ideals. Regularly repeated sporting practices play a part in masculinising the bodies of young men, particularly through soccer and rugby in the UK. Closely tied in to these practices are heroic fantasies of competitive manliness and virility through varied sporting heroes.

The other key feature of the muscular ideal, especially in Britain, is that it has been shaped by the protestant work ethic and the cultural link, increasingly evident in the late-nineteenth and earlier-twentieth centuries, between strenuous work and current ideals of manliness (Petersen, 1998). In industrial Britain this produced the embodiment of industrial, masculine bodies that were necessary to undertake hard and dangerous work in steel making, coal mining, ship building, etc. (Walkerdine and Jimenez, 2012). The male body of the industrial worker had to be honed and disciplined to withstand the strenuous rigours of the work within a social context of economic insecurity produced by regular, international fluctuations in the labour markets (Walkerdine and Jimenez, 2012). Also, these working-class embodiments were passed down from generation to generation and often from father to son.

Aging Men's Loss of Physical Strength and Muscle in Later Life

Drummond has already alerted the reader to the ways that body size, physical strength and musculature play a significant part in the construction of a young/middle-aged man's masculine identities (Drummond, 2007). Also, those younger, masculine identities are powerfully influenced, real and imagined, by the symbolic promise of the muscular, manly ideal in Western culture, as I was by Charles Atlas.

Labouring, in the working years, for the male industrial worker, became a way of honing and disciplining his working body to withstand the strenuous rigours of hard and, sometimes, dangerous labour (Walkerdine and Jimenez, 2012). As some industrial workers' bodies hardened and matured, their bodies became associated with the ideals of physical toughness, robustness and invulnerability (Petersen, 1998). However, as men age they lose muscle size and muscle strength (Drummond, 2007). This sometimes comes as a challenge to their masculine identities and their sense of what they can do with their bodies, especially after their early training in fitness, sport and strength. These losses present difficulties to some aging men who find it difficult to come to terms with the shifting nature of their changing bodies. Some men still cling on to the preservation of an internalised ideal of muscle and strength and often perceive any changes to these ideals as subordinating deviations.

Other aging men find alternative ways around physical deterioration. Some aging men can develop a wider understanding of the loss of muscle size and strength and seem to come to terms with the physical changes that are a part of the aging processes. While others, like Robert and Hanif, develop transgressive, rebellious approaches, where they challenge established attitudes and refuse to conform to conventional, gendered norms associated with masculinised, aging bodies.

Robert's Embodied Agency and his Transgressive, Aging Body

Aging men's bodies, like Robert's, are not just disappointing and deteriorating bodies. They can also play a significant role in initiating personal and social change as agency works through the transgressive bodies (Tulle, 2008) of some aging men.

To understand more precisely what Robert had to grapple with between the ages of 13 and 60, a life course perspective needs to be taken to indicate some of the most important embodied features of his life. At about 13 and 14, Robert was powerfully influenced by the symbolic promise of the muscular, manly ideal in Western culture. In his case he felt particularly vulnerable and insecure about his adolescent body as a growing, white, working-class boy. He comments:

DJ: When did you become conscious of your body?

Robert: Probably about thirteen or fourteen when I thought I was too thin.

DJ: Did you worry about what the others would think of you?

Robert: I suppose I did really. I must have done if I thought I was too thin. But really I wasn't too thin – it was really how I should be.

But I suppose I thought I was too thin because I used to go to the pictures – the kids' matinee – and watch people like John Wayne and thinking that everybody should be like him, you know.

Measuring himself against the culturally idealised, masculine, bodily norms represented by John Wayne (8), Robert saw himself as personally inadequate and wanted to be tougher and more physically robust. His embodied position at that time of his life was also shaped by girls' preference for 'bigger guys':

But you see in them days all the pin ups for the girls were all sort of bigger guys.

The pervasive, post-Second World War, military culture also influenced Robert in his desire for a more muscular, tougher body. His impressions of that time go like this:

I suppose with it just being after the war the men had come back from the war and you was trying to look up to them because they had to be tough. Same as the blokes in the First World War. They had to be tough so you thought that was how you had to be. It's understandable. So you didn't have time for weaklings otherwise we wouldn't have won the war.

From the later ages of 19 and 20, Robert began to exercise and consciously work on his body to 'build it up'. He started by using a Bullworker (9) and getting involved in a Karate class. Here are Robert's comments on this period of his life:

Robert: ... well how that came about was a friend of mine, he gave me a Bullworker. He gave me one because he was interested in Karate and he did a Karate class and he got me to go as well and he gave me this Bullworker because he said that I needed to build myself up. I thought it were alright myself and so I got a Bullworker. In fact I've still got one – an old one.

DJ: And do you use it now?

Robert: Sometimes, yeah. Mostly first thing in the morning. So I started off with a Bullworker and doing the Karate and things like that.

At this time of his life, Robert seemed to be conventionally following bodily ideals of physical toughness, strength and body size within the dominant culture of masculinity. This physical tendency was also reinforced by the industrial work regime that honed, shaped and disciplined his body as a platelayer[2] lifting and shovelling mainly in outdoor work (Walkerdine and Jimenez, 2012). There is often a long history of working-class embodiments like Robert's, passed down through generations, from father to son. In Robert's case this is exactly what happened to him. His father worked as chief shunter for British Rail[3] and Robert followed him, choosing outdoor work and working for British Rail as well.

Historically, working-class men like Robert had to be 'strong enough to do your job'. They needed bodies that would withstand the stresses and strenuous rigours of the work that they were doing (Walkerdine and Jimenez, 2012). They could not afford for their bodies to cave in and let them down at key moments of their wage-earning labour. However, despite their good intentions, industrial accidents were frequent and Robert was no exception to this general trend.

Robert's life turned upside-down in 1989 when he was in his late 40s. This is his account of what happened:

> I was shovelling and somebody dropped a jack because a train was coming and I sort of caught it on my shovel. We were tense anyway and it was cold and the accident injured my neck. So I went to the doctor's and he sent me to the hospital and then I got a letter from the railway saying, 'Do not report for duty. Just collect your wages every Thursday from the wages' office'.

This accident changed the narrow, habitual way of working in Robert's life and as he says, it gave him a 'broader outlook' on society and culture and world politics. This is Robert's commentary on what he did after his accident:

> ...because then I packed up my regular sort of employment and I only did part time jobs and went on courses and various things like that, including educational courses like geography and religious studies as well as trying out acting in a local theatre.

With these gradual shifts and changes of outlook came more independent questioning of the social context that he inhabited. What became clearer from my interviews with Robert was his commitment to moving on with change through inventive adaptation and creative improvisation, 'not trying to stop the same', or desperately clinging onto the past. His advice to other aging men went like this:

> ... well they do need to move on because it's no good trying to do what you did in 1955 when the year is 2006. You've got to accept change whether you like it or not and it's no good saying that things were better years ago and all that sort of thing.

Robert had begun to critically reflect on his own embodied life. This involved a careful dismantling of the common myth of bodily invincibility. He says this:

> ... as you get older you realise that life is very fragile and you are not indestructible. When you are young you think you are going to go on for ever and ever. But you are destructible and I think you do realise that because over the years you get to know more and more people who died.

This conscious awareness of mortality and bodily fragility leads Robert on to take up a transgressive perspective on the loss of bodily strength in old age.

Some aging men find alternative ways around the loss of physical strength and physical deterioration. Robert seems to be one of these men who, alongside his 'broader outlook' on life, struggles to come to terms with and develop a wider understanding of the physical changes that are an integral part of the aging process. I want to quote the whole of Robert's key commentary on not fitting into the traditional, masculine model of building physical strength, especially when younger. Robert's commentary starts with his disappointment at not being able to lift the piece of rail track that Robert now uses as a substitute for a Bullworker:

> Robert: ... and whether I'll be able to lift it up again I've no idea but I'm still pretty agile and that's more important as you get older than being able to lift rail track up above your head.
>
> DJ: Do you think that being agile is now more important than being physically strong?
>
> Robert: Yeah. But when I was younger I think it was probably the other way round. I thought that being stronger was more important but, I suppose, as you get older strength doesn't count, does it? Especially in this modern world it doesn't count so much. At one time – thirty or forty or fifty years ago – you had to be strong or you wouldn't survive but today you don't have to be, but you still have to be agile and fit.

Robert's embodied agency is seen here in the way he sees through the supposed necessity of a strong, muscular, masculine body, and he is also beginning to understand how bodily needs and capabilities change with age and that agility and fitness might prove more appropriate bodily values in a contemporary, aging world.

In Praise of 'Weak' Bodies for Aging Men: Exploring Hanif's Embodied Agency

In the 1950s and early 1960s in post-war Britain there was an extremely polarised binary system of gender relations (Segal, 1990). Despite a few women and men who risked crossing the gendered divide, there was, generally, a rigid segregation of male wage-workers operating exclusively in the public sphere and female, unpaid, domestic workers in the private sphere.

Binary opposition (e.g. masculine/feminine; strength/weakness; white/black etc.), particularly at that time in the early 1960s, seemed so 'natural', fixed and inevitable that most people did not question this conventional way of thinking and understanding (Hatchell, 2007). So when he was young at 23 and working in Britain it seems possible that Hanif took for granted the 'strength/weakness' gendered dichotomy that probably seemed so fixed and natural.

It took the later gendered and sexual disruption of gay liberation, feminism and the queering of gender relations to provoke a broader unsettling of gender relations in Britain. Some men's traditional, centre-stage position as male breadwinner, provider and head of the family household were all in the process of being undermined. As a result, the normative ways of being a man were beginning to become desta-bilised.

Within this process of destabilisation there was a dawning recognition of hidden diversities amongst British men, such as ethnically and racially diverse men, disabled and aging men. Not much focused attention had been given to these diverse and varied men like Hanif.

The surprising feature of Hanif's interviews with me is his open and honest admission that he has always had a 'weak' body and that even from the age of nine or ten, he recognised that:

I was very young and weak. I wasn't a very well-built lad.

There is usually some hint of unmanly shame or streak of humiliation in such a disclosure usually associated with a memory of the gendered binary of 'strength' (masculine) and 'weakness' (feminine), but here

Hanif is able to be relatively undefensive about his open admission. Later, Hanif explains his position more fully:

> DJ: You describe, in the interviews, having a weak body and not being physically strong so has that helped or hindered you as a man through your lifetime?
>
> Hanif: A bit of both. I think being weak has kept me out of a lot of trouble but, on the other hand, there are things which if you were a bit stronger you would want to do things. But on the balance of probability I probably think that being weak has overwhelming benefits for me.
>
> DJ:'Can you explain what those benefits are?
>
> Hanif: The benefits are, you know, that once you are in a weaker situation you don't become too aggressive towards others. I think that some people with heavily built bodies are very insulting and very rude to other people.

In an attempt to be balanced, Hanif accepts and tolerates 'weakness' not as an effeminising threat to his manhood but as a help to being non-aggressive and keeping himself out of trouble. His acceptance of his more gentle and peaceful body gives a clear and pointed example of embodied agency. Hanif is revealing his own self-actualised power in trusting his peace-making body and connected mental strength. He refuses to conform, in a transgressive way, to conventional gendered norms of muscular, strong, aggressive bodies.

However, I want to dig a little deeper into the historical legacies and social forces that have played a part in shaping Hanif's commitment to peaceful, non-aggressive, masculine identities. I can never show a fully comprehensive picture of what has helped him to accept his 'weak' body but I can sketch in some indications of what might have contributed to his present acceptance. First, I will try and establish some key features of Hanif's historical background and then I will make specific references to some linked features of his personal, life story.

Historical background

Colonial Relations in Pakistan.   Hanif spent twenty-two years living in Pakistan before he came to Britain in 1962. He had a limited experience of living in 'that part of Pakistan that was directly ruled by the British.' Hanif experienced, to some degree, the supposed superiority of white, imperial, masculine bodies and the way he was defined as feminine and subordinated as an inferior, colonised, native boy and man (Connell, 2000).

Sinha puts it like this:

'Colonial masculinity' – a politics that informed both colonisers and colonised – illustrates the multiple ways in which masculinity cemented relations of power in the colonies (Sinha, 1995). It constituted a hierarchy of masculinities in which an elite 'white' masculinity presided above both loyal – but simple – 'martial' or 'manly' races and clever-but-treacherous feminised or effeminate native men. (Sinha, 2007)

Asian Communities in Britain and Asian Masculinities. Asian communities in the 1960s and 1970s in Britain were considered as relatively 'unthreatening, law abiding and unproblematic' (Alexander, 2000). Hanif, during his life course, experienced his community in that general way. He was also constructive in his attempts to build a more active community through setting up a Pakistani Friends' League in the late 1960s and later becoming a county councillor in 1985. Hanif's political activism seems to question this unruffled depiction of Asian men's masculinities as 'passive and hyper-feminised' (Alexander, 2000).

More recently, some young Asian men have started to assert themselves much more vigorously, through violence, criminality, drug taking, sexual exploitation and Islamic fundamentalism. However, there are many exceptions to this generalisation. In the global climate of Islamaphobia after 9/11 in the US, Hanif was a part of setting up a moderate Pakistani Muslim community group specialising in youth groups, that explored the diversity of different Muslim gatherings and organisations in Britain, rather than allowing themselves to being lumped all together as fundamentalists or terrorists.

Partly positioned as patriarchal in his Asian family's structure, the wider, gender relations' movements in the UK have undermined, to some extent, his old position as unchallenged head of the household. When I interviewed him he certainly came across as gentle and caring (see the reference to tenderness and caring' in the personal, life story section below).

Comments About Hanif's Religion. At 67 Hanif asserted the importance of religion in his everyday life. He said:

...in fact it's my faith activity which has kept me going.

Religion seemed to offer Hanif the possibility of a future life of deeper contemplation, and although he was occasionally guilt-ridden about not starting his religious studies early enough in his life, he was also aware that being close to his family was also a major part of bringing religion into his life.

I asked Hanif how long he spent praying each day. His answer went like this:

> ...in the morning prayer the minimum requirement is three verses from the qur'an and you can finish that within ten minutes. Right. Then you go on to afternoon which, these days, is two o'clock but in winter time it is one o'clock and that takes you...if you come to mosque for prayers with the rest of the congregation then by the time you left home it would take you half an hour but your actual prayers will only last about fifteen or twenty minutes. Then there is the late afternoon and that only takes you ten minutes. And then you've got evening prayers when the sun sets. That only takes you about seven or eight minutes and then there is the late night prayer which is round about half past nine/ten o'clock time. That takes you a good forty minutes.

Since his early retirement, Hanif has been able to engage more personally in communal prayers at the mosque and at home. That seems to have provided him with a closer and more intimate link with members of his family.

Personal Life Story

Added to this historical background, there are also some more personal episodes and general comments that help to explain Hanif's relation to his physical body.

1. Physical Problems.   I asked Hanif a question about how he felt about his body now:

Hanif: I've got a lot of physical problems with my body.

DJ: Such as?

Hanif: If I start from my head to toe. I've got glaucoma and I use two medications for that. And then I've got diabetes and I take tablets for that. I have to be regular and punctual with that. I've got to be very careful with my diet but sometimes we neglect that. And then

I've got angina and I take some tablets for that. I think walking more would probably make me a lot fitter.

2. *Disc Problems and a Bad Back:*. Hanif was a bus driver but he developed disc problems in his back that prompted an early retirement from work through ill health. Here is Hanif's description of his disc problem:

> I brought the bus back to the garage and I got up from the seat and I felt no pain in my back or anything but when I got up from the seat I couldn't straighten up myself. I tried but I couldn't. I stood there for a while and there were a lot of other buses coming into the garage but I couldn't stand up. I was bent down. I went to the timekeeper and gave him my card and I sat in my car and I came home. And the next day I got up and I couldn't sit down. I couldn't put my shoes on. I couldn't wash my face. I thought how am I going to work? My back was completely packed up and I wanted to put an empty milk bottle outside my house and I got the bottle in my hand. There was an English woman walking back and I said to her: 'Excuse me can you put this bottle on the floor for me?' and she said: 'What's wrong?' And I said that I had a bad back and there was nobody at home so she put the bottle down for me. And for a long time – I think about three months – it took for me to recover from that. But I fully recovered and then it came back in 1985/86 and I was admitted to hospital and I had a scan and the scan showed there was some disc problem.

Looking back over these examples of historical background and personal life stories it is intriguing how Hanif became accustomed, in age, to his weak and physically frail body, with his disc problems, angina, diabetes and other difficulties.

But what it does not show is that Hanif was also a self-defined 'mental fighter' who recognised that he did not want to fight through his fists. As we have seen from aspects of the historical backgrounds, Hanif had to combine old and new gendered discourses in being partly patriarchal and partly 'feminine', gentle and contemplative within his family's rituals and prayers at home and in the mosque. As Hanif comments:

> My experience is that if you are not gentle; if you are not tender; if you are not caring you are in danger of losing your own family and your own children, and of losing yourself above all.

Hanif possessed a transgressive aging body because his masculinity was not insulted or threatened by having a 'weak' body. He did not need to display or defend his bodily strength. He saw that a 'weak' body could help him in developing a more peaceful and non-aggressive body.

Discussion

Aging men are often viewed through the prism of illness or a regime of pill-taking (Hazan, 1994; Fleming, 1999), and are closely tied in to poor health and inevitable decline. Of course, it is true that aging men's bodies do deteriorate and a major part of dealing with old age is learning to manage successive waves of loss: loss of work identities and status; loss of sexual potency and decreased muscle mass and strength (Wolpert, 2011) and so on.

Although aging is a challenging process, many aging men are not feeble or helpless. Too much of the research on aging has used a 'reductionist, biomedical model, assuming that illness, disability and emotional distress are inevitable consequences of the biological processes of aging within the individual' (Lee and Owens, 2002). But aging men's bodies are not just disappointing or decaying bodies. They can also play a significant role in initiating personal and social change. Some aging men, like Robert and Hanif, relate to their aging bodies in a different way. Their bodies become active agents of change and begin to defy conventional, gendered assumptions and norms embedded over a long period of time in their bodies.

In Robert's case, it is possible to observe his bodily development very clearly throughout his life. The reader meets him, first of all, measuring himself negatively against the culturally idealised, masculine, bodily norms of dominant masculinities. But later, a physical injury at work wakes him up to a broader outlook on society and culture. Through independent questioning and critical reflection he begins to recognise the importance of inventive adaptation and applying what Kate Davidson calls a 'best fit' attitude to his current, embodied experiences (Davidson, 2013). From this standpoint Robert is able to see through the common myth of bodily invincibility and develops a more conscious awareness of his own mortality and bodily fragility. In his key commentary exchange with me, he is now able to put agility and fitness in his body above his early and conventional need for bodily strength. In doing this the reader sees the struggle that Robert has lived through to come to terms and start to accept the physical and masculine identity shifts and changes that are an integral part of the aging process for aging men.

In terms of social agency, there are still huge gaps in our knowledges about the everyday lives of aging men. Aging men still do not seek help from or consult their GPs. Also, many very lonely, aging men do not confide enough with other men or do not risk emotional disclosure to another human being about a troubling problem.

Future research and innovatory social practices are urgently needed to investigate social network strategies that attract aging men to want to join. This does not just need traditional, social agencies to do something about this but perhaps it needs the ingenuity and determination of retired, aging men to build some informal social groups for themselves. However, aging men are an extremely diverse group of men and perhaps that diversity (ethnically, racially, alternative sexualities, and in terms of different social classes, disabilities etc.) needs to be fully acknowledged before future participatory schemes can be initiated and developed.

Important questions about a more engaged future for aging men still recur:

...who shall take the lead in correcting biased and stereotypic generalizations about elderly men? Will men assume responsibility for taking the lead themselves? (Kaye and Kosberg, 1997)

9
Conclusion

Aging Men's Vantage Points

Over the last 30 years in the UK, second-wave feminism and gay, lesbian and transgender liberation have undermined the normative assumptions of the male-dominated research paradigm of science, reason and objectivity. Taken for granted dualisms (mind/body; reason/passion; culture/nature; male/female) were inherited from the enlightenment (Ramazanoğlu and Holland, 2002), and an unequal, gendered opposition was constructed between objectivity (men's sphere) and subjectivity (women's sphere).

Male-dominant forms of scientific reason have constituted themselves in opposition to what is outside reason (e.g. passion, sensuality, desire, subjectivity and bodily concerns). As a result, women have been subordinated through these dualisms by being primarily associated with irrationality, hysteria and bodily issues. Feminists have rightly critiqued these 'either/or' dichotomies and shown how narrowly restrictive they are in the lives of women.

Feminist standpoint ('the view that knowledge is shaped by social position': Hearn, 2007) epistemologies grew out of their subordinated 'vantage point on male supremacy' (Hartsock, 1983) and their challenges to objectivist, male-dominated knowledges. As all knowers are positioned as 'situated' (Haraway, 1991; Johnson et al. 2004), the claim to objectivity masks the way that where one stands shapes what one can see and how it is understood (Pease, 1998). For example, some aging men's vantage points (of being companioned, divorced, isolated, or being adventurous travellers, workless or loving grandfathers) affect the knowledges they can produce and the counter-hegemonic challenges they can make to the established, social order.

Although frequently socially invisible (Thompson, 1994) aging men's lives are characterised by rapid, sometimes traumatic changes mainly experienced in their fragmented bodies, and they sometimes go through a restless confrontation with shifting ambivalent identities and selves. However, aging men's contradictory positions in later life, often hovering between social/heterosexual privilege and the social oppression of ageism, make their progressive movements towards a gender equality standpoint very problematic.

In their youth, aging men were often privileged and empowered, in heterosexual terms and also through the possession of social power. Earlier over-emphases on career, work success, competition and selfish sexual relations often produce an unquestioning conformity to male supremacy. Although gender relations are changing, there are still legacies of privilege that benefit some aging men. Of course, some aging men, frequently positioned at the top of business and political hierarchies, can be very privileged indeed.

This privilege often co-exists with ambiguity and loss in aging men's lives. Ageism, segregation from the social mainstream and severe marginalisation also occur. But one of the central changes in aging men's lives is bodily deterioration and disruption, particularly the loss of bodily strength and the diminishing of sexual potency.

I have personally learnt a great deal from feminism and gay, lesbian and transgender liberation about having the courage 'to speak their truth' (Ramazanoğlu and Holland, 2002) even though, as a 75-year-old aging man I am much more contradictorily and problematically positioned. However, I do believe an aging man's standpoint is possible if grounded in some of the social realities and experiences that confront aging men in an everyday sense and if a critical position is taken to monolithic assumptions of male power. From a position of men of lesser power, bodily fragility and marginalised masculinities, some aging men become more critically aware of the damaging limitations of some youthful masculinities. Out of this critical awareness can emerge knowledges that are about a self-critical positioning and even produce ideas about the possibility of gender equality and an anti-patriarchal viewpoint as in Ray's life course commentary.

In this final chapter I want to offer a few more points about aging men's contradictory positioning. Over many years I have struggled to find forms of analysis that are more sensitively responsive to the varied and constantly changing transitions that many aging men live through. I have rejected the distant abstractions and totalising systems of some 'objectivist' research. Over-determined, universalist notions of patriarchy that view men as a monolithic, homogeneous category with a unified set of interests, cannot capture the contradictory, changing dynamics of the moving lives of aging men.

It seems to me that a social, postmodern approach (Nicholson and Seidman, 1995) to understanding aging men has got a great deal to recommend it. The assumption that aging men are rational, stable, unitary subjects has been undermined like other conventional notions by postmodernism and instead can be viewed, through a postmodern lens, as fractured, diverse and dynamically shifting subjects. Also, the central contradiction surrounding aging men of being both privileged and oppressed is also something that postmodernism can deal with. With its emphases on multiple and changing subjectivities, difference, ambiguity and its refusal to look for epistemological absolutes (Haywood and Mac an Ghaill, 2003), postmodernism creatively disrupts the universalising tendencies of modernity. Producing new knowledges from the margins can shape some aging men to become more actively visible and vocal in their local and global worlds.

The Key Themes of the Book

The key themes of the book are explicitly acknowledged and examined here. They are the possibility of change for aging men (60–75); the central importance of aging bodies in men's attempts to confront and sometimes to reflect on unsolved dilemmas; aging men's contradictory relationship to patriarchy and power; the continuing movement of aging men's lives and often their refusal to remain passive and static; the attempt to explore the emotional intricacies of aging men's lives through prioritising conversational intimacy in the research processes rather than information about 'outer selves.'

The Possibility of Change

Change is one of the most distinctive features of aging men's lives. Instead of conforming to the popular stereotype of being couch potatoes, many aging men face a contradictory and continuously shifting set of realities including retirement and loss of work, a loss of bodily strength and sexual potency, confronting disability, becoming a grandfather and perhaps sorting out new relationships within the family.

Robert, one of the research participants, embraced change for aging men. His advice to other aging men went like this:

> Well they do need to move on because it's no good trying to do what you did in 1955 when the year is 2006. You have got to accept change

whether you like it or not and it's no good saying that things were better years ago and all that sort of thing.

Aging Bodies

Discussion of old bodies is sorely lacking (Calasanti and Slevin, 2006) in the literature on gender and aging. But it is only when the researcher attends to the small details of old bodies that the reader gains a more rounded representation of the everyday lives that aging men lead. That is why I have prioritised the accounts of the intimate sensations and experiences of inhabiting a particular, aging body. Also it is why I have included participants' narratives of disability, recovery from colon cancer, industrial accident, marathon running, asthma and many chronic illnesses.

It is also through physical injury and bodily disruption that sometimes provokes a confrontation in later life with masculine identity reassessment. It is through the physical shocks and dislocations in aging men's lives that the dominant ideals of masculinity and gendered expectations begin to become destabilised and unsettled and more open to possible changes.

Contradictory Relations to Patriarchy and Power

Aging men, in Western culture, inhabit an ambiguous, social category (Spector-Mersel, 2006; Whitehead, 2002). Many aging men are still privileged (e.g. heterosexual, white, middle-class, able-bodied, rich, aging men) but simultaneously they are marginalised by ageism and bodily fragility. Thus, in many aging men's lives, there is a contradictory mixture of some legacies of masculine and heterosexual privilege and power interacting with some reductions in aging men's social and bodily power.

This argument is made even more complex because, in their lives, there are other intersections of class, race, sexual orientation, ethnicity, disability and other social forces mingling with age relations. So, for example, one of the gay research participants has lived through a lifetime of grappling with the poverty and social oppression of growing up in a mining community in South Wales along with individual and institutional homophobia. Another research participant has had to cope with an ambivalent class relation mixed with a brutal racism epitomised by an offensive insult shouted out by a fellow councillor:

Why don't you get on your banana boat and get back to your own country?

Aging Men on the Move

Aging men are on the move in old age. However much we impose popular assumptions and stale stereotypes onto them about being caught in static and fixed positions, a great deal more internal and external movement is taking place in their half-hidden lives. Robinson and Hockey in their study of 'Masculinities in Transition,' talk about 'mobile masculinities' and major shifts that include the 'life times of the older participants' involved in their investigation (Robinson and Hockey, 2011).

The Emotional Intricacies

In this study I have opted for a five-interview approach that prioritises conversational intimacy and an atmosphere and relation of relaxed trust that provides a positive background for the investigation of emotional intricacies in the lives of the research participants.

Instead of focusing on factual information and the 'outer self' I have deliberately explored what the participants felt about subjects like fear, anxiety, their own sense of physical vulnerability, and I have supported any attempt to re-assess masculine identity reconstruction.

Here is an example of emotional intricacy taken from the interviews with Brian:

> DJ: What do you fear most as an aging man?
>
> Brian: Disability. Not least because I've got my wife to look after...I remain fit and these things enable me to not only enjoy the life that I've got but enable me to do a whole host of things that perhaps if I was disabled I would not be able to enjoy. Inability as well as disability, I think, are the two things.

Structural Immobility

The aging process is commonly seen as a passive and static condition with aging men as the unchanging inhabitants (Hazan, 1994: 74). Hazan goes on to say that a 'structural immobility' is imposed on the aged 'and stands in absolute contradiction to their personal experience and sensibility, for they are in fact undergoing rapid and important changes in roles, identities, abilities and bodily functions that influences their self-perception and their capacity to handle everyday affairs.' Perhaps when aging men are conceived as people in constant motion and movement is it possible to appreciate more of the full, complex subjectivities of aging men and catch further glimpses of their contradictory variety?

Part of the problem of trying to capture aging men's lives, in a research study, is that many of them are not rigidly anchored in one, fixed place, time and context – although some are. Aging men are perpetually on the move in old age. Robinson and Hockey (2011: 4), in their study of 'Masculinities in Transition', talk about 'mobile masculinities' and that description fits many aging men's lives. But it is not just about shifts in time and place. It is also about 'change', emancipatory possibilities and sometimes about political transformation as well. This potential for change in aging men still seems to be largely neglected in academic research on men and masculinities. Although there are significant signs that substantial work is being done in the aging masculinities' field (Kampf, Marshall and Petersen, 2013; Sandberg, 2011; Calasanti and Slevin, 2006; Biricik and Hearn, 2009), and a one day seminar on 'Studies of Aging Masculinities; Still in their Infancy?' organised by the Centre for aging and biographical studies at the Open university in February 2013, some researchers seem to ignore the crucial point that the meanings of masculinity are changed and re-negotiated over time. Or, to put it another way, aging can facilitate changes in masculine identities (Arber, Davidson and Ginn, 2003).

Theorising Aging Men

If, as researchers, we aim to do justice to aging men's subjective subtlety and ambiguity, then we need to acknowledge that one of the dominant forms of studying and analysing men and masculinities – through the concept of hegemonic masculinity – is largely unable to deal with aging men's shifting and contradictory realities. As Hearn remarks:

> ... the social-constructionist hegemonic masculinity frame is too weak for taking on board the complexities of aging. (Hearn, 2012)

The concept of hegemonic masculinity (HM from now on) was derived from (Connell, 1983; Carrigan, Connell et al. 1985: Connell 1987). However, some of the ways that HM has been interpreted have presented difficulties for understanding aging men. The widespread and often imprecise application of the term has often degenerated into HM being seen as a list of negative traits or characteristics in men (Collier, 1998). This 'blanket descriptor of male power' (Whitehead, 2002: 88) has created barriers to recognising aging men as active, nuanced, masculine subjects. The contradictory mixture of privilege, pain, power and fragility to be found in aging men's lives has not been adequately acknowledged, particularly when it is viewed from an HM perspective.

HM as a concept and other major ways of theorising men and masculinities have paid too much attention to younger and middle-aged men and also have not done justice to the frequent shifts, disruptions and destabilisations encountered by many aging men in their embodied selves. Frequent life-changing events like coping with grandchildren, severe illnesses, adaptations, reflecting on death, breakdown, hospitalisation, supporting your daughters and sons, loss of job security and status, the death of a spouse, forging new relationships with wives and partners, all provoke adjustments in later life.

Alternative Forms of Enquiry into Aging Masculinities

Over the last twenty years I have searched for alternative forms of exploration and analysis that might begin to capture more adequately the everyday, fragmentary realities of aging men's lives. This I have done through what I call critical autobiography, (Jackson, 1990; 2001; 2003) and through biographical research (Jackson, 2016).

Critical autobiography is a mode of social enquiry that investigates the dynamic interaction between social forces, contexts and personal narratives. It is not intended to be individualistic or narcissistic (See Church, 1995; Jackson, 1990). As Hearn comments about my use of critical autobiography in researching men and masculinities:

> ... [he] uses his own life as a resource to theorise his male selfhood and gendered construction of boys and men more generally. (Hearn, 2007)

Therefore, in my critical autobiographical work, gendered insights mingle with a world of interior complexity and greater emotional depth in this alternative form of research.

Biographical, narrative research has developed a qualitative research methodology (Roberts, 2002; Chamberlayne, Bornat and Wengraf, 2000) that again offers more space for collaborative interaction between the researcher and the researched. The research method, using oral history interviewing strategies, seeks to understand the changing embodied experiences and outlooks of aging men in their daily lives set within a social and historical context. The strength of qualitative methods is seen in the way that they allow the researcher to delve deeper into masculine identities and subjective complexities (Emslie, Hunt and O'Brien, 2004).

So, I am suggesting that if researchers want to explore the intimate sensations of aging bodies, 'the motives, emotions, desires' (Jefferson, 2002) of the internal complexity of aging men's lives and the possibility of a greater emotional depth, then they might need to consider using these alternative forms of enquiry.

The Changing Meanings of Men and Masculinities in Aging Men's Lives

There is an urgent need to 'reinvent aging' (Kampf, Marshall and Petersen, 2013) but still the aging processes are viewed in largely deficit terms (Gullette, 2004) or as Lewis Wolpert puts it:

... there is, at times, a lack of respect for the experience and knowledge of the old. (Wolpert, 2011)

Now, in 2016, things are beginning to change in the recognition that there is a need to 'specifically explore men's aging as a central analytical tool for reconceiving masculinity' (Kampf, Marshall and Petersen, 2013; Thompson, 1994; Hearn, 1995; Arber, Davidson and Ginn, 2003; Calasanti and Slevin, 2006). A detailed study of aging men's lives has the subversive potential to change the conventional meanings of men and masculinities. Some researchers on men and masculinity issues seem to ignore the crucial point that the meanings of masculinity are significantly changed and re-negotiated over time, space and different contexts.

The loss of social power, economic productivity (although social productivity might increase with age), bodily strength, sexual potency and status that aging men encounter in old age weakens some aging men's attachments to patriarchal relations (Silver, 2003). Admittedly, other aging men cling on to old, defensive routines and identities and sometimes refuse to acknowledge their increasing fallibility and fragility. However, these changes and losses can open emancipatory possibilities in moving beyond obsessive concerns with work, success, ambition, competitive individualism, an over-emphasis on sexual relations and achievement. It has even been suggested that some aging men develop a critical self-reflexiveness on how power operates in gender relations (Meadows and Davidson, 2006). From this innovatory perspective on old age a tentative movement can sometimes be discerned, in some aging men, towards 'an aging men's anti-patriarchal standpoint', (Calasanti and Slevin, 2006) like Ray's discovery, as one of the research participants, that a more compassionate, relational model of masculinity is more valuable to him, as an aging man, than a competitive, self-aggrandising, masculine identity.

Earlier over-emphases on career, work and sexuality are often demoted (Silver, 2003). In their place come a fresh focus, for some, on 'seeking connections with others' (Thompson, 2006), a quest for deeper intimacy and sometimes an interest in mending broken relations within the family. Although some aging men are still struggling with pensioner poverty, managing bodily pain or sedated in non-stimulating, residential 'homes', other aging men can begin to reflect on changing their lives as men. This time for reflecting back on their lives and stock-taking can represent a movement away from the egotistical, self-aggrandising, masculine self. Sometimes it also brings with it a new concern for caregiving (Kramer and Thompson, 2005), particularly with ill spouses, and occasionally seems to unlock fresh energy for re-making family connections and a frequent desire to participate in 'emotion work of relational concerns' (Thompson, 2006).

Aging Men as Active, Complex, Human Subjects

The men interviewed in this research study offer challenges to the negative and restrictive assumptions and stereotypes about aging men. It is important to remind ourselves of the robust diversity and surprising complexity that exists within the social categories of the old and the disabled.

Here are just a few examples from my nine chapters. First, Roy opposes a penetrative, predatory model of male sexualities saying:

> ... affection is more important to me than coming [and that] hugging, kissing and holding [is better than an orgasm].

Brian shows what caring for an ill spouse feels like when he talks about having to 'hover' around his wife. He defines 'hover' in this way:

> By 'hover' it is being available and available to her quite quickly at times without necessarily being intrusive. So if she's getting out of the car then the walking frame is parked adjacent to the door. I've opened the door. I've put the brakes on and she'll swing herself round and get hold of the hand door. So the 'hovering' turns into action. If she

stands up then I can go to her and just catch her arm. But if, as she gets out of the car, I get hold of her arm and start pulling her out of the car then that's intrusion.

Hanif, a Pakistani Muslim, speaks up in praise of 'weakness' for aging men. He says acknowledging his 'weakness' has unexpected advantages for men like him in that his acceptance of his body has kept him out of trouble and moved him towards valuing his non-aggressive, peace-loving personality.

Also, Peter, in interrupting the interviewing process while I was at his home, taught me to reassess my research methods in relation to working with disabled, aging men. Initially I was in a rush wanting to get the interview completed. But he stopped what I was doing, saying that he was becoming too stressed and tense. His valuable intervention helped me to slow down and begin to appreciate the confusion and bodily irregularity that he was facing as a disabled man. By the end of the first interview I had been, as a social researcher, shaken awake into relating to Peter as a more fully rounded human being rather than seeing him, exclusively, as a 'tragic victim' of Parkinson's disease.

Aging Men as Researchers

I am a pensioner activist and writer. I have worked for the last ten years on an independent, self-funded, research project from a small pension without any research grants, administrative support or access to a university library. Over the years I have assembled my own small library on men, masculinities and aging men. From these I have learnt a great deal as well as from regular dialogue with my friends. Moreover, I have also received the help of some academics who have generously given me their time.

However, writing and studying from the margins has helped me to generate some of my own specific knowledge and insights about aging men and perhaps given some of my ideas a sharper clarity. My experience over the ten years has convinced me of the importance of encouraging other aging men and women to pursue their own personal, political and social investigations as researchers.

Therefore I want to make a claim for pensioner-led research counting as a serious approach to research. Aging men and pensioners should be able to initiate their own styles of researching and produce their own research agendas but through their interaction with the non-aged as well. Also, there is a rich potential treasure house of future research to be done on aging men, recognising that research on aging men is still in its infancy (See Tarrant and Watts, 2014). A list of future research possibilities is to be found in the 'Endnotes' section of this book after this chapter.[1]

Most of the research on aging has been done by the non-aged. 'The world of older individuals needs to be studied from the inside' (Silver, 2003). Therefore it is important to get aging men to become researchers themselves, so that aging men's insights, experiences, knowledge, hidden resources might be recognised and validated in working with the non-aged. Also aging men's resources need to be used in creating and controlling their own independent research agendas and designs.

Notes

1. Introduction

1. There has been a debate about how to name 'aging men'. Toni Calasanti (2004) wants to use the term 'old' rather than 'older' or 'aging' men for political reasons. She goes on to say:

   'Whereas "old" is socially constructed, reified and stigmatized, using the term "older" conveys that old people are more acceptable if we think of them as like the middle-aged.'

   Although I have some sympathy and respect for Calasanti's position, I have decided to use 'aging men' rather than 'old men'. This is because 'old' suggests a fixed position that does not convey any notion of change or fluidity. I have chosen 'aging' because it suggests some kind of shifting movement and flexibility across a continuing lifetime and the more dynamic possibility of change and difference.

2. Western culture, sometimes equated with Western civilization, is a term used very broadly to describe a heritage of social norms, ethical values, traditional customs, belief systems and specific artefacts and technologies that have some origin or association with Europe. This term has come to apply to countries whose history is strongly marked by European immigration, such as the countries of the Americas and Australasia, and is not restricted to the continent of Europe.

3. This book reaches out to a variety of audiences:

   (A) The aging process for many ordinary people is a place of frequent change, life review and critical re-assessment of a lifetime's experience and events. Therefore, any older people who are sorting out the meanings of a lifetime's experience or younger people who are starting to reflect on age, might be very engaged in this book as active readers or members of a wider reading group.

   (B) The thoughtful, community activist who is especially engaged in social policy and changing practices.

   (C) The academic who is interested in critical work on the changes in aging men's embodied lives.

   (D) Older people who are curious about the UK as an aging society and culture and who want to explore a book that offers a creative challenge to worn-out notions of age and aging bodies.

3. Aging Men's Embodied Selves: Rethinking Aging Men's Relationships with their Changing Bodies

1. A gendered identity, or selfhood, is not innate or essentialised. It is now well recognised that 'selfhood' is something that is socially produced through the narratives and social interactions people use to make sense of their lives.

4.   A Historical and Cultural Analysis of Aging Men's Sexualities in the UK

1. Arrested for the criminal offence (at that time) of homosexuality in 1954. However, Lord Montagu always denied this charge. The media controversy might have led to the decriminalisation of homosexuality in 1967.
2. John Wayne was a very successful, U.S., film actor, specialising in action/adventure films mainly from the 1930s to the 1970s. He epitomised rugged, frontier masculinity (Kimmel, 1996) and was often hero-worshipped by young boys.
3. The Bullworker is an isometric exercise device used for strength training originally sold in the early 1960s. Exercises are performed by pushing inward on the contractible cylinders or by pulling the cables outwards away from the cylinders. The resultant compression of the internal spring creates the desired resistance; the Bullworker returns to its original position when pressure is released.
4. The reference to dancing here perhaps contains an erotic ambivalence for Robert being both an opportunity for close, sensual contact within a rule-bound, social convention.

8.   Exploring Aging Men's Embodied and Social Agency in a Free Market Economy Context

1. Agency is a term used by poststructuralists, feminists and postcolonial theories to denote self-actualised power usually of the individual or 'subject' (Wright, 2007).
2. Platelayer is a railway employee whose job is to inspect and maintain the quality of the railway track and look out for any wear and tear on the line.
3. British Railways (BR) which from 1965 traded as British Rail, was the operator of most of the rail transport in Great Britain between 1948 and 1997. It was formed from the nationalisation of the 'Big Four' British railway companies and lasted until the gradual privatisation of British Rail, in stages between 1994 and 1997.

9.   Conclusion

1. Here are a few suggestions for future research on aging men:

   - How can aging men's health and well-being be improved?
   - How can GPs and hospitals communicate more clearly and effectively with aging men?
   - How can we support aging men to use their initiatives in building social networks, especially in retirement?
   - How can social agencies combat loneliness and social isolation in the lives of aging men through designing social networks that appeal to aging men?
   - How can we change the cultural barriers, like homophobia, competitive rivalry, fears of seeming effeminate, that prevent aging men from developing intimate friendships with other men?

- Do aging men have trouble expressing their feelings? If so, what can be done about this?
- An investigation is needed into aging men's violences and abuses and in different social contexts.
- How does elder abuse affect the everyday lives of aging men?
- How can the state support grandfathers in caring for grandchildren?
- Much more research is needed on aging men's bodies particularly from a life course perspective.
- More bodywork classes for aging men are needed in contexts where they feel comfortable.
- More research is needed to map ethnically and racially diverse, aging men's embodied lives and experiences.
- More gender-sensitive research needs to be done on aging men with disabilities such as Parkinson's disease, Alzheimer's and other experiences of dementia.
- More research attention needs to be focused on the aging lives of gay men.

Bibliography

Alexander, C. (2000) *The Asian Gang: Ethnicity, Identity, Masculinity.* Oxford. Berg.

Annandale, E. and Hunt, K. (2000) *Gender Inequalities in Health: research at the crossroads,* in Annandale, E. and Hunt, K. (Eds.) *Gender Inequalities in Health.* Buckingham. Open University Press.

Applegate, J. and Kaye, L. (1993) *Male Elder Caregiver,* in Williams, C. (Ed.) *'Doing Women's Work; Men in Non-traditional Occupations.'* London. Sage Publications.

Arber, S. and Ginn, J. (1995) *Connecting Gender and Aging : A Sociological Approach.* Buckingham. Open University Press.

Arber, S., Davidson, K. and Ginn, J. (2003*) Gender and Aging: Changing roles and relationships* Maidenhead, Open University Press.

Ashe, F. (2007) *The New Politics of Masculinity: Men, power and resistance.* Abingdon. Routledge.

Atkinson, R. (1998) *The Life Story interview.* London. Sage

Barnes, C. (1990) *Cabbage Syndrome: The social construction of dependency.* London: Falmer Press.

Barnes, C. (1997) *The Social Model of Disability: A sociological phenomenon ignored by sociologists,* Paper presented at British Sociological Association Conference, April 1997.

Benhabib, S. (1995) *Feminism and Postmodernism* in Nicholson, L. (Ed.) *Feminist Contentions: A Philosophical Exchange.* London.

Bernard, M., et al. (2000) *Women Aging: Changing Identities, Challenging Myths.* London. Routledge.

Beynon, J. 2002. *Masculinities and Culture.* Buckingham, Open University Press.

Biggs, S., Phillipson, C., Money, A. and Leach, R. (2006) *The Age-Shift Observations of Social Policy, Ageism and the Dynamics of the Adult Lifecourse.* 'Journal of Social Work Practice': Vol. 20. No. 3, 239–52.

Blaikie, A. (1999) *Aging and Popular Culture.* Cambridge. Cambridge University Press.

Blake, V. (2009) Ongoing work on a psychosocial approach to men and masculinity. (I'm indebted to Vic for some thoughtful insights during our weekly conversations about men and masculinities).

Blakemore, K. and Boneham, M. (1994) *Age, Race and Ethnicity*: A Comparative *Approach.* Buckingham. Open University Press.

Bornat,J. (1994) *Reminiscence Reviewed.* Buckingham. Open University Press.

Bourdieu, P. (1980) *Le sens pratique.* Paris. Les Editions de Minuit.

Bredenkamp, S. (2007) *Disability,* in Flood, M., Gardiner, J., Pease, B. and Pringle, K. (Eds.) *International Encyclopedia of Men and Masculinities.* London. Routledge.

Brod, H. (1987) *The Making of Masculinities: The New Men's Studies.* (Ed.) Allen and Unwin.

Bury, M. (1982) *Chronic Illness as biographical disruption.* 'Sociology of Health and Illness', Vol. 4: 167–82.

Calasanti, T. (2003) *Masculinities and Care work in Old Age* in Arber, S., Davidson, K. and Ginn, J. (Eds.) *Gender and Aging.* Open University Press.

Calasanti, T. (2004) *Feminist Gerontology and old men*. Journal of Gerontology, 598, 305–14

Calasanti, T. and King, N. (2005) *Firming the floppy penis; class and gender relations in the lives of old men*, in 'Men and Masculinities', 8 (1), pp. 3–23.

Calasanti, T. and Slevin, K. (eds.) 2006. *Age Matters: Realigning feminist thinking*, New York: Routledge, Taylor and Francis Group.

Carrigan, T., Connell, R. and Lee, J. (1985) *Towards a New Sociology of Masculinity*, 'Theory and Society', Vol. 14 (5), pp 551–604.

Chamberlayne, P., Bornat, J. and Wengraf, T. (2004) *The Turn to Biographical Methods in Social Science*. Abingdon. Routledge.

Charmaz, K. (1995) *Identity Dilemmas of Chronically Ill Men*, in Sabo, D. and Gordon, D. (Eds.) *Men's Health and Illness: Gender, power and the body*, pp. 266–91), Thousand Oaks, California. Sage Publications.

Church, K. (1995) *Forbidden Narratives: Critical Autobiography as Social Science*. Gordon and Breach publishers.

Cohen, T. F. (1992) *Men's Families, Men's Friends*, in Nardi, P. M. (Ed.) *Men's Friendships*, Sage Publications.

Collier, R. (1998) *Masculinities, Crime and Criminology*. London. Sage Publications.

Collinson, D. (2003) *Identities and Insecurities: Selves at work*, in 'Organization', Vol. 10 (3): 527–47. London. Sage Publications.

Connell, R.W. (1983) *Men's Bodies*, in *Which Way is up?* Sydney. Allen and Unwin Australia.

Connell, R.W. (1987) *Gender and Power*, Cambridge, Polity Press.

Connell, R.W. (1995) *Masculinities*. Cambridge. Polity.

Connell, R.W. (2000) *The Men and the Boys*. Cambridge, UK, Polity Press.

Connell, R.W. and Messerschmidt, J. (2005) *Hegemonic Masculinity: Rethinking the concept*. 'Gender and Society', Vol. 19 (6): 829–59.

Connell, R. and Wood, J. (2005) *Globalization and Business Masculinities*, in 'Men and Masculinities', Vol. 7 (4): 347–64.

Corker and Shakespeare, (2002) *Disability/Postmodernity: Embodying disability theory*. London. Continuum.

Davidson, K. and Meadows, R. (2010) *Older Men's Health: The Role of Marital Status and Masculinities*, in Gough, B. and Robertson, S. (Eds.) *Men, Masculinities and Health*. Basingstoke. Palgrave and Macmillan.

Davidson, K. (2013) *The Health and Caring Paradox*, in Kampf, Marshall and Petersen (Eds.) *Aging Men, Masculinities and Modern Medicine*. Abingdon. Routledge.

Drummond, M. (2007) *Age and Aging*, in Flood, M., Gardiner, J., Pease, B. and Pringle, K. (Eds.) *International Encyclopedia of Men and Masculinities*, London. Routledge.

Ducharme, F., Levesque, L., Lachance, L., Zarit, S., Vezina, J., Gangbe, M. and Caron, C. (2006) *Older Husbands as Caregivers of their Wives: A descriptive study of the context and relational aspects of care*. 'International Journal of Nursing Studies', Vol. 43: 567–79.

Dutton, K. (1995) *The Perfectible Body: The Western Ideal of Physical Development* London. Cassell.

Emslie, C., Hunt, K. and O'Brien R. (2004) *Masculinities and Aging Men: A qualitative study in the west of Scotland*, 'The Journal of Men's Studies', Vol. 12, (3), pp. 207–26.

Epstein, D., Johnson, R. and Steinberg, D. (2004) *Blairism and the War of Persuasion: Labour's passive revolution*. London. Lawrence and Wishart.

Fawcett, B. (2000) *Feminist Perspectives on Disability*. Harlow. Pearson Education Limited.

Feldman, H., Goldstein, I., Hatzichristou, D., Krane, R. and McKinlay, J. (1994) *Impotence and its Medical and Psychocorrelates: Results of the Massachusetts male aging study*. 'Journal of Urology', Vol. 151: 54–61.

Femiano, S. and Coonerty-Femiano, A. (2005) *Principles and Interventions for Working Therapeutically with Caregiving Men: Responding to challenges* in Kramer, B. and Thompson, E. (Eds.) *Men as Caregivers*. New York. Prometheus Books.

Fennel, G. and Davidson, K (2003) *The Invisible Man? Aging men in modern society.* 'Aging International', Vol. 28 (4), pp. 315–25

Figueroa, M. (2004) *Male Privileging and Male Under Performance in Jamaica*, in Reddock, R. (Ed.) *Interrogating Caribbean Masculinities*. Kingston. University of the West Indies Press.

Finkelstein, V. (1993) *The Commonality of Disability*, in Swain, J., Finkelstein, V., French, S. and Oliver, M. (Eds.) *Disabling Barriers-enabling Environments*. London. Sage Publications.

Fleming, A. (1999) *Aging Men in Contemporary Discourses on Aging: Absent bodies and invisible lives*. 'Nursing Inquiry', Vol. 6, 3–8.

Flood, M. (2007) *Men's Movement*, in Flood, M., Gardiner, J., Pease, B. and Pringle, K. (Eds.) *International Encyclopaedia of Men and Masculinities*. Abingdon. Routledge

Foucault, M. (1978) *The History of Sexuality, Volume One. An Introduction*. Harmondsworth. Penguin.

Foucault, M. (1980) *The Confession of the Flesh*, in Gordon, C. (Ed.) *Power/Knowledge: Selected interviews and Other Writings, 1972–1977*. Hemel Hempstead. Harvester Wheatsheaf.

Fracher, J. and Kimmel, M. (1987) *Hard Issues and Soft Spots: Counselling Men about Sexuality*. In Kimmel, M. and Messner, M. (Eds.) *Men's Lives* (Fourth Edition). Boston. Allyn and Bacon.

Gabb, J. (2008) *Researching Intimacy in Families*. Basingstoke. Palgrave Macmillan.

Geertz, C. (1973) *The Interpretation of Cultures*. New York. Basic Books.

Gerschick, T. and Miller, A. (1994) *Gender Identities at the Crossroads of Masculinity and Physical Disability*. 'Men and Masculinities', Vol. 2: 34–55. Sage Publications.

Gerschick, T. (2005) *Masculinity and Degrees of Bodily Normativity in Western Culture* in Kimmel, M., Hearn, J. and Connell, R.W. (Eds.) *A Handbook of Studies in Men and Masculinities*. Sage Publications.

Giddens, A. (1992) *The Transformation of Intimacy: Sexuality, Love and Eroticism in Modern Societies*. Cambridge. Polity Press.

Gilligan, C. (1982) *In a Different Voice: Psychological theory and women's development* Cambridge, Massachusetts: Harvard University Press.

Ginsberg, T.H., Pomerantz, S.C. and Kramer-Feeley (2005) *Sexuality in Older Adults: Behaviours and preferences* in 'Age and Aging,' Vol. 34; 475–80.

Glaser, B. and Strauss, A. (1967) *The Discovery of Grounded Theory: Strategies for Qualitative Research*. Chicago. Aldine Press.

Gott, M. and Hinchcliff, S. (2003) *Sex and Aging: A gendered issue*, in Arber, S., Davidson, K. and Ginn, J. (Eds.) *Gender and Aging: Changing Roles and Relationships*. Maidenhead. Open University Press, pp. 63–78.

Gough, B. and Robertson, S. (2010) (Ed.) *Men, Masculinities and Health.* Basingstoke: Palgrave Macmillan.

Graham, M. (2007) *Gay Masculinities,* in Flood, M., Pease, B., Gardiner, J. and Pringle, K. (Eds.) *International Encyclopaedia of Men and Masculinities.* Abingdon. Routledge.

Grosz, E. (1993) *Bodies and Knowledges: Feminism and the crisis of reason* in Alcoff, L. and Potter, E. (Eds.) *Feminist Epistemologies.* New York. Routledge.

Gullette, M.M. (2004) *Aged by Culture.* Chicago. The University of Chicago Press.

Hall, S. (Summer, 2011) *The Neoliberal Revolution.* 'Soundings: A Journal of Politics and Culture', (46).

Hanlon, N. (2009) *Caregiving Masculinities: An Exploratory Analysis,* in Lynch, K., Baker, J. and Lyons, M. (Eds.) *Affective Equality: Love, Care and Injustice.* Basingstoke. Palgrave Macmillan.

Hanlon, N. and Lynch, K. (2011) *Care-Free Masculinities in Ireland,* in Ruspini, E., Hearn, J., Pease, B. and Pringle, K. (Eds.)*Men and Masculinities Around the World: Transforming Men's Practices.* New York. Palgrave Macmillan.

Haraway, D. (1991) *Situated Knowledges: The Science Question in Feminism and the Privilege of Partial Perspective,* in *Simians, Cyborgs, and Women: The Reinvention of Nature.* London. Free Association books.

Hartsock, N. (2004) (Ed.) *The Feminist Standpoint: Developing the ground for a specifically Feminist Historical Materialism,* in the *Feminist Standpoint Theory Reader.* New York. Routledge.

Hatchell, H, (2007) *Gender,* in Flood, M., Gardiner, J., Pease, B. and Pringle, K. (Eds.) *International Encyclopedia of Men and Masculinities.* London. Routledge.

Haug, F. et al, (1987) *Female Sexualization.* London. Verso.

Hawkes, G. (1996) *A Sociology of Sex and Sexuality.* Buckingham. Open University Press.

Haywood, C. and Mac an Ghaill, M. (2003) *Men and Masculinities.* Buckingham. Open University Press.

Hazan, H. (1994) *Old Age: Constructions and Deconstructions.* Cambridge. Cambridge University Press.

Heaphy, B., Yip, K. and Thompson, D. (2004) *Aging in a Non-heterosexual Context,* in 'Aging and Society,' Vol. 24: 881–902.

Hearn J. and Sandberg, L. (2008) *Aging Men, Aging and Power: Masculinities theory and alternative spatialised theoretical perspectives.* Sextant.

Hearn, J. (2006) *The Implications of Information and Communication Technologies for Sexualities and Sexualised Violences: Contradictions of sexual citizenships,* in 'Political Geography,' Vol. 25, 944–63. Elsevier Ltd.

Hearn, J. (2007) *Methods, Methodology and Research,* in Flood, M., Gardiner, J., Pease, B., Pringle, K. (Eds.) *International Encyclopedia of Men and Masculinities.* London. Routledge.

Hearn, J. (2012) (Ed.) *Male Bodies, Masculine Bodies, Men's Bodies.* London: Routledge, Taylor and Francis Group.

Hearn, J. (1995) *Imaging the Aging of Men,* in Featherstone, M. and Wernick A. (Eds.) *Images of Aging: Cultural representations of later life.* London. Routledge.

Hockey, J. and James, A. (2003) *Social Identities Across the Life Course.* Basingstoke. Palgrave Macmillan.

Holdsworth, A. (1988) *Out of the Doll's House: The story of women in the twentieth century.* BBC. Booklet.

Holland, J., Ramazanoğlu, C., Sharpe, S. and Thomson, R. (1998) *The Male in the Head: Young people, heterosexuality and power*. London. The Tufnell Press.

Hollway, W. (1984) *Gender Difference and the Production of Subjectivity*, in Henriques, J., Hollway, H., Urwin, C., Venn, C. and Walkerdine, V., *Changing the subject: Psychology, social regulation and subjectivity*. London. Methuen.

Hollway, W. (2006) *The Capacity to Care*. Hove. Routledge.

Hollway, W. and Jefferson, T. (2000) *Doing Qualitative Research Differently*. London. Sage Publications.

Holter, O. (2007) *Men's Work and Family Reconciliation in Europe*, 'Men and Masculinities', Vol. 9 (4), 425–56

Hope, D.P. (3rd February, 2002) *Courting and Conquering the Feared P—ny*. Published in 'Jamaica Gleaner'.

Howson, R. (2007) *Marginalised Masculinities*, in Flood, M,. Gardiner, J., Pease, B. and Pringle, K. (Eds.) *International Encyclopaedia of Men and Masculinities*. Abingdon. Routledge.

Hunt, S. (2007) *Body image*, in Flood, M., Gardiner, J., Pease, B., and Pringle, K. (Eds.) *International Encyclopaedia of Men and Masculinities*. Abingdon. Routledge.

Jackson, D. (2007) *Ageism*, in Flood, M., Gardiner, J., Pease, B. and Pringle, K. (Eds.) *International Encyclopedia of Men and Masculinities*. London. Routledge.

Jackson, D. (2008) *Aging Men's Embodied Selves: Rethinking relationships of change*, in 'Auto/Biography Yearbook 2008'. British Sociological Association Auto/Biography Study Group. Nottingham. Russell Press.

Jackson, D. (1990) *Unmasking Masculinity: A critical autobiography*. London, Unwin Hyman and Routledge Revivals.

Jackson, D. (2001) *Masculinity Challenges to an Aging Man's Embodied Selves Struggles, Collusions and Resistances (An exploration in critical autobiography)*: Auto/Biography: 'A British Sociological Association Study Group Journal', Vol. ix, 107–15.

Jackson, D. (2003) *Beyond One-dimensional Models of Masculinity: A life-course perspective on the processes of becoming masculine*. Auto/Biography: 'A British Sociological Association Study Group Journal', Vol. xi, 71–87.

Jackson, D. (2014) *Aging Men are Changing Men: Emancipatory Possibilities for Aging men*, in Tarrant, A. and Watts J.H. (Eds.) *Studies of Aging Masculinities: Still in their infancy/*. London. Centre for Policy on Aging. The Open University

Jefferson, T. 2002. *Subordinating Hegemonic Masculinity*. Theoretical Criminology, Vol. 6 (1), 63–88.

Johansson, T. (2007) *Intimacy*, in Flood, M., Gardiner, J., Pease, B. and Pringle, K. (Eds.) *International Encyclopaedia of Men and Masculinities*. Abingdon. Routledge.

Johnson, R. et al. (2004) *The Practice of Cultural Studies*. London. Sage Publications.

Johnson, R. and Walkerdine, V. (2004) *Transformation Under Pressure: New Labour, class, gender and young women*, in *Blairism and the War of Persuasion*. London. Lawrence and Wishart.

Jones, K. (2003) *Education in Britain: 1944 to the present*. Cambridge. Polity Press

Josselson, R. (1995) *Imagining the Real: Empathy, narrative and the dialogic self*, in Josselson, R. and Lieblich, A. (Eds.) *The Narrative Study of Lives*. London. Sage Publications.

Kampf, A., Marshall, B. and Petersen, A. (2013) *Aging Men, Masculinities and Modern Medicine*. Abingdon. Routledge.

Katz, S. (1996) *Disciplining Old Age: The formation of gerontological knowledge*. Charlottesville. University Press of Virginia.

Katz,S. (2000) *Busy Bodies: Activity and the management of everyday life*. 'Journal of Aging Studies'. Vol. 14 (2).

Katz, S. and Laliberte-Rudman, D. (2004) *Examplars of retirement: Identity and Agency Between Lifestyle and Social Movement*, in Tulle, E. (Ed.) 'Old Age and Agency.' New York. Nova Science Publishers.

Kaufman (1994) *Contradictory Relationships to Patriarchy and Power*, in Brod, H. and Kaufman, M. (Eds.) *Theorising Masculinities*. California. Sage Publications.

Kaye, L. (1997) *Informal Caregiving by Aging men*, in Kosberg, J. and Kaye, L. (Eds.) *Elderly Men*. Springer Publishing Company.

Kaye, L. (2005) *Service Utilization and Support provision of Caregiving Men* in Kramer, B. and Thompson, E. (Eds.) *Men as Caregivers*. New York. Prometheus Books

Kaye, L. and Applegate, J. (1994) *Aging Men and the Family Caregiving Orientation* in Thompson, E.H. (Ed.) *Aging Mens Lives*. Sage Publications.

Kaye, L. and Applegate, J. (1995) *Men's Style of Nurturing Elders*, in Sabo, D. and Gordon, D. (Eds.) *Men's Health and Illness: Gender, Power and the body*. Sage Publications.

Kimmel, D. (1979) *Life-history Interviews of Aging, Gay men*. International journal of aging and human development, Vol. 10 (3), 1979–80.

Kimmel, M. (1996) *Manhood in America*. New York. The Free Press.

Kontos, P. (2004) *Embodied Selfhood: Redefining agency in Alzheimer's Disease*, in Tulle, E. (Ed.) *Old Age and Agency*. New York. Nova Science publishers.

Kosberg, J. and Kaye, L. (1997) (Eds.) *Elderly Men Special Problems and Professional Challenges*.' Focus on Men. New York. Springer Publishing Company.

Kramer, B. (2005) *Men Caregivers: An overview* in Kramer, B. and Thompson, E.H. (Eds.) *Men as caregivers*. Amherst, New York. Prometheus books.

Kramer, B. and Thompson, E. (2005) (Eds.) *Men as Caregivers*, New York: Prometheus Books.

Laliberte-Rudman, D. (2006) *Shaping the Active, Autonomous and Responsible, Modern Retiree: An analysis of discursive technologies and the links with neo-liberal, political rationality*. 'Aging and Society'. Vol. 26: 181–201

Lawler, S. (2008) *Identity: Sociological Perspectives*. Cambridge. Polity Press.

Lee, C. and Owens, G. (2002) *The Psychology of Men's Health*, Buckingham, Open University Press.

Levine, M. (1990) *The Life and Death of Gay Clones*, in Kimmel, M. and Messner, M. (Eds.) *Men's Lives*. Fourth Edition. Boston. Allyn and Bacon.

Mac an Ghaill, M. and Haywood, C. (2007) *Gender, Culture and Society: Contemporary femininities and masculinities*. Basingstoke. Palgrave Macmillan.

Mac Rae, H. (1998) *Managing Feelings: Caregiving as emotion work*, in 'Research on Aging' Vol. 20: 137–60.

Marsiglio, W. and Greer, R. (1994) *A Gender Analysis of Aging men's Sexuality: Social, psychological and biological dimensions*, in Thompson E.H. (Ed.) *Aging men's lives*. Thousand Oaks, Sage Publications.

May, T. (1999) *Reflexivity and Sociological Practice*. 'Sociological Research Online', Vol. 4, (3).

Meadows, R. and Davidson, K. (2006) *Maintaining Manliness in Later Life: Hegemonic Masculinities and Emphasised Femininities*, in Calasanti, T. and Slevin, K. (Eds.) *Age Matters: Realigning Feminist Thinking*. New York: Routledge, Taylor and Francis Group.

Morgan, D. (ed.) (2005). *Class and Masculinity*, in Kimmel, M., Hearn, J. and Connell, R.W. (Eds.) *The handbook of studies on men and masculinity*. Thousand Oaks, California. Sage Publications.

Morgan, D. (2002) *You Too Can Have A Body Like Mine*. London, Routledge.

Muller, J.H. (1999) *Narrative Approaches to Qualitative Research in Primary Care*, in Crabtree, B. and Miller, W. (Eds.) *Doing Qualitative Research*. London. Sage Publications.

Mutchler, M. (2000) *Young Gay Men's Stories in the States: Scripts, sex and safety in the time of AIDS*, in 'Sexualities', Vol. 3: 31.

Nicholson, L. and Seidman, S. (1995) *Social Postmodernism: Beyond Identity Politics*. Cambridge. Cambridge University Press.

Nurse, K. (2004) *Masculinities in Transition: Gender and the Global Problematique*, in Reddock, R. (Ed.) *Interrogating Caribbean Masculinities*. Kingston. The University of the West Indies.

Oberg, P. (1996) *The Absent Body: A social gerontological paradox*, in 'Aging and Society', Vol. 16: 701–19.

Oliver, M. (1983) *Social Work with Disabled People*. Basingstoke. Macmillan.

Oliver, M. (1996) *Understanding Disability: From theory to practice*. Basingstoke. Macmillan.

Paterson, K. and Hughes, B. (2000) *Disabled Bodies* in Hancock, P., Hughes, B., Jagger, E., Paterson, K., Russell, R., Tulle-Winton, E. and Tyler, M. (Eds.) *The Body, Culture and Society: An Introduction*. Buckingham. Open University Press.

Pease, B. (1999) *Researching Profeminist Men's Narratives: Participatory methodologies in a postmodern frame*, in Fawcett, B., Featherstone. M., Fook, J. and Possiter. A (Eds.) *Practice and Research in Social Work*. London. Routledge.

Pease, B. (2000) *Recreating Men: Postmodern Masculinity Politics*. London. Sage Publications.

Petersen, A. (1998) *Unmasking the Masculine: 'Men' and 'Identity' in a sceptical age*. London. Sage Publications.

Plummer, K. (1995) *Telling Sexual Stories*. London. Routledge.

Plummer, K. (2005) *Male Sexualities*, in Kimmel, M., Hearn, J. and Connell, R.W. (Eds.) *The Handbook of Studies on Men and Masculinities*. Thousand Oaks. Sage Publications.

Polkinghorne, D.E. (1988) *Narrative Knowing and the Human Sciences*. Albany. SUNY Press.

Potts, A., Grace, V., Vares, T. and Gavey, N. (2006) *Sex for Life? Men's counter-stories on erectile dysfunction, male sexuality and aging*, in 'Sociology of Health and Illness', Vol. 28 (3), pp. 540–55.

Ramazanoğlu, C. and Holland, J. (2002) *Feminist Methodology: Challenges and Choices*. London. Sage Publications.

Redman, P. and Mac an Ghaill, M. (1997) *Educating Peter: The Making of a History Man*, in Steinberg, D., Epstein, D. and Johnson, R. (Eds.) *Border Patrols: Policing the Boundaries of Heterosexuality*. London. Cassell.

Roberts, B. (2002) *Biographical Research*. Buckingham, Open University Press.

Robinson, V. (2007) *Heterosexuality*, in Flood, M., Gardiner, J., Pease, B. and Pringle, K. (Eds.) *International encyclopaedia of Men and Masculinities*. Abingdon. Routledge.

Robinson, V. and Hockey, J. (2011) 'Masculinities in Transition', Basingstoke, UK, Palgrave Macmillan.

Rosenthal, G. (1993) *Reconstruction of Life Stories: Principles of selection in generating stories for narrative biographical interviews*, in Josselson, R. and Lieblich, A. (Eds.) 'The Narrative Study of Lives', Vol. 1. London: Sage, pp. 59–91.

Russell, R. (2001) 'In Sickness and in Health: A Qualitative Study of Elderly Men who Care for Wives with Dementia.' Journal of Aging Studies: 15 (4): 352–67.

Russell, R. (2004) 'Social Networks Among Elderly Men Caregivers' in Thompson, E. (Ed.) 'The Journal of Men's Studies', Vol. 13, Number 1.

Ruspini, E.H et al. (2011) (Eds.) 'Men and Masculinities Around the World: Transforming Men's Practices.' New York. Palgrave Macmillan.

Ruxton, S. (2009) *Man Made: Men, masculinities and equality in public policy*. London, Coalition on Men and Boys.

Saint-Aubin, A. (2004) *Opening the Books on Aging Men: Are all the old men white and all the widowers heterosexual?* in 'Journal of Men's Studies', Vol. 13, (1).

Sampath, N. (1997) *Crabs in a Bucket: Reforming Male Identities in Trinidad*, in Sweetman, C. (Ed.) *Men and Masculinity*. Oxford. Oxfam

Sandberg, L. (2007) *Ancient Monuments, Mature Men and those Popping Amphetamine: Researching the lives of aging men*. Nordic Journal for Masculinity Studies. Vol. 2, (2), 85–108.

Sandberg, L. (2011) *Getting Intimate: Old age, masculinity and (hetero) sexual subjectivity*. Linkoping. Linkoping University Press.

Sandbrook, D. (2006) *Never Had It So Good: A history of Britain from Suez to the Beatles*. London. Routledge.

Schiavi, R. (1999) *Aging and Male Sexuality*. Cambridge. Cambridge University Press.

Scott, A. et al. (1995) (Ed) 'Gender and Social Support Networks in Later Life'. Buckingham: Open University Press.

Segal, L. (1990) *Slow Motion: Changing masculinities, changing men*. London. Virago Press.

Segal, L. (2013) *Out of Time: The Pleasures and the Perils of Aging*. London. Verso.

Seidler, V. (1989) *Rediscovering Masculinity: Reason, language and sexuality*. London. Routledge.

Serrant-Green, L. and McLuskey, J. (2008) *The Sexual Health of Men*. Oxford. Radcliffe Publishing.

Shakespeare, T. (1994) *Cultural Representation of Disabled People: Dustbins for disavowal* in 'Disability and Society', Vol. 9 (3): 283–99

Shakespeare, T. (1999) *When is a Man Not a Man? When He is Disabled*, in Wild, J. (Ed.) *Working with men for change*. London. University of Central London Press.

Shiers, J. (1988) *One Step to Heaven?* in Cant, B. and Hemmings, S. (Eds.) *Radical Records: Thirty years of Lesbian and Gay history*. London. Routledge.

Shippy, R., Cantor, M. and Brennan, M. (2004) *Social Networks of Aging, Gay Men*, in Thompson, E.H. (Ed.) 'The Journal of Men's Studies,' Vol. 13, (1).

Shuttleworth, R. (2006) *Disability and Sexuality Towards a Constructionist Focus on Access and the Inclusion of Disabled People in the Sexual Rights Movement*, in

Teunis, N. and Herdt, G. (Eds.) *Sexuality Inequalities: Case studies from the field.'* Berkeley. University of California Press.

Schutze, F. (1992) *Pressure and Guilt: The experience of a young German soldier in World War Two and its biographical implications,* 'International Sociology', Vol. 7 (2): 187–208; Vol. 7 (3): 347–67.

Silver, C. (2003) *Gendered Identities in Old Age: Towards (de)gendering?* in 'Journal of Aging Studies', Vol. 17, 379–97.

Sinha, M. (2007) (Ed.) *Colonial and Imperial Masculinities.* Abingdon: Routledge.

Sipes, C. (2005) *The Experiences and Relationships of Gay Male Caregivers who Provide Care for their Partners with AIDS,* in Kramer, B. and Thompson, E. (Eds.) *Men as Caregivers.* New York. Prometheus books.

Skeggs, B. (1997) *Formations of Class and Gender.* London. Sage Publications.

Slevin, K. (2008) *Disciplining Bodies: The aging experiences of older heterosexual and gay men.* 'Generations'.

Smith, S. and Watson, J. (2001) *Reading Autobiography: A guide for interpreting life narratives.* Minneapolis. University of Minnesota Press.

Solimeo, S. (2008) *Sex and Gender in Older Adults' Experience of Parkinson's Disease.* 'Journal of Gerontology' Social Sciences: Vol. 638, No. 1, S42–S48.

Sparkes, A. (2004) *Bodies, Narratives, Selves and Autobiography: The example of Lance Armstrong* in 'Journal of Sport and Social Issues', Vol. 28, No. 4, pp. 397–428.

Sparkes, A. and Smith, B. (2002) *Sport, Spinal Cord Injury, Embodied Masculinities and the Dilemmas of Narrative Identity.* 'Men and Masculinities': Vol. 4 (3): 258–85.

Spector-Mersel, G. (2006) *Never-Aging Stories: Western Hegemonic Masculinity scripts.* 'Journal of Gender Studies', Vol. 15: 67–82.

Staudacher, C. (1991) *Men and Grief.* Oakland. New Harbinger Publications, inc.

Steedman, C. (1996) *About Ends: On the ways in which the end is different from an ending.* 'History of the Human Sciences', Vol. 9 (4), 99–114.

Steinberg, D. and Johnson, R. (2004) *Blairism and the War of Persuasion.* London. Lawrence and Wishart.

Stoller, E. (2005) *Theoretical Perspectives on Caregiving Men,* in Kramer, B. and Thompson, E. (Eds.) *Men as Caregivers.* New York. Prometheus books.

Thomas, C. and Corker, M (2002) *A Journey Around the Social Model,* in Corker, M. and Shakespeare, T. (Eds.) *Disability/Postmodernism: Embodying disability theory.* London. Continuum.

Thompson, E.H. (2006) *Images of Old Men's Masculinity: Still a Man* in 'Sex Roles', Vol. 55; 633–48.

Thompson, E.H. (1994) *Older Men's Lives.* Thousand Oaks. Sage Publications

Thompson, E.H. (2000) *Gendered Caregiving of Husbands and Sons,* in *Intersections of Aging: Readings in Social Gerontology.* Los Angeles. Roxbury Publishing Company.

Thompson, E.H. (2005) *What's Unique About Men's Caregiving?* in Kramer, B. and Thompson, E.H. (Eds.) *Men as Caregivers.* New York. Prometheus books.

Tolson, A. (1977) *The Limits of Masculinity.* London, Tavistock Publications.

Torres, M. (2007) *Subordinate Masculinity,* in Flood, M., Gardiner, J., Pease, B. and Pringle, K. (Eds.) *International Encyclopaedia of Men and Masculinities.* Abingdon. Routledge.

Townsend, J., Godfrey, M. and Denby T. (2006) *Heroines, Villains and Victims: Older people's perceptions of others,* in 'Aging and Society,' Vol. 26, 883–900

Tulle, E. (2004) *Old Age and Agency*. New York. Nova Science Publishers.

Tulle-Winton, E. (2000) *Old Bodies*, in Hancock, P., Hughes, B., Jagger, E., Paterson, K., Russell, R., Tulle-Winton, E. and Tyler, M. *The Body, Culture and Society*. Buckingham. Open University Press.

Tulle, E. (2008) *Aging, The Body and Social Change: Running in Later Life*. Basingstoke. Palgrave Macmillan.

Vacha-Haase, T., Wester, S. and Christianson, H. (2011) *Psychotherapy with Aging Men*. New York. Routledge.

Vincent, J. (2003) *Old Age*. London. Routledge.

Wagner, D. (1997) *Breaking New Ground: Older men and the workplace*, in Kosberg, J. and Kaye, L. (Eds.) *Elderly Men: Special Problems and Professional Challenges*. Springer Publisher Company.

Walker, K. (1998) *'I'm Not Friends the Way She's Friends': Ideological and behavioral constructions of masculinity in men's friendships*, in Kimmel, M. and Messner, M. (Eds.) *Men's Lives*. Fourth Edition. Boston. Allyn and Bacon.

Walkerdine, V. and Jimenez, J. (2012) *Gender, Work and Community after De-Industrialisation: A psychosocial approach to affect*. Basingstoke, UK, Palgrave Macmillan.

Walters, T. (1999) *On Bereavement: The culture of grief*. Buckingham, Open University Press.

Watson, J. (2000) *Male Bodies: Health, culture and identity*. Buckingham. Open University Press.

Weedon, C. (1987) *Feminist Practice and Poststructuralist Theory*. Oxford. Blackwell

Weeks, J. (1977) *Coming Out: Homosexual Politics in Britain, from the Nineteenth Century to the Present*. London. Quartet Books.

Weeks, J. (2004) *Labour's Loves Lost: The legacies of moral conservatism and Sex Reform*, in Steinberg, D., Johnson, R. (Eds.) *Blairism and the War of Persuasion*. London. Lawrence and Wishart.

Whitehead, S. (2002) *Men and Masculinities*. Cambridge. Polity.

Williams, C. (1993) *Introduction*, in Williams, C. (Ed.) *Doing 'Women's Work: Men in non-traditional occupations*. Sage Publications.

Williams, R. (1977) *Marxism and Literature*. Oxford. Oxford University Press, pp. 121–27.

Wolpert, L. (2011) *You're Looking Very Well: The surprising nature of getting old*. London. Faber and Faber Ltd.

'Women in Work': Trades Union Congress, (2012).

Wright, M. (2007) Agency in Flood, M., Gardiner, J., Pease,B. and Pringle, K. (Eds.) in *International Encyclopedia of Men and Masculinities*. London. Routledge.

Index

The manufacturer's authorised representative in the EU is Springer
Nature Customer Service Centre GmbH, Europaplatz 3, 69115 Heidelberg,
Germany. If you have any concerns regarding our products, please
contact ProductSafety@springernature.com

Printed and bound by CPI Group (UK) Ltd, Croydon, CR0 4YY
23/04/2026
02095621-0001